D0195597

Bless This Mess

Bless This Mess

*A Modern Guide
to Faith and Parenting
in a Chaotic World*

Rev. Molly Baskette
AND Ellen O'Donnell, PhD

CONVERGENT
NEW YORK

Copyright © 2019 by Molly Baskette and Ellen O'Donnell

All rights reserved.

Published in the United States by Convergent Books, an imprint of Random House, a division of Penguin Random House LLC, New York. convergentbooks.com

CONVERGENT BOOKS is a registered trademark and its C colophon is a trademark of Penguin Random House LLC.

Library of Congress Cataloging-in-Publication Data
Names: Baskette, Molly Phinney, 1970– author. | O'Donnell, Ellen, author.
Title: Bless this mess: a modern guide to faith and parenting in a chaotic world / Molly Baskette and Ellen O'Donnell.
Description: [New York] : Convergent, [2019]
Identifiers: LCCN 2018060430 (print) | LCCN 2019001813 (ebook) | ISBN 9781984824134 (ebook) | ISBN 9781984824127 (pbk.)
Subjects: LCSH: Parenting—Religious aspects—Christianity. | Child rearing—Religious aspects—Christianity.
Classification: LCC BV4529 (ebook) | LCC BV4529 .B37725 2019 (print) | DDC 248.8/45—dc23
LC record available at https://lccn.loc.gov/2018060430

ISBN 978-1-9848-2412-7
Ebook ISBN 978-1-9848-2413-4

PRINTED IN THE UNITED STATES OF AMERICA

Cover design by Sarah Horgan

10 9 8 7 6 5 4 3 2 1

First Edition

For Carmen Grace and Rafael James Phinney Baskette,
who have ruined my life for the better, and to
my beloved Peter, partner in many a parenting crime.

—Molly

For Luke Myles and Jonah Michael O'Donnell Weyant: I love
you to the moon and back a megabajillion times plus some.
And for Eric, who loves us without conditions
and who always has my back.

—Ellen

Contents

On Children

Kahlil Gibran

Your children are not your children.
They are the sons and daughters of Life's longing for itself.
They come through you but not from you,
And though they are with you yet they belong not to you.
You may give them your love but not your thoughts,
For they have their own thoughts.
You may house their bodies but not their souls,
For their souls dwell in the house of tomorrow,
which you cannot visit, not even in your dreams.
You may strive to be like them,
but seek not to make them like you.
For life goes not backward nor tarries with yesterday.
You are the bows from which your children
as living arrows are sent forth.
The archer sees the mark upon the path of the infinite,
and He bends you with His might
that His arrows may go swift and far.
Let your bending in the archer's hand be for gladness;
For even as He loves the arrow that flies,
so He loves also the bow that is stable.

Before We Begin

In July 2004, toting my firstborn in a sling, I (Ellen) walked into a small, sweaty service at First Church Somerville, Massachusetts, a United Church of Christ where Molly Baskette had been pastor for less than a year. A once-dying congregation in a funky, gentrifying neighborhood, First Church was about to make a remarkable turnaround. Dozens of young people were beginning to show up, joining the older Protestant forebears of the church, attracted by the authentic, raw, and soulful worship style and the engaging sermons Molly preached (liberally peppered with personal stories).

This was a welcome change of pace for me. I had grown up steeped in Catholicism, but had left the Church at the start of the millennium over the sex abuse crisis and the Church's reluctance to adopt more progressive policies. Although I felt disappointed by my old faith, I was not ready to leave Christianity behind completely. Religion had been formative for me, for better and for worse, and I still wanted my three-month-old, Luke, to grow up knowing how to look for the good in a world that could be so hard, but without all the baggage of the religion I had grown up with.

I was in graduate school for clinical psychology at the time, working at a residential home for children and adolescents outside Boston. During Luke's naptimes, I was writing a dissertation on what makes for good parenting. I was voraciously reading hard-core parenting research, but also mainstream parenting books, memoirs like Anne Lamott's *Operating Instructions* and first-wave "mommy blogs." I even dipped into the work of Dr. James Dobson; about the only resource on Christian parenting at the time. But none of my research provided practical guidance on raising a spiritually grounded Christian kid in a liberally minded family. So I did what any good doctoral student would do. I ditched the books and googled a list of churches to try on for size. Typing in "liberal Christian churches," I saw a picture of Molly and a rainbow flag. First Church Somerville was the first and last church I visited.

When I came into that first service, there were only two kids in the congregation, and one of them was Molly's two-year-old, Rafe. He was in a local family daycare, and soon I started Luke there as well. So began a carpool that lasted four years and a friendship that has lasted many more. It was also the start of this book.

Seeing each other at the difficult liminal moments of the carpool pickup and drop-off, when a kid was melting down or simply refusing to put on shoes (or even clothes!), Molly and I began to share our own stories, which really meant being totally vulnerable with each other about the often manic challenges of balancing home, mommyhood, and careers. We each brought different viewpoints and ideas to the table. I could provide Molly with much-needed perspective from the science of child development, and Molly could provide me with spiritual practices and pastoral guidance. Psychology was not enough. Spirituality was not enough. Each of us had something the other needed for the hard, messy, on-the-job training of raising children.

Avid readers both, we realized we could provide the world

with the parenting book we longed for and that didn't yet exist: a book that combined the best of what psychology, science, and Christianity have to offer, a book that was inclusive, and that encouraged the idea that parents are their children's first and best spiritual teachers (but also that they are not alone in this calling!).

Time passed. We each had second kids (Molly's Carmen and my Jonah, whom you'll hear more about soon). I finished my PhD and became a child psychologist at Massachusetts General Hospital. Molly faced and defeated cancer and saw her church grow in health and strength, as the Sunday school enrollment expanded from three kids to eighty in just a few years. Today, 40 percent of the congregation of First Church Somerville is gay, lesbian, transgender, or bisexual. There are families with two moms, or stay-at-home dads; kids who are adopted, multiracial, or were born from IVF (in vitro fertilization) or IUI (intrauterine insemination). Molly eventually left Somerville and now serves First Congregational Church in Berkeley, California, a United Church of Christ (UCC) whose tagline is "The Motley Pew." She wrote and published a couple of other books. And finally this one got born!

From the beginning, we conceived our book as a go-to for credible scientific research on child development and parenting, digested into lay terminology. We hoped it would inspire open-minded Christian parents with practical ideas and a heavy dose of humor (we believe that God, first among us, loves a good laugh), as well as provide real-world insights to help the stressed-out and/or bewildered family that sometimes just needs a friend to say it's OK.

Most of all, we wanted to make our own experiences— our triumphs, disappointments, brokenness, foibles, and mistakes—the foil for it all. So many parenting books make it all sound so eeeeeasy. And it's not. Parenting is like a highly competitive endurance sport that is always pushing us to new and sometimes frightening levels.

In this book, you'll get guidance on the topics we ourselves have struggled with over the years: how to talk to kids about money, their bodies, God, ethics, disability, and difference; how to pray together as a family and bring other spiritual practices into the home; how to fight fair; how to stress less (*really*); how to embody an ethic of service to others; how to live a deep generosity and gratitude practice; how to really know our kids and have a more expansive understanding of who God made them to be, in Her image rather than our own. And we set out to prove that it is totally possible to be a well-informed, progressive Christian parent.

To that end, you may have already noticed we usually use *She* in reference to God—not because God has a gender, but because so many of us, even those raised in a progressive church or in no church at all, default to male language for God, our cultural factory settings. Using *She* is an attempt to put a thumb on the scale of patriarchy, to jog us out of old images and tropes. Besides, new data suggest that girls who have direct experience with female clergy grow up with higher self-esteem and attain better employment. If female clergy can do that for girls, what can a female God-image do for them?

As the book developed, we found ourselves writing in one voice, meeting the goal of a perfect marriage of spirituality and psychology. As already mentioned, we will be sharing a lot of our own stories—our successes and our failures (with minor editing and, of course, permission from our children—trying to keep those therapy bills to a minimum). We are firm believers in "good enough parenting," meaning parenting is a process, and perfection an impossible goal. We have tried to learn from our mistakes and from each other, and we hope you, beloved reader, will feel permission to be imperfect out loud yourself as you join us on this journey. No doubt about it, parenting is hard! The good news is that if it *is* hard, you're probably doing it right.

A Word about How to Read This Book

We know you are busy and exhausted, like every parent. Even if you *mean* to, it is hard to read a whole entire book, so this one is organized into three parts. Part I, "Foundations," provides a theoretical framework for all that follows. It introduces themes, ideas, and terms from psychology and theology that will come up again and again: a way of thinking about your parenting and your kids through a modern scientific as well as time-honored Judeo-Christian spiritual lens.

Part II, "The How-Tos," gets into the nitty-gritty of challenges and issues most parents (including us) face along the way. Each chapter covers an ongoing conversation—a unique topic that is likely to come up again and again in the life of your family—from toddlerhood through the teen years. You'll find main ideas in bold throughout each of these chapters, some practical applications by ages and stages, and a simple end-of-chapter prompt to help you carry these nuggets into your daily life. If your prayers these days sound like Anne Lamott's first essential prayer—namely, "Help!"—go ahead and dive into the practical Part II. We won't stop you.

Part III, "Singular/Sacred Stories," uses personal narratives about unique parenting situations to illustrate a universal truth: the mix of joy and terror that is being a parent. We both learned a lot in graduate school, but our best stuff comes from the people we are privileged to meet in our work: families facing everything from garden-variety challenges to unimaginable obstacles. We want to share some of their wisdom with you, because spiritual parenting is about much more than having the right words or techniques. It is driven by wisdom and faith, and those things are learned in shared testimony rather than in textbooks.

Consider this your new bathroom book! (Let's be honest: it's the only place you get You Time these days.) Knowing there's not one "right" way to read this book—just as there's no one "right" way to parent your unique-in-all-the-world children—go ahead and get started.

PART I

Foundations

CHAPTER 1

Spiritual *and* Progressive Parenting

Not an Oxymoron

Some years ago we stumbled on a satirical *New Yorker* piece that read: "A recent study has shown that if American parents read one more long-form think piece about parenting they will go f*cking ape shit." It went on to describe the all-too-familiar and all-too-frustrating experience of reading popular parenting books, even when they are based on really sound psychological science.

The ideas are many: good parenting is all about supportiveness. No, wait, it's all about grit and resilience. Nix that, it's about nature versus nurture. Free-range kids, helicopter moms. Tiger-mothering or attachment parenting.

Does the world really need *another* parenting book?

We think so.

Once, Molly came to Ellen in tears. Frustrated and overwhelmed with how to parent strong-willed three-year-old Rafe, Molly had resorted to spanking, which went against everything she believed in as a parent and a Christian—but none of the other methods she used had worked. She had read lots of books and articles and watched videos, but none offered the spiritual and empirical guideposts she needed in one holistic approach to be the kind of parent she longed to be: kind, funny, and easygoing yet firm, always on the floor, playing games, doing messy crafts, singing with her children, deftly engaging their deep theological questions, providing a loving and supportive but never hovering or stifling presence as they grew. Instead, she was becoming the mother she'd always feared she'd be: repeating the same mistakes her own mother made, impatient, a yeller, a control freak with lapses into temper. How could things be unraveling so?

Until now, many of the spiritual and psychological guideposts for raising kids have been on seemingly opposite ends of the field. On the spiritual side, there are numerous "Christian parenting" books, but many of them encourage a body-negative theology, strict gender roles, and a fundamentally pessimistic worldview, not to mention a "spare the rod and spoil the child" mentality. That form of parenting doesn't hold up to what psychological science teaches us ultimately works for our kids or families, and doesn't fit with our experience or with the type of parents we want to be. We imagine that you, like us, have no interest in raising "real boys" or perfectly compliant girls.

And while there are plenty of great secular parenting books out there, none, by definition, gives guidance on Christian spirituality. (Why would they? They're secular.) Popular parenting books based on the science of developmental and clinical psychology give short shrift to religion. At the far end of the field, those books tell us our kids don't need religion and that it may even be bad for them, leading to increased risk-taking behavior like underage drinking and unprotected sex (a misread of the research that we'll clear up in a bit). Few recognize that spirituality is good for our kids and families, and none acknowledges that parenting at its best can be a deeply spiritual experience.

Good-Enough Parenting

So what does make for good parenting? Or what we prefer to call "good-enough parenting"? Sound psychological science on child development has plenty to offer in this department. So does a deeply rooted spirituality, **because parenting is a spiritual practice, taking us to our highest highs and our lowest lows, while helping us mature alongside our kids.** Our goal in this book is to curate the best of what psychology *and* an open, inquisitive, LGBTQ-affirming Christianity has to say about both the red-letter days and the deep joys of childrearing. A marriage of the scientific and the spiritual can help us raise whole, healthy kids who will grow up to be more fully who God intends them to be: autonomous and emotionally intelligent adults, each with their own unique personality and calling.

We don't claim to have the magic wand. Parents often assume that Ellen has a secret weapon to "fix" whatever ails their child and family emotionally. And the parents in Molly's church sometimes come to her as the "paid religious professional," the only one with answers to their kids' or their own probing spiritual and theological questions. But you don't always have a pastor or a psychologist in your back pocket or at daycare drop-off. Even if you did, she would tell you there is no instant fix or "right" answer. Our kids and our families are complicated and messy. We have a lot of wisdom and experience to guide us, but few quick-and-easy solutions.

As regular churchgoing faces precipitous decline, this book acknowledges that more and more of our children's spiritual learning, active or passive, is happening in the home. **Our assumption in writing this book is that *you* are your child's first and best spiritual teacher.** You are the one they will come to with big questions about life, death, God, faith, and doubt. You are the one they will need when life throws more at them than they can handle. You are, in fact, their first God-figure (don't let it go to your head).

You know your children better than any professional. You are the expert who has logged countless hours in discovering who they are—but to be an expert also takes humility and the ability to take a step back to get a wider lens.

As a minister who lets good research guide her pastoring, and as a clinician who is a lifelong person of faith, we want to give you a way to let *both* Christian spirituality *and* sound psychological science shape your parenting and the conversations you have with your kids across ages and stages: conversations about social concerns, sexuality, violence, generosity, justice, and issues of right and wrong in an often morally confused and confusing world. There is a way of being an informed, effective, and loving Christian parent; a way of weaving all of those things into the fabric of your family's life; a way to talk to your kids about God and Jesus that is authentic and perfectly in tune with *all* of your family's values. We know it can be done because we are living it.

And spoiler alert: even with our advice and strategies, you will never be the perfect parent. You will never have the perfect child, suitable for humble-bragging about on social media. No matter how hard you try, things will go wrong that are out of your control: learning disabilities, health challenges, unexpected losses, and hard seasons. It's why this book is titled *Bless This Mess*. God doesn't need to bless what's already working. It is in our pain, our need, our helpless crying out that God is able to draw near and bless us *and* the messes we find ourselves in.

Letting Go of Fear and Reaching for God

About a year after we met at church, Ellen put Luke in Rafe's daycare. Carpooling little ones, we began to see a lot of each other's messes, both literal and figurative. Ellen would arrive for pickup and find Molly unshowered and running late because her three-year-old was taking twenty minutes to put on his socks (and those were days when he *wanted* to put them on). It was an epiphany for her that even a minister didn't always know what to do with a strong-willed little person.

On that day pretty early on when Molly admitted to Ellen that she had resorted to spanking out of frustration, she was a bit shocked to have Ellen admit that she, a child psychologist and parenting expert, had "put" (read: thrown) two-year-old Luke onto his bed for a time-out with a lot more force than necessary. Ellen had shocked herself with her own strength . . . and anger. It wasn't an intentional move. She had not been drawing on any of her field expertise in parenting or child development. She had not been *thinking* at all, or at least not with anything other than her reptilian brain. The toss—heck, even the "time-out" that justified it—was driven entirely by impulse and emotion. Our kids know where *all* of our buttons are. Let she who is without buttons cast the first stone.

From there, the floodgates opened. Now fully vulnerable with each other, we confessed *all* of our parenting regrets and questions, our mistakes and fears. We also started sharing what we each knew. We lingered at drop-off or met up for coffee to get to the bottom of thorny parenting conundrums. Molly would ask Ellen, "Is this normal?" Ellen would ask Molly, "How do I answer that?"

Ellen's ideas about parenting strategies and human development meshed perfectly with Molly's understanding of what

God *really* wants for and from parents, children, and families. And Molly's way of talking to children and teens about the really hard stuff related to ethics and spirituality, how humans are made, and what we are called to be and do in the world (a way that leaves room for questions and avoids platitudes) fit perfectly with what Ellen knew about children's cognitive, emotional, social, and moral development and potential.

Revealing our parenting fears and our shame to each other, letting it out of the shadows and into the light, has brought us both more strength, wisdom, resiliency, perspective, and stamina. But just like having faith, letting go of fear is not a "one and done." It's a lifelong process and practice. **Every day, in every challenging moment of parenting, we can choose again to release fear, or its conjoined twin, anger.** Both fear and anger are forms of control, and releasing either one requires surrender, something admittedly very hard for humans to do. It also involves a lot of humility and asking for help—including help from God, who might not feel present in our lives often enough.

We don't buy into the platitude that "God doesn't give us more than we can handle." There is too much evidence in all of our personal and professional lives that life gives us more than we can handle every single day, often in the form of our kids, and the *mishegas* that comes with them: temper tantrums, stitches, messes, learning disabilities, life-threatening illness and injury, cancer, parents dying too soon, financial struggles, divorce, addiction, school shootings, bullying, sexism, racism, and other forms of discrimination.

Yet the reality is this: God is there for us in our parenting struggles. She might show up as a moment of breath, a pause before we do something we'll regret. She might show up in the preposterously funny thing our five-year-old does in the midst of a ballistic tantrum that undermines our anger or tears with laughter, or as our best psychologist or pastor friend admitting that she has messed up too—big-time. She might show up as comforting words from our ancient and holy texts, proof positive that children have always driven their parents mad, or as some much-needed advice from our own dad or aunt or sibling on the other end of the phone, if we just make the call. If we let Her in by just asking to be present and part of our lives, **God will make us stronger even (or especially) in our weakest parenting moments.**

This book is no substitute for a vital community of faith, a community to teach and love you in good times and support and love you in hard times, but it may be a first step toward finding one. In the meantime, we hope it offers you practical, just-in-time support for the good, the bad, the messy, and the holy of childrearing. God willing, this book will help you ease your anxious grip on your kids, knowing that they belong to Someone Else who has their highest good in mind: the God who made them (and us, and you), imperfect and still beloved, just as we are, and as we are *all* becoming. As the inimitable Anne Lamott says, "God loves us just as we are—and loves us too much to let us stay that way."

Reclaiming Christian Faith—or Finding It for the First Time

If you aren't currently part of a community of faith, you probably don't have many conversations about how to raise your kids to be spiritual beings. Cocktail party conversation about faith and religion tends much more toward cultural and political criticism, at least in the progressive Northeast and Northern California, where we practice and preach. Even if you do go to church as a family more often than on Christmas and Easter, you are more likely to drop the kids off in Sunday school and dash out right after service to get to the next sports game than to spend time talking with others about ways to bring your faith home to the Monday-through-Friday slog. Why don't we talk with other parents about how to be more faithful families? We are all short on time. But we suspect something deeper is at work here.

As a child psychologist, Ellen spends a lot of time with parents talking about really hard stuff. She sits with families from around the world who are facing devastating diagnoses: kids with type 1 diabetes; life-threatening, disfiguring burns and amputations; parents with cancer. Families facing the challenges of learning disabilities, autism spectrum disorders, anxiety, depression, and divorce. Yet rarely do parents volunteer information about their spiritual or religious beliefs and practices. This appears to be particularly true for Christian families from the United States, where Christianity seems to have become all too synonymous with conservatism, closed-mindedness, anti-intellectualism, and a punitive parenting style that is contrary to anything you will read in the *New York Times* parenting section.

In Ellen's hospital work, only the families from far across the world are quick to share how their faith sustains them through the often terrifying task of being responsible for a little person's life. Parents from the United States are much more likely to talk about personal religion in the past tense. This is as true of newcomers to Molly's church as it is of parents in Ellen's practice. They tell us what tradition they grew up in and how they left it. They explain the bits and pieces they've chosen to continue and that they are a "spiritual but not religious family." We get it. There are good reasons for skepticism regarding the religion we grew up with and the harm it has caused the world.

But you still want your kids to believe in a higher power, a force of love in the universe that has their best interests at heart. You want them to feel the essential goodness of the world in spite of how chaotic and scary it can seem, and to understand their purpose in leaving the world better than they found it. In short, you long for them to have a grounding faith that will sustain and orient them even when you are not around.

There's a way in which we can allow our real spiritual hunger and our religious roots to shape our parenting and nurture our children's moral development and happiness, without ignoring the difficult parts of religion or being asked to believe things that are obviously false. If we invest in our progressive faith, it will be there to draw on not just in times of emotional distress or emergencies but for the everyday joys and slogs of being family. If we learn our sacred stories and do our spiritual practices often until they are as intuitive and common as brushing our teeth, maybe we will turn to God more easily and naturally when we need Her most, and we will be better able to receive Her strength when we find ourselves in a difficult parenting moment. And we will raise a generation of kids who have an even more expansive and reliable faith than the one we were given.

Enter a new parenting paradigm from our ancient Christian faith, and a vintage proverb that has not gotten nearly enough press.

CHAPTER 2

Spare the Rod and Spark the Child

A New Parenting Proverb

For millennia, many people raised a single biblical banner when it came to parenting: "Spare the rod and spoil the child." It's no wonder, with this tagline and its implications of discipline, authoritarianism, and permission for corporal punishment, that even those of us who consider ourselves believers strongly consider ditching the Bible as archaic and out of touch with modern parenting philosophies.

Besides, there are plenty of messages out there that religion might actually be *bad* for our kids. To look at just a few recent parenting headlines: *Study Finds That Children Raised without Religion Show More Empathy and Kindness; Raising Children without Religion May Be a Better Alternative, Suggests New Research; Growing Up Godless Is a Good Thing.*

The last time you were at the end of your parenting rope, what words did you reach for to help? The Bible? Probably not. When you needed more support, you likely turned to the Amazon bestseller list or to your go-to parenting blog. Hopefully they helped get you through that tough time—God can work through authors as well as the ether.

But where to start? A quick search on Amazon yields 207,370 books on "parenting." Ecclesiastes 12:12 mourns, "Of making many books there is no end, and much study is a weariness of the flesh." Sometimes we try to solve a spiritual problem with an intellectual solution, and all that does is turn us into head cases. Even when the intellectual solutions are sound and based on good research, their wisdom often flees us when we are flooded with anger or exhaustion. At best, we are often left utterly confused by conflicting messages from so many different parenting experts, trying to figure out how it all applies to our particular kid at that particular moment.

When you are entirely overwhelmed—when you are about to raise your hand in anger, or surrender!—you don't need a parenting expert or a new theory or approach any more than you need a wooden spoon hanging on the wall at the ready for doling out discipline. You need God. Someone stronger than you, from whom you can draw the *right* kind of strength.

Helpful or not, a full 13,667 of those parenting books on Amazon fall into the category of "Christian parenting." A lot of that literature seems to fit into one of two theologies: either our kids are raw material put into the world for us to shape into our masterpieces, or they are fundamentally flawed and in need of our stern correction. Are those really our only choices?

Christianity has lost its "cool" in more ways than one. Look at some of the discouraging (and arguably biased) research that suggests that religion is bad for our kids. It's scientifically accurate. There *is* some evidence that secular teenagers are less likely to succumb to peer pressure than religious teens. White teens who are secular are less racist than their Christian peers. Secular grown-ups are less vengeful, less nationalistic, less militaristic, less authoritarian, and more tolerant, on average, than religious adults. But a lot of the research driving those headlines preaching that religion is bad for our kids are referencing a particular *kind* of religion, and a particular kind of parenting that tends to go with it.

As an example, a University of Chicago study found that

children raised in nonreligious households are kinder and more altruistic than children raised in religious households. The parents of children who refused to share their stickers in a version of something called "The Dictator Game" were both Christian and Muslim. They were also far more punitive and judgmental, by their own report, than the secular parents. They tended to adhere to parenting attitudes and to employ parenting practices proven ineffective in research on instilling prosocial values and fostering positive behaviors in children.

Meanwhile, the children raised in secular families were being taught to live by the principle of empathetic reciprocity. In other words, "Do unto others as you would have them do unto you," the Golden Rule, made famous by Jesus in his Sermon on the Mount. **The secular parents may not have been raising their kids with religion, but they *were* raising them spiritually.** They were teaching their kids to live in a Christlike way, acknowledging that we are each part of something much bigger than any one of us alone, which puts the collective good before individual wants.

There is, in fact, a lot of *good* research on the protective powers of spirituality: its ability to buffer teenagers against substance use, unprotected premarital sex, depression, and anxiety and to forge resilient kids and families. Research overwhelmingly suggests that spiritual people are emotionally and physically healthier on average than nonspiritual people. Much of this research comes out of psychologist Lisa Miller's lab at Teachers College, Columbia University. She defines spirituality as "an inner sense of a living relationship to a higher power (God, nature, spirit, universe, the creator, or whatever your word is for the ultimate loving, guiding life-force)." Spirituality is a sense of connection to something bigger, a higher power and a plumb line for daily guidance. For Christians, that plumb line is Jesus.

"In all cases," Dr. Miller points out, "what makes spirituality meaningful is *personal choice and ownership*" rather than rigid rules or doctrine. She argues that children are born with a natural proclivity toward spirituality, and that the parents' job is to foster its development as much as the development of language, learning, and social skills. Take Ellen's Jonah, age eight, calling Ellen back to his bedroom for the umpteenth time. He was having trouble falling asleep and explained that he had made up a "game" where he made a "thankful wish" anytime his bedside clock had a repeating pattern of numbers. At 8:08 it was "I'm thankful for the planet." At 9:09 it was "I'm thankful for my family." Ellen told Jonah these sounded like prayers of thanks, and they started saying them together at bedtime.

So how do we as parents raise a spiritually grounded child, without all the heavy baggage of religion? **It begins (and middles and ends) with two key parenting practices:**

1. Getting to know the child you've been given.

2. Letting go of fear and holding on to faith, in order to parent that child into becoming the person God intends them to be.

Relinquishing Control to Discover the Child God Gave You

To be a parent is to be afraid a lot of the time. For some parents this is more true than for others. Some of us have the privilege of fearing only for our children's academic success, financial independence, and happiness. Others have to fear for their children's literal safety from bodily harm, be it from bullets on the street, from a system that might take their children from them, from an abusive relationship, or from a life-threatening illness.

We want to protect our kids and ensure that they will survive and thrive—it's our job, after all. And because we know from personal experience and from the headlines that parents lose their children every day—literally and figuratively—to abuse, drunk drivers, accidental shootings, intentional shootings in schools and movie theaters and dance clubs or at the hands of police, to sexual assault or alcohol or drugs, to suicide . . . how can we not be afraid?

The natural fear that accompanies being responsible for raising tender beings to adulthood can often make us feel helpless and out of control. **And that feeling of helplessness in turn can make us more angry, authoritarian, and controlling.** Remember from Chapter 1 how Molly and Ellen admitted to each other that their feelings of helplessness had made them give way to temper? Even if we don't spank, we may punish excessively, set rules on the spur of the moment without thinking them through, and make decisions for our kids with no input from them. And we yell . . . a lot.

Who among us has not felt out of control as a parent: standing in the frozen food aisle with our fractious two-, four-, or eleven-year-old or, in the privacy of our own homes with no other witnesses, feeling the urge to use power over our child before they overpower us?

What if, before she had resorted to spanking, Molly had taken a deep breath? The word *spirit* and the word *respiration* come from the same root. What if, before tossing Luke into time-out, Ellen had looked at the fire in his eyes and seen her own stubborn determination—the one that has gotten her through some pretty big challenges in life? What if each of us, in our weakest moments, had lifted our arms in prayer instead of in anger? Given *ourselves* a time-out to listen to God, instead of continuing to scream at a child who had obviously stopped listening?

Is there another proverb we can live by, out in the wilderness, beyond "Spare the rod and spoil the child"? Is there a better plumb line for holy parenting that doesn't require us to ditch everything we now know about how children actually develop and how we want to parent them? Something to hold on to when we are anxious and afraid? Something that allows us to feel a strength beyond ourselves that we can trust in and lean on? And that our children, in turn, can draw on when we are not with them?

There is. It goes like this:

> *Train children in the right way, and when grown, they will not stray.*
> —PROVERBS 22:6

A lot hangs on that phrase "in the right way." Does it mean raise our children the way *we* think they should be? According to our rigid hopes, or unmet needs, or unconscious projections? No. The original Hebrew suggests that "in the right way" actually hews more closely to "according to *their own* nature and temperament." It is akin to going along with the grain of wood rather than working against it.

Our job as parents is to discover who our children are, then love them further into being. Every child is distinct, perhaps shockingly different from their siblings (how can that be, with all that shared DNA?), and every one is, as the psalmist says, "fearfully and wonderfully made." Our greatest joy as parents may be to get to know the person God has given us to raise, whether by birth, adoption, or some other circumstance. But it can also be our undoing, because we worry that if we do in fact let our kids "be who they are," they won't make it, whatever that means for our family and values. They'll get lost or overwhelmed. They won't make it to college—or maybe to tomorrow. Our kids consistently ruin the illusion of who we imagined we'd get when we put in our order at the divine deli.

But here is some good news. Our children still have lots of time and opportunity to keep revealing themselves. We do not yet know what they will become. Let us mightily resist the fear that all will end in disaster. Be patient. There is much more story to be told.

By having a proverb that really aligns with what we intuitively know to be true about (1) who our kids are and (2) the kind of parenting they deserve, we can come back to that strong spiritual baseline more quickly, even when under pressure or about to blow our top. We will be more comfortable living with our families in the messy middle. And we'll gain an ear to filter through all the noise of the myriad parenting experts and advice from friends, relatives, teachers, coaches, pastors, preachers, and the media.

Before we start talking about what to *do*, let's take a moment to really think about whom we've been *given*, and what we really mean when we say that our children are a gift from God.

Getting to Know the Child You've Been Given: How Understanding Temperament Might Just Help You Hold Your Temper

Before having her second son, Ellen worked on a study of temperament with the psychiatrist Carl Schwartz, a student of renowned Harvard psychologist Jerome Kagan. Kagan piloted a groundbreaking longitudinal study of the role of temperament in child development. He and his team spent more than two decades following a group of babies into young adulthood to scientifically study the innate biological determinants of personality and behavior and the ways that parenting, privilege or lack of it, and life experience shapes people.

Temperament is a person's nature: a pattern of innate traits and emotional proclivities they have when they enter the world; while shaped by nurture, this pattern remains relatively stable over time. People of faith might describe it as "how God made you."

Kagan defines temperament along a spectrum of reactivity, from *low reactive* to *high reactive*. From birth, people have different qualities in different degrees. About 20 percent of babies are considered high-reactive. Those babies are born with a neurochemistry that makes their amygdalae, the part of the brain responsible for the fight-or-flight response, more "excitable" than others. High-reactive infants startle more easily, are more restless, cry more often, and are just generally less easygoing. Kagan calls them *inhibited*.

Let's call them, without any judgment, more *intense*. Intense inhibited babies are more cautious and fearful when faced with new situations, and as children and teenagers they are more prone to anxiety. Even as adults, they have higher resting heart rates. They may be more introverted. Walking around feeling raw and exposed all the time is hard work, and these children may be prone to retreating for self-preservation.

Another 40 percent of the babies Kagan and his colleagues have studied fall into a category he calls *low reactive* or *uninhibited*. They are, to so many parents, the elusive "easy" babies, seemingly always smiling and letting their parents sleep through the night. When presented with new people or situations, these babies show hardly any change at all in heart rate. Their amygdalae are far less reactive. As toddlers, they approach new playmates with ease. Extroverted and affable, they are always up for adventure. At age eleven, more low-reactive kids than high-reactive kids describe themselves as "happy most of the time." As adolescents they laugh at their own mistakes and engage in casual banter with an unfamiliar female examiner (Ellen) even when she presents them with challenging tasks from an IQ test.

Ellen clearly knew Jonah would be different from his big brother. In fact, she was eager to see how this new personality would unfold. But she still woke in a panic the first night in the hospital with newborn Jonah when she sent him to the nursery at ten p.m. and hadn't heard a peep from him by five a.m. She called the nurse to find out what terrible thing had happened to the baby! Years earlier, her firstborn, Luke, could be heard screaming down the hallway every two hours, their "zero-to-sixty" baby.

Ellen sometimes feared she was a tone-deaf mother for not being able to figure out her first baby's cries. But when Jonah came along she realized Luke was just more intense than his little brother, a little more on the inhibited end of the temperamental spectrum. And he and Jonah were going to need different parenting, from babyhood on up.

Here again is our new proverb: **"Train children in their own way, and when grown, they will not stray."** "In *their* own way" is a helpful reminder that every child is born with their own baseline temperament. Yet by the time they reach age seven, 50 percent of high-reactive (intense) babies are *not* any more fearful or anxious than their low-reactive peers. Kagan points out that what we really inherit is a temperamental *bias*. High-reactive babies are still high-reactive children, teenagers, and adults if you put them through an fMRI scan or any number of other tests. But they don't necessarily look that way in real life. Certain situations or conditions might bring out their intensity, but many of them have learned how to be calm-ish, as a rule. This is where the *training* part of our proverb comes in: the nurture side of the equation.

Temperament is not the same as personality. It's a set of innate proclivities that may or may not be expressed in how a person behaves in the world. People are not biologically or divinely determined so much as they are *inclined* or *constrained*. This jibes with our Christian faith. There is a lot of room for movement even within the "grain" of each person.

What this means for us parents is that we would do well to keep our expectations for our kids in check (and beware of giving ourselves too much credit for the baby who sleeps through the night and blame for the one who doesn't). That said, we still have a big role to play in helping our children learn to harness their temperament so that they can be the best version of themselves, and to develop their own unique personality to its fullest.

One other thing. It is tempting to equate *low-reactive* with "easy" and *high-reactive* not just with "intense" but with "difficult." Yet Kagan's research cautions against this. Not only do some of those intense babies grow to be calmer children, teenagers, and adults, but many of them also turn out to be quite high-achieving. At least in middle-class homes, high-reactive children tend to be more concerned with academic achievement and go on to achieve higher levels of education (on average) than their low-reactive peers. A certain amount of anxiety is a good thing. Too little anxiety and humans lack motivation. Too much anxiety and we are paralyzed into inactivity. Just the right amount of well-managed anxiety makes for driven, often highly successful people. And that intensity also often goes along with a sensitivity that, if harnessed, makes for incredibly thoughtful and empathic people who are capable of amazing things.

Of course, low-reactive babies have their own strengths and weaknesses. Their natural curiosity may spur creativity and learning with none of the burden of worry or overstriving for achievement. They are often the calm amid the storms of family conflicts or other crises. But they may also wander too far afield and get lost. If too uninhibited, they may throw caution to the wind and act impulsively, even dangerously.

So what makes the difference? What makes some intense babies remain intense for their whole lives—while others at least appear more easygoing? How does one easygoing baby, willing to take risks, turn out to be an innovator or inventor or leader, while another never finds his way or, worse yet, allows his impulses to be his own undoing? This is where nurture comes in, in all of its complexity. Parenting is only one piece of an amazingly tricky puzzle. Who we become is shaped and sharpened over time by the people who raise us, by all the experiences we have, and by the skills we gain to manage and channel our temperamental biases. It's an amazing, even divine, mystery that we know only a little about.

Temperament is a theme you will see us come back to again and again: getting to know the person you have been given. Our job as parents is to find our child's "grain" and go with it, because going against that grain is frustrating for the carpenter and in the end wrecks the wood.

The central question becomes: **Who is this child I've been given? How is she like me? How is he different from me? How does their temperament fit (or not) with all the different temperaments in our family?**

While we often feel acutely that our kids are a reflection of us (and this is why we want to sit on them when they misbehave in the frozen food aisle), they are *not* us. They are different from us—sometimes very different indeed. And we suffer from that discordance. Maybe they clam up, or they never *shut* up. They are slobs or anal-retentive stressballs. They are opinionated or shy, angry or timid, goofy or serious-as-a-heart-attack. They are nerds whose best friends are books, or kids who get an

A in social life and a C in everything else. They are risk takers always up for the next adventure and consequent trip to the emergency room, or rigid routine followers who insist on eating foods of a single color.

Maybe we think our kids should be more like us, or more like we want them to be, or more like what our mother-in-law thinks they should be, forgetting that it is natural and right that they be *exactly who they are*. This doesn't mean we are to let our children run amok. We are there to put up rails, tame their worst impulses, and help them become more resilient in their anxieties and fears so that they can function as well as possible as adults. But when we cross the line into making our children over into our image—**when we get too caught up in how our children behave and how what they do reflects on us as parents, we become what psychologists call *ego-involved*.** Their successes and failures become *our* successes and failures. Think of the hovering dance mom or hard-driving soccer coach dad. But also think of how much it matters to you what grades your child gets, how popular she is, which college he attends. Does it matter *too* much? Does it risk harming your baseline peace or your closeness to your kid? Does it communicate to them that who they fundamentally are is wrong, or bad, or not enough?

We are all ego-involved in our children's character, behavior, and achievements (or lack thereof) to some extent, and for good reasons. Natural selection has shaped human parents to feel intense love and affection toward their children, and to be emotionally invested in them such that we want to stay near them, provide for them, and protect them from threats. Even though for most of you reading this book there may be little competition for actual survival, the cues are everywhere in our society that we (and our children) have to compete to succeed, and therefore survive.

The important thing to remember is that ego-involvement

is bred by fear, and it often leads us to be more controlling as parents. It robs our kids of the chance to make and learn from their own mistakes, to take full credit for their own successes and full responsibility for their own failures, and to discern how those mistakes and failures impact themselves and others connected to them.

How do you keep your own ego-involvement in check, so as not to allow your self-esteem as a parent, or even as a person, to hinge on your child's choices? When we are able to see who our kids *really* are, and to support their natural gifts, passions, and proclivities rather than making them into "our little masterpieces," we are co-creators with God in raising amazing kids into full-flowered adults.

Self-differentiation from our children—knowing where we end and they begin—gives us the filter we need to parent in a way that both nurtures and guides. To put a twist on a favorite parenting metaphor, it allows us to watch their wings grow, and to care for them until they are ready to fly on their own, knowing they can always come back to the nest for rest when they need it. When we love the kids God has given us for who they are, *and* we help them grow into the Way of Jesus, a way of kindness, responsibility, generosity, and love, they will know that they can roam, and they can always come home.

What Our Kids Really Need: A Parenting Holy Trinity

You may be wondering why it's so bad to be controlling of our children's choices and behaviors. After all, we *do* know better what is right for them, at least most of the time. Maybe you're even about to close this book, thinking: "This is crazy. Kids can't just run free to be whoever they want and to do whatever they want without any sense of right and wrong."

Or you may be thinking, "I'm not controlling. I don't spank. I've read all the parenting books and I know punishment doesn't work as a long-term strategy. Instead, I praise them for the things I want to see more of. We use positive reinforcement in our house." But praise in itself can be a means of control, with guilting or expressions of disappointment as its shadow side. Even when you *think* you're not being controlling, you probably are. Ugh.

Just what is so bad about control? Let's start with what our kids really need. As much as we are prone to become ego-involved in their achievements, most of us know deep down that our children don't really need to win every trophy or get into an Ivy League school to grow into happy and thriving adults. In fact, most of us know by now that winning every game or being told "There are no winners or losers here" actually *undermines* our kids' self-esteem. But why?

A huge body of research into human behavior suggests that even the laziest among us are active beings with plenty of agency. We are motivated to explore and master the world around us. If you need convincing, take your toddler to the beach and put her in the sand or at the water's edge and see what she does. Take your nine-year-old on a hike and let him scramble up a cliff to get a God's-eye view of Creation. Say yes when your teenager tells you they want to take a summer mission trip overseas to learn where and how people so outwardly different from them live, and increase their empathy for others in the process.

Self-determination theory is based on the assumption that human beings are born with *intrinsic motivation* to explore and master their worlds and, in so doing, gain

new skills for survival as well as for pure enjoyment. We feel competent when we master something new. Think of the smile that breaks through the stern face of concentration when a baby finally manages to grab that toy just beyond her reach. Self-determination theorists acknowledge that rewards and punishments shape human behavior. But unlike behaviorists, they don't assume that contingencies (such as rewards or guilt or pressure or threats) are necessary to *drive* human behavior.

Self-determination theory tells us that what human beings really need are three key things, all of which foster intrinsic motivation:

1. **To feel autonomous:** Humans need to feel that we are in control of our own behavior and make our own choices. To feel autonomous is to experience agency in the world. Psychologists refer to this as experiencing an *internal locus of control*. To take a spiritual bent, we need to experience free will, be it over choice of juice box flavor or whether to take honors algebra instead of regular old seventh-grade math.

2. **To feel competent:** We also need to feel that we are effective in interacting with our environment. Think of competence from a child's perspective. Give a ten-year-old who loves to read a toddler book and she will toss it aside. Too easy. Give her *War and Peace* and she will look at you wide-eyed. Too hard. But give her a "just right" book that challenges her enough to feel increasingly competent, and she will read it cover to cover.

3. **To feel related to those around us:** People need warmth and affection. We need to feel that we have a safe and secure base from which we can venture out to

explore our world, and to which we can return when necessary. This is the core of attachment theory. It doesn't mean we keep our kids literally attached to us, but suggests that we give our kids the confidence to eventually be independent of us and the ability to self-soothe. Relatedness is part of what allows even the child hysterically crying at school drop-off to eventually be coaxed into leaving, knowing you will be there at the end of the day just as you always are.

When we have these three needs met, we are psychologically healthier. We are curious and competent explorers, motivated to master the world around us, try new things, and know we have a safe and secure base to return to.

When we don't have these needs met, we are prone to depression. We lack motivation, drive, and the competence to do much of anything. We feel helpless and hopeless and lonely, disconnected from those around us.

Alternatively, when we feel that our autonomy is being undermined, we may push back, rebel, and act out, struggling to maintain our sense of control and competence even at the expense of feeling connected to those around us. This is the underpinning of that occasionally reliable but really quite awful parenting tool, reverse psychology. If your teenager seems to feel an overwhelming need to do the exact opposite of everything you say, ask yourself if perhaps you have been falling into the trap of being just a teensy bit too controlling.

Are you beginning to see the problem with controlling parenting? When we undermine our children's need for autonomy, we undermine their intrinsic motivation—their desire and drive to explore and master new things. We also risk having them rebel, or do the right thing for the wrong reasons. If we rely only on rules and consequences without any explanation of *why* it is important to us that they do X and not Y, without involving them at all in the decision of whether and how to meet our expectations, there is a good chance they will meet those expectations only when we are around, and won't when we aren't.

How to Meet Those Three Needs

Are you throwing your hands up in despair? "Another parenting book telling me I'm doing it all wrong!" Not at all.

Again: there is no one right way to parent. But there are spiritual and empirical guideposts we can follow to be the parents our children need us to be.

At the beginning of the Creation myth in Genesis, God said, "Let us make humans in our own image," and God took a fistful of dirt and breathed life into it. That is what we are made of: God and dirt, both holy and essential ingredients for human life. As parents, we are the ones in the best position to help our kids unearth themselves, while keeping grounded ourselves. Just as getting to know God in all Her complexity is a lifelong process, so is getting to know our children. One of God's names in the Bible is YHWH, which can roughly translate to "I Am Myself." From the beginning, God is modeling that we, made in God's image, are individuals.

To parent is to walk the fine line between knowing, loving, and accepting our children for who they are while at the same time communicating our values and expectations, and challenging them to be and become their best selves. Our spiritual calling as parents is to love our kids the way that our Parent God loves us. But we also have to prepare them to live in the world as adults, with enough boundaries and challenges offered as they grow to foster in them strength, resilience, and empathy. How do we do that?

What if your bent is not toward authoritarian parenting but its opposite? Right now, in twenty-first-century America, the idea that our children are gifts to be cherished, nurtured, and loved is so pervasive that we don't usually stop to think about what that means. Sometimes, it is the belief that our children are gifts that leads us astray. Far from needing to rule the roost ourselves, we let our children run the show. They are not just precious gifts from God—they have become the gods. Taken to an extreme, this understanding can risk us raising narcissistic children who threaten to grow into socially aggressive teens and entitled adults. We fail to see their flaws and foibles; we make excuses for their behavior, or enable it, by failing to do the necessary (and painful) up-front work to set limits or let them experience the natural consequences of their behavior (like letting the kid who didn't finish his homework miss the birthday party).

As Proverbs 19:19 warns, "If you effect a rescue, you will only have to do it again."

We *do* believe that children are a gift from God. We also believe that they have a complex core of temperament, personality, genetic programming, and predisposition, which then emerge into the soup of a specific family with its culture and stories, in a specific environment and geography, at a specific time in human history. All of these powerfully influence and shape our children, temperament be damned.

We all want our kids to be happy, and let's be honest: we get a little dopamine hit every time we get to say yes to their insistent need or want. It's certainly a lot easier than saying no. **But ancient wisdom (and a whole lot of research) suggests that if we let the short-term happiness win every time, we**

will make our kids miserable in the long run: because we will not have taught them the power of recovering from disappointment (grit, resilience), delaying gratification (perseverance), and considering the needs of others (empathy).

Worse yet, research on human nature, parenting, and child development tells us that if we veer too far one way or the other—being either overly controlling or overly permissive—our kids will be *less* happy than if we can find a middle way. Proverbs 19:18 says: "Discipline your children while there is hope. If you don't, you'll be a willing participant in their deaths." Setting clear limits and boundaries for our kids is a form of life-saving love.

Let's revisit ye olde "spare the rod." The whole proverb goes like this: "Those who spare the rod hate their children, but those who love them are diligent to discipline them" (Proverbs 13:24). A progressive translation yields this: "If you don't give correction, you hate your child; loving parents give their children structure and discipline." Wait, what? I hate my kid if I'm not willing to be a hardass? And just down the road in Proverbs 15:32 it says, "Those who reject discipline hate *themselves.*"

Anyone who has ever let their three-year-old stay up way too late at a party knows exactly the real-life struggle in follow-through. Providing structure and setting healthy limits is hard work and no fun, but when we consistently apply them, our job as parent gets a hundred times easier. We know that if we weather the storm of the immediate and relatively short-term tantrum, the following day will be calmer and our toddler happier. Likewise, we know that if we are too friendly with our teens, and dependent on their positive opinion of us, we risk putting them in real danger.

Proverbs 9:10 also tells us that "The fear of the Lord is the beginning of wisdom." This, like discipline, is largely a foreign concept to our culture. Many of us are allergic to authoritarianism when we are its subjects. But early on, if we are not "formed" by strong structures, limits, and traditions, we ourselves become big babies, and even dangerous ones. Here's what we want to know: How can I be authoritative without being authoritarian? How can I be strong *and* loving?

A friend of Molly's pastors a large city church. People across the mental health spectrum worship there every week. The pastor regularly welcomes homeless addicts and mentally ill folks as the modern embodiment of Jesus Christ, who himself was homeless and spent most of his time with vulnerable people at the margins of society. But she also has to set limits for folks who trample boundaries and defeat the ability of other worshippers to be safe and worship peacefully. She has a tagline that says, "All people are welcome, but not all behaviors are welcome." This is a good mantra for our families!

Having authority and *being* authoritarian are two different things. Or as Ellen's graduate school advisor, Wendy Grolnick, PhD, puts it, **to be in control is very different from being controlling.** You may have experienced that moment when you've gone around the bend, following your recalcitrant kid from room to room, hammering at them verbally, mercilessly taking your own bad mood out on them, and trying to *make* them behave. You take away one privilege after another: "No screens! No sleepover! No dessert!" And when that fails, you lay on the guilt: "You're making me crazy!" Colossians 3:21 wryly urges, "Parents, do not provoke your children, lest they become discouraged."

Having authority, providing structure, and setting limits for our kids doesn't mean we never admit our own mistakes or say sorry. It does not mean we are not vulnerable with them. Susan Stiffelman's excellent book *Parenting without Power Struggles* deftly illustrates the difference between the parent who is a calm captain of the family ship and the parent who is a dictator and must overpower her children because she has effectively lost control.

Inclusive Christian parenting calls us to a middle way: parent and child in a mutually respectful but clearly structured relationship. The word *obedience* literally means "to give ear to, to lean forward and listen." Ellen Davis, a professor of Hebrew scriptures who taught Molly all about the book of Proverbs in seminary said, "Obedience to your superior is an act of kindness to yourself."

Theologian Richard Rohr says it is probably a good idea to err on the side of being a little conservative when our children are young—to give them something good to rebel against, since it is in our nature to push back against boundaries. Think of the child who wants one more scoop of ice cream, minute on the playground, or bedtime story. Evolutionary psychologists will tell you it is *essential* for adolescents to push back against boundaries. If we didn't, we would probably never venture out to leave the nest and procreate.

So how do we find this middle way? Researchers have identified three dimensions that make environments particularly supportive of people's needs for autonomy, competence, and relatedness, and Dr. Grolnick expanded and applied this work to parenting. We will return to these three guideposts throughout this book. The three dimensions that support children's innate needs, foster intrinsic motivation, and are most likely to help them to adopt and internalize values that guide their behavior are the following:

1. **Autonomy support (versus control)**

2. **Structure**

3. **Involvement**

These three elements are our Holy Trinity of Parenting. Dr. Grolnick describes autonomy-supportive parenting this way: "Parents provide choices for children and encourage their children to initiate their own activities. The goal of autonomy-supportive parenting is to facilitate a sense of self-initiation in children and to support their active attempts to solve their own problems." Christians may try to follow the Golden Rule, but the radical community organizer Saul Alinsky coined the Iron Rule, paraphrased thus: *Never do for your children what they can do for themselves.*

To be autonomy-supportive does take time. It requires being thoughtful, explaining the reasons and rationale for our parenting decisions and limits, and considering our child's point of view: knowing our child's world, and being present when it matters.

The second element, structure, is not the same as rules. Structure means expectations are clear and we ensure that our kids are aware of the potential consequences of their choices. It also means consistently following through on the limits or consequences we have set.

Structure provides a necessary "swaddle" that helps our children understand where the limits are and feel secure— not only physically but emotionally and spiritually. Our limits communicate to our children, from toddlerhood on up to adulthood, right ways of living: take turns, persevere, listen as well as speak, be gentle with the vulnerable ones, be respectful to older ones, be generous, and, above all, be kind, even to enemies (while still respecting yourself).

Finally: involvement. "Quality is more important than quantity" in the time we spend with our kids is a cliché for a reason. Involvement doesn't have to mean being home every day after school until bedtime. It means making sure that, somewhere in that window, you look your child in the eye and ask them an open-ended question about their day, then take time with the answer. Involvement means warmth, availability, and a parent's knowing what is most important for and to their child at a given moment in time.

Autonomy support, structure, and involvement are intertwined and essential. To be involved without being autonomy-supportive is to be a helicopter parent, ever present without allowing our kids to make their own decisions lest they screw up. To be involved without providing structure is to be a best friend and not a parent, with no limits or guidelines to provide a compass for your child. And to be structured without being involved or offering autonomy support is to risk being an authoritarian tyrant.

We'll never get the Holy Trinity of Parenting perfectly right. Remember that "good-enough parenting" means always juggling, and often dropping one of the balls, only to pick it up again. This is what you'll see in our stories in the chapters that follow: our attempts to let temperament and the Holy Trinity of Parenting, together with our learnings from the Way of Jesus, be our parenting guideposts. That, and remembering that there is a much more powerful Parent always drawing near to us and our children.

BIG IDEAS

- To be in control as a parent is different from being controlling. Neither controlling, authoritarian parenting nor out-of-control, emotional, or passive parenting is likely to help our children become who they are meant to be.

- When you're angry at your child, ask yourself if what you really are is afraid. If you're afraid and feeling out

of control, start here: Breathe. Pray. Call a human angel
to your aid.

· There is an alternative to the biblical proverb "Spare
the rod and spoil the child." It is "Train your children
in their own way, and when grown, they will not stray."
Both science and spirituality teach us that our primary
job as parents is to get to know and love the children we
have been given.

· Our children come into the world both already made
and still becoming. Each member of our families
has their own unique temperament and personality
and yet will continue to grow and change. The key is
to be loving and connected to our children without
becoming ego-involved and making them an extension
of ourselves—or a projection of who we wish we were.
We allow them to make mistakes, within reason,
and experiment with their autonomy and natural
consequences.

· The parenting trinity is **autonomy support** (fostering
intrinsic motivation and instilling values rather than
obedience by allowing our kids to feel a sense of choice,
competence, and understanding of their actions),
structure (within certain clear limits and with full
knowledge of the potential consequences of their
choices), and **involvement** (always with you alongside
them, to the degree that they need, so that you can
catch them when they fall and teach them to stand
back up again on their own).

Prayer

God, help me to see and love my children for who they
really are, just as You made them. Help me to keep
growing into the parent I long to be, while knowing You
love me just as I am. Give me the courage to make my
kids unhappy in the short term for their long-term grit,
resiliency, and joy, and for the good of the world.

Amen.

PART II

The How-Tos

CHAPTER 3

How to Be "Good"

A New Way of Talking about Goodness and Badness

Take a minute to think back on your favorite movies from childhood or adolescence. Chances are there was a good guy and a bad guy, the popular group and the outcast, a bully and a victim, maybe a hero. From *Cinderella* to *The Outsiders*, *The Karate Kid* to every John Hughes movie ever made (we have them memorized), Hollywood knows how to capitalize on the human need to put people into categories in order to make sense of the world around us, at least for two hours at a time.

Arguably, the best movies acknowledge that the categories aren't always so clear or fixed. Sometimes the bad guy reveals himself to be good after all, or at least conflicted. But by the time the lights come back up, it's often clear who is who, and it all gets tied up with a neat feel-good bow.

Movies succeed because they appeal to the universal struggle of figuring out the good guys from the bad, right from wrong. And there's no doubt that thinking in categories can be useful. Most schools now have antibullying programs. Many of them give kids the heuristic of "bullies, bystanders, and upstanders" to help them decide who and how to be when confronted with tough choices. The goal is to give them the tools they need to go from being bystanders to upstanders— kids who speak up rather than allow bullying to continue, who include rather than exclude—in short, good guys.

To be an upstander is to say something when they see a bully harassing or hurting a peer: if not right then and there, at least to tell an adult afterward, even if there are repercussions for snitching. To be a bystander is to freeze, to do nothing, and by doing nothing to be complicit with the bullying.

The best of these programs recognize that being an upstander isn't easy. When faced with a threat, humans do one of three things: fight, fly, or freeze. It's an instinctive reaction, one that is incredibly difficult to press "pause" on in order to consciously think and *decide* how to react when under stress. The best programs give kids more than one strategy to stand up to bullying and lots of opportunities to practice when the pressure is low and their amygdalae are quiet.

In large part, these programs seem to work. School-based bullying prevention programs have been found to decrease bullying by up to 25 percent. And even though cyberbullying is an increasing problem, overall rates of bullying decreased between 1990 and 2009. Still, more than one out of five students report being bullied. And this leaves out the more innocuous heartbreak of being left out or left behind by peers. Who are the bystanders and upstanders when your kid isn't invited to the sleepover or your teen is left out of a party?

No bullying prevention program can fully prepare our kids to make the really hard decisions: the ones where the "right" choice is not so obvious and where it's so much more messy and complicated. Striving to be an upstander is a good rule of thumb, and strategies like being on the lookout for the "Double D" of "dangerous and destructive" behavior are helpful shortcuts to making good choices. But in practice, reality is so often more complicated, and the "right thing" is so much harder to do than it is in theory. Even if it seems crystal clear from the outside, we know the inside perspective is often much murkier.

Once, Ellen's Luke, age nine at the time, came home distraught because he had witnessed a peer being teased on the bus (the den of all grade school evil). Having learned all about bullies, upstanders, and bystanders in social skills time at school, he tearfully told Ellen, "I don't know what I was!" He knew he wasn't the bully, but was he a bystander? He thought so. But was that awful? Was he a "bad kid" for having done nothing, when the truth was he was frozen in fear that if he spoke up the teasing might turn on him? Was there still time to be an upstander? It was so confusing!

Consider the following situations with which we all have first- or second-hand experience:

- You're on a playdate with your best friend and your toddlers. Your child doesn't feel like sharing a toy, and your bestie's child bops yours over the head.

- On a family road trip you learn that your nine-year-old took a pack of gum from the last rest stop, now sixty miles in the rearview mirror.

- Your twelve-year-old finds out that her friend recently tried cutting, but only once and the friend swears she probably won't do it again.

- Your fourteen-year-old goes to her first teenage party in the town you just moved to. She tells you there will be parents at the party, but when she arrives, it's entirely unsupervised and some kids are already drunk. She wants to call you for a ride home, but her new friends let her know that if she does that, she'll be friendless come Monday.

· Your sixteen-year-old is hanging out in a mixed group of friends and the clown of the group starts a routine. Your son is filming it on his cellphone when things take a turn and the clown starts harassing one of the girls in the group. Your son has video of the whole thing.

· Your seventeen-year-old saw that his childhood friend posted a meme on social media with a quote about the escape of suicide. They don't really speak to each other anymore and he's unsure whether the post is serious.

Progressive theology gives the ultimate example of a person capable of complex moral reasoning: Jesus. Jesus wasn't a fan of black-and-white answers and often answered people's questions with more questions. He expected them to wrestle their own way to truth, recognizing that each of us has a moral compass that will tell us the right thing to do, if we get quiet and listen.

The Development of Moral Reasoning

If we are to deal with moral complexity with our kids in an age-and-stage-appropriate way, we first need to take a quick look at the development of moral reasoning. Psychologists have been observing and researching children's moral development since the field of child psychology was born. Pioneers like Jean Piaget and Lawrence Kohlberg agreed that kids shift as they age from concrete "black-and-white" thinking about right and wrong, which creates absolutes regarding good and evil, often locating them in specific people or types ("cops and robbers"), toward an ability to consider other people's perspectives and experiences and to recognize moral complexity. Children also, as they grow, move from fear of punishment and desire for reward toward being guided by an internal sense of justice.

The basic consensus was that, until about age nine, children are very rule-bound. They follow the rules because they fear being punished if they don't. They expect other people to follow the rules or be punished, too. They assume the robber must be a bad guy who *should* go to jail.

At an older age and a higher level of moral reasoning, the fifteen-year-old might refuse to shoplift with his friends not only because he might get in trouble with his parents if he does, but also because he knows they would be disappointed in him. If he has internalized his parents' values, he might even recognize that it hurts the store owner financially when people steal.

At the highest level of moral reasoning (which Kohlberg believed only 10 to 15 percent of even adults achieve) it becomes much more complex. When might it be justified to steal? Your twenty-seven-year-old needs an expensive cancer medication, so you fudge her age on your health insurance forms so it will be covered, knowing neither you nor she can afford it otherwise. Is that really stealing? Even if it is, is it morally wrong in a country with a broken and unjust healthcare system?

Or something even more of us have likely done: lied about our small tweenager's age to get the more discounted ticket, so we can better afford the family outing. Is that really *bad* when we might use the money we saved to, say, feed hungry kids instead of corporate America?

People don't necessarily progress through these stages of moral reasoning in a linear fashion. We may reason complexly in one situation and then revert to binary "right and wrong" justice-seeking in another. And it turns out that our kids may be capable of more complex moral reasoning well before Piaget thought they were. **Our goal as parents should be to help our kids learn how to engage in complex moral reasoning:** so they can use it to make deliberate decisions about how they will act in the world, and so they can better understand how and why other people do what they do.

Scaffolding and Using Our Stories

While Piaget and Kohlberg may have underestimated what our kids are capable of, understanding the development of moral reasoning helps us talk with our kids about moral dilemmas in an age-appropriate way. But let's not stick only to the topics we think our children can handle. They can handle more than we think, and soon, they may *have* to. At this moment in culture and technology, it is nearly impossible to shield even our youngest from the constant barrage of news streaming into their consciousness via social media, theirs and ours. They need our guidance to decode what they are hearing.

We can draw on the stories they hear, as well as those they experience on the schoolyard, together with our spiritual understanding of goodness and badness (and that ancient, potent word: *sin!*) to help our kids grow in the complexity of their moral reasoning.

In the 1930s, the psychologist Lev Vygotsky theorized that child development occurs in context, and that cognitive development (in other words: thinking, thinking about thinking, and moral reasoning) depends on language. In other words, **we learn how to reason through moral dilemmas by talking them through—first with others, and later with ourselves.**

Vygotsky also proposed one of Ellen's favorite concepts in child psychology: the *zone of proximal development* (ZPD for

short). The ZPD is the distance between where kids find themselves in terms of development and the next level they may
move to with guidance from adults or more capable peers.

Think of a puzzle as an example. You don't want to give
your preschooler a toddler puzzle that's too easy for them to
complete, or a thousand-piece puzzle of the Eiffel Tower. The
ideal puzzle is one they can nearly do on their own but need
an older guide present to suggest rotating this piece or trying
that one instead. By completing enough of these "just right"
puzzles, they will gain the skills to take on a more challenging
one. From the ZPD came another concept: *scaffolding.* Scaffolding is what adults do to help kids move from the zone they are
in to the next, more challenging one.

Just because our younger children naturally spend lots
of their time in black-and-white thinking doesn't mean they
aren't capable of more complicated moral reasoning. In fact,
there is good evidence that they are very capable (even before
Piaget's magical age of nine) and that parents have quite a bit
of sway over their moral development. We can use our stories—
hypothetical, biblical, and real-world moral conflicts heard on
the news or lived by us and our kids—to scaffold our children's
moral development.

Good Guys versus Bad Guys and the Fallacy of Redemptive Violence

When Molly's kids were young they used to listen to "Mama's
stories" on the radio (aka NPR) as they drove around town doing
errands. They always wanted to know who "the bad guy" was.
At the tender age of two or three, they were already schooled in
**the myth of redemptive violence: the story at the heart of
human culture that says there are two clear sides in every**

clash, one all good and the other all evil, and the good side is permitted to use violence to vanquish evil. There's nothing wrong with violence per se, this myth upholds—as long as *you're* the good guy. And naturally, each of us identifies as the good guy.

This myth fuels every one of our conflicts, from large-scale global battlegrounds like the complex mess in the Middle East, to the shouting match you had with your spouse when you thought the kids were asleep. If I'm on the side of "right," then I must be good and justified in my actions. The myth is the basis for nearly every movie and bedtime story and has perpetuated ancient feuds between humans for thousands of years. No one can remember how the argument started, but both sides know exactly *who* the bad guy is.

The myth deeply satisfies our core need to locate all evil outside of us, in other human beings (the woman who cut you off in traffic, the other guy's political candidate), so that we can feel OK about ourselves. It also gives us a sense of safety. But it's a false sense of safety. As Ellen's six-year-old Jonah asked once, after far too much screen time, "Why does the good guy always win?" Ellen's answer: "The good guys don't always win in real life, probably because it is often very confusing just who the good guy is."

Because kids begin trying to separate out who is good from who is bad at a very young age, it seems as if humans might have come with these factory settings. Could it be God who has installed them? We don't think so—or at least, God didn't intend for us to stay stuck in those early settings as we grow.

It is developmentally important for young kids to ask the good-guy/bad-guy question. They are trying to get essential information about the world and the way it works for their own physical survival and moral clarity; they need to know that they are safe, and that the bad guy isn't coming for them. And it fits with their naturally dichotomous moral thinking at this age. But that doesn't mean we should answer them in ways that reinforce a good-guy/bad-guy false binary. These are the ultimate "teachable moments." Guiding kids toward the highest level of moral reasoning starts now.

Whenever Molly's kids asked the question "Who's the bad guy?" (at least a dozen times a day, it felt like), she would reaffirm, "There are no good guys and no bad guys. God made everything and everybody and called it good. But then God gave us choices, and none of us chooses good all the time. Everybody is a little bit of each, mixed together. Some days, the good gets the upper hand. Some days, the bad. And most of the time, there's more going on than we can see."

You might think this answer is as much an oversimplification as the myth of redemptive violence, or that this might be too much for little brains to process and understand. But it also happens to be true. Think about a couple days ago, when you, a basically good person, picked that fight. Or you took something that didn't technically belong to you when nobody was watching. Or you ignored the person in need who asked you for something you could provide. You are a mixed bag of good and bad feelings, motives, and choices—and so is everybody else. You'll recognize this as a basic theology of God's goodness, our free will, and the thorny and elusive nature of sin, a concept that theologian Paul Tillich put into shorthand as "separation from God, self and others."

Factory settings or no, even younger children can understand that morality is complex and human beings are, too. Ellen's son Jonah, age six, was at the theater watching *Star Wars: The Force Awakens* with the family. Han Solo and Ben/Kylo Ren (who even has two names to demonstrate his two natures) are on the bridge in an epic patricidal struggle. Jonah, eyes focused on the screen, whispered, "Don't choose the dark side."

He understood intuitively that people are not good or bad, but choices are, and so are circumstances. Sometimes people make bad choices because their hand is forced by the situation they are in, or because of what they have learned from our family systems, or an expectation someone in authority has for them, or because of their own biochemistry.

Children's black-and-white thinking appeals to a very human need to have clear sides so we can get out of the messy middle. It's hard to live with the ambiguity of a gray area, and it feels threatening to our survival. But all the psychological theories of moral development share a few things in common. They all assume that individual people are constantly evolving, growing, learning from, and being shaped by their environment and experiences. They are all built on ideas of human agency and the ability to change, even if that growth is not always linear or unidirectional. And in every single one of these theories, black-and-white thinking is considered immature thinking.

Incidentally, the fundamentalist wing of every major religion, Christianity included, is immature religion, because it still trucks so much in black-and-white thinking, separating people into good and evil. The primary purpose of this kind of "fast-food" religion is to gratify our egos and salve our fears by creating in-groups and out-groups, with the out-group at best scapegoated and marginalized, and at worst killed en masse.

Jesus himself did not go in for dualistic thinking. He was always blurring the boundaries, unmasking the "good" religious people of his day, and lifting up society's castoffs as the real examples of morality. His example challenges us to refrain from thinking of ourselves as only good—or ever thinking we know who the "bad guy" is. We are all works in progress. God is not done with us, and we all have the capacity to change.

Here is what we know from psychology, from the Bible, and from our own everyday experience of being human. People have choices. Those choices do not occur in a vacuum. There are all sorts of influences and constraints operating on us. And yet our favorite protagonists are people who made difficult choices and took noble action in spite of constraints and challenges. They are stories of people behaving in unexpected ways.

The Prodigal Child: Repentance, Redemption, and Reconciliation

The Bible is rife with antiheroes: including bad parents, rebellious teenagers, wild children, thieves, compulsive liars, alcoholics, murderers, and the worst, whiners. And these are the "good guys" in the cast of characters.

There is the hero of Hebrew scripture, Jacob, who cheated his dopey brother out of both his blessing and his birthright by masquerading as him to his blind father. It takes him a couple decades to go home and beg his brother's forgiveness.

There are Jacob's eleven sons who sell their younger and favored brother Joseph as a slave, then tell Jacob that he was eaten by wild animals, which almost kills the old rogue. They are reunited with Joseph years later when they arrive starving in Egypt only to have Joseph, now powerfully protected by the pharaoh, feed them and give them everything they need.

There is the classic story of the prodigal son, who asks for his inheritance early, as if his father were already dead, and spends it on booze and women, and when his life is in the crapper (literally: he is mucking out pig barns for a living), he finally goes home to trade pig slop for a clean bed.

This whole cast of characters is there to remind us that

human beings can and do change—and that change often comes as a result of suffering, as well as simple maturing, taking our souls more seriously.

Each of us is beloved from the get-go by the God of infinite second chances, a God who is able, even when we can't see it happening just yet, to change us from the inside out. There are no lost causes, and no bad seeds. (Remember this when your child turns fifteen and becomes temporarily unrecognizable to you.)

This is why we do our kids a huge disservice with "one strike and you're out" policies, such as school policies related to drug possession or fighting. These policies are unhelpful for two reasons. First, in parenting and raising kids, the punishment should always fit the crime. Suspending kids from school makes sense if they have done something that hurt another person in their community, no question. And if it was extremely serious, or there is a credible risk of repeat behavior, expulsion may be appropriate.

But we've heard cases of expelling a four-year-old from preschool for pushing on the playground. Or a high schooler for cheating on a final. Or an underage college student for being caught with marijuana. Or at home: grounding a preteen indefinitely for not being where she told her parents she was going to be. None of these leaves any room for repentance, redemption, or reconciliation. One-strike policies leave no room for change. And such consequences reinforce the "separation from others" aspect of sin by further isolating the sinner, leaving them no way back to the community or self they wronged.

"One strike and you're out" policies, with their black-and-white thinking, cut deeply across the grain of how human beings develop over time. All of the research on cognitive and moral development tells us that human beings are hands-on learners. We learn best through experience, not from being told what to do or what not to do and then being held to rigid expectations.

Kids love to experiment. We are sure that, like us, you have at some point walked into your kitchen to find a kid making slime or trying out a new "special recipe." They don't want us to tell them that baking soda and vinegar combined will erupt everywhere; they want to find out for themselves. One of Ellen's go-tos in therapy with kids and teens is to ask them to "experiment," to try out different ways of solving problems to see if they get a different outcome, one that makes them happier or is more effective than what they've been doing. Teenagers with diabetes don't take their insulin to prevent long-term complications; that timeline is too long to intrinsically motivate them. But they might be willing to try checking blood sugar and adjusting their medication before a big game to see if it helps them play better. Sometimes letting our kids experiment also means letting them fail or suffer the consequences of their poor choices (within reason). A hangover can be a quick cure for drinking too much; a comment about their bad breath from a friend can be more effective than nagging at getting them to brush their teeth.

When Bad Things Happen to Good People: Understanding Evil

When Molly's daughter, Carmen, was in second grade, her school went into lockdown, a precautionary measure after a nearby bank was robbed at gunpoint. It shook Carmen to the core, and in her fear she reverted to black-and-white thinking. Did they catch the bad guy? she asked. Would a different robber come in her house and kill her family? Could they get a gun to be ready for the next time?

Her questions became an opportunity to nuance the situation, to empower her by pushing back against her reptilian-brain anxiety, and to guide her out of the myth of redemptive violence with its good-guy/bad-guy archetypes. Molly talked with her about probability overestimation: how unlikely it was that they would experience a home invasion in their relatively low-crime neighborhood, and how our feelings are not always good barometers of the level of threat.

Molly asked questions to humanize the perpetrator and give him dimension and complexity: Why might he have done such a thing? What motivated him? Was it addiction or poverty? Was it peer pressure? Could Carmen imagine being at the mercy of those forces? And they also used it as an opportunity to talk about unconscious bias and systemic racism: How likely was Carmen to assume the perpetrator was a young black male, even though he turned out to be white? And then to be afraid of other young black males walking down the street? The news and entertainment media have a vested interest in literal black-and-white thinking, where the "bad guys" are often portrayed as African American or Arab.

This may seem like a heavy conversation to have with a second grader. And to be fair, we have both been asked by our exasperated kids on more than one occasion, "Why do you have to make everything so complicated?" But phrased in age-appropriate terms, challenging Carmen to think about the situation with empathy and curiosity, while also reassuring her that she was safe, Molly's conversation with Carmen that day was a good example of scaffolding moral development.

There is also a good argument that age seven or eight (for most typically developing kids) is the perfect time to begin to complicate things. While they may still be prone to good-guy/bad-guy concrete thinking, they are also increasingly aware of just how big a world we live in. As Ellen's Luke existentially exclaimed when he was eight and battling bedtime anxiety, "The universe is just so *big* and we are so *tiny!*"

Second- and third-graders are also increasingly aware of other people's perspectives and needs. This can manifest itself very sweetly in their care for younger siblings, grandparents, and friends. Ellen's Jonah, age eight, washed his hands at the pool unprompted the other day after eating a snack with peanut butter so he could safely go say goodbye to a buddy with a nut allergy.

But it can also manifest itself in a sudden peak in anxiety as they realize that there are many people in the world, and their intentions are not always good. Jonah, who shares the anxious temperament of the rest of the family but is also the most laid-back of the crew, has been increasingly worried at nighttime. He wonders if someone might break into the house, asks "Why do there have to be weapons in the world at all?," and wants to get a dog to train to sniff out the bad guys and keep him safe.

The conversation about choices and context allows our kids to imagine other possibilities when they are frightened and overwhelmed by the world. Maybe the robber that day near Carmen's school was a sociopath bent on self- and other-destruction. Sin and evil are real, and our kids already know that. But it is equally or more possible that he needed money to feed an addiction, an illness that made his thinking disordered and for which he needed help. This wouldn't preclude the possibility of violence against innocents but would make it far less likely. Kids are very apt to overestimate the probability of evil in the world and fear that something bad will happen to them or the people they love, without us counterbalancing the equation.

Talking about choices also allows our kids to feel a sense of control in scary situations. They can choose to look for the helpers, in the wise words of Mr. Rogers. Carmen could appreciate the police who rushed to the bank, as well as her principal for making the call to shelter in place that, while frightening, was meant to keep the students safe. Our kids can even choose to try to do something about the evil they see in the world. Jonah is in the midst of writing a letter to his state senator asking that guns be made illegal.

SOLVE Your Problems with Role Play

Talking about our Christian values when our kids face scary situations and tough decisions can be a powerful tool, but only if we've spoken about those values often with them, and modeled them. Some tools from psychology can help, too. Molly eased Carmen's anxiety by challenging her to think about how complex the situation was. Psychologists refer to this as *cognitive restructuring*. One of Ellen's other go-to tools for older kids and teens facing tough decisions is the SOLVE acronym for problem solving. Here's how it works:

> *S* **is for Select a Specific Problem:** Be *really* clear about
> what exact problem you are trying to solve. Example:
> Your teen wants to go to a party where she knows there
> will be underage drinking.
>
> *O* **is for Options:** Brainstorm as many solutions as
> possible without evaluating them or dismissing any.
> Example: She cannot go, she can go and drink, she can
> go and not drink, she can go and pretend to drink, she
> can go and use you as an excuse to bail if things get out
> of hand. (Note: This is where kids need help and can
> exercise autonomy—put every idea on the table, even the
> ones you hate.)

L **is for Likely Outcome:** Once all of the options are on the table, it's time to consider what is likely to happen if you choose each one. The key here is that **there is no perfect option. If there were, there wouldn't be a problem to solve in the first place.** Each option will have some good and bad mixed in.

V **is for Very Best One:** Choose the best of the imperfect options and try it out. Which option is most likely to solve the problem? Example: Your teen decides she will go to the party and won't drink. She'll pretend to, however, to avoid pressure or judgment.

E **is for Evaluate**: Debrief. How did it go? Was the problem solved? Did things work out mostly OK? Would you do it the same way the next time? If it fails, can you go back to your list of options and try the next best one? Example: She went to the party, but her friends knew she was faking. She then chose to drink, and now she's feeling tipsy and worried things are getting out of hand. But she remembers that you gave her the option of using you as an out. She fakes a text message from you that she has missed curfew and you are on your way.

Problem solving, like story sharing and moral reasoning, is a muscle that needs practice to stay strong. If we weave moral stories into our family conversations on a regular basis—even when they are seemingly far removed from us—and practice problem solving with our kids when we can, they'll have these skills in their toolbox when they need them. More often than not they'll be upstanders. They may even become one of the 15 percent of adults who reach Kohlberg's highest level of moral reasoning! Though we'll settle for getting them home safe—good-enough parenting, and good-enough kids.

When Our Kids Choose Wrongly

As our kids get older and make increasingly complex moral decisions, they will sometimes choose wrongly in a way they come to regret, or choose differently from the way we would. The fact that every one of us makes good and bad choices reminds them (and, even more important, us) that all is not lost. They can choose again (and again), and choose differently next time. Of course, the possibility of them choosing wrongly in a way that is irreversible is the root source of all parent anxiety. And it can make us controlling even when we know we need to let them experiment.

Our job as parents is to give our kids the information and practice they need to make wise choices most of the time, which will hopefully keep their bad decisions from being ruinous ones. We gradually lengthen their rope, and work hard to manage our anger when they make a bad choice. This is not to say we can't or shouldn't show them we're disappointed. We need to tell our children when their choices conflict with our values if we want them to internalize those values as their own. But the point is that we are disappointed in their choice, not in *them*. One bad decision, even one hundred bad decisions, does not a bad person make.

Holding on to this basic tenet, we will better be able to stay calm enough to use our children's own decisions, experiences, and stories to help them wrestle with the ambiguity of right and wrong—especially as they get older and the questions get harder. We can help them forge new neural pathways and think about human nature and choices in terms of gray areas. We can talk through scenarios and situations with them to help prepare them for how they might act when they see someone being teased or bullied or (God forbid) when they are in serious danger themselves. We can guide them toward making the best decisions they can and to know to ask for help when the best choice isn't clear.

We need both real and imaginative practice to prepare us to be able to overcome that fight/flight/freeze response. This is the reason we've all seen the "tips and tools for intervening" if we see someone being harassed. We know we can't rehearse every difficult decision our kids will face ahead of its happening. We also know that the toughest decisions don't have a clear-cut right-and-wrong answer. What we need are tools to guide our kids when we aren't there.

If we had a magic wand, one of its parenting powers would be to ensure that our children make the "right" decision every time, especially as the questions, situations, and decisions get harder and scarier. But child development research tells us that if we want to raise truly moral humans, they need to be able to think, reason, *and* sometimes make mistakes.

There's a basic tenet of psychology that tells us, "The best predictor we have of future behavior is past behavior." But here's the rub: even past behavior is a very poor predictor.

First: past behavior is a better predictor of future behavior in the *short* term than it is over the long term. For example: parents of toddlers, the likelihood that your three-year-old will throw another tantrum next week is much greater than the likelihood he will throw one when he is thirteen. (Though it's not impossible.) Which is just to say: people do change.

Second: high-frequency habitual behaviors (e.g., behaviors that happen a lot) are more predictive than low-frequency behaviors. If your fifteen-year-old just plagiarized an essay for the first time, she is not a chronic cheater . . . yet. This is why Ellen often finds herself steering anxious parents *away* from therapy. It's when bad behavior becomes a pattern that parents might need to worry. If your toddler hits her baby brother now and then, don't worry too much. But if it's every day multiple times a day, worry more.

Third, and most important: past behavior predicts future behavior best when it happens in a moral vacuum. A person is far less likely to make the same "bad" choice again in the future if they have gotten negative or corrective feedback about their decision. Giving calm, rational corrective feedback about poor decisions is critical to the job description of parent. Remember Proverbs 19:18: "Discipline your children while there is hope. If you don't, you'll be a willing participant in their deaths."

What It Really Means to Sin . . . and to Apologize

The popular books *Masterminds and Wingmen* and *Queen Bees and Wannabes* (which Tina Fey turned into the hilarious movie *Mean Girls*—watch it with your tweenagers as part of their formal training in emotional intelligence) have given us important archetypes for understanding our children as social creatures. Unfortunately, the catchy titles of Rosalind Wiseman's books have been co-opted so that even parents label kids—*mean girl, queen bee, wingman, lax bro*. Wiseman never meant for these to be understood as fixed identities. The major developmental task of adolescence is identity formation. Trying on social roles is part of this formation as they figure out not so much *who* they want to be but *how* they want to be in the world.

When Luke came off the bus the day of the bullying incident, confused whether he was an upstander or a bystander, he wasn't so much worried he had made a bad decision. He worried he was marked for life (or at least for the rest of grade school). Here's an even better example. About a year after that, Ellen got the dreaded call from the principal. There had been

another incident on the bus. Luke and a friend had been repeat-
edly teasing another boy about his hearing impairment. The
nature and repetition of the teasing fit the school's definition
of "bullying."

There was no doubt this time. Luke was the bully. Ellen did
not follow her own advice. She did not stay calm. She did not
focus on the behavior rather than on her child. She feared all
was lost. She had raised a mean kid. Worse than the bystander
he had been at nine, at ten he was a bully. Where had she gone
wrong? She lectured Luke on all the people he loved with disability or difference, reminded him about all the kids she works
with in her practice.

Then Luke burst into tears. The words tumbled out in a
rush to explain that the teasing on the bus was rampant. Everyone was teasing and being teased. This group of ten-year-old
boys were trying to be funny. But they hadn't yet learned where
funny crosses the line into mean, or how to stop themselves
when they were over the line. Luke was being teased, too, for
a physical attribute he was quite sensitive about. He had said
what he said about the other boy's hearing to deflect attention
from himself, and he picked up on the first difference he noticed. His choice to deflect deeply hurt the boy, but it hurt Luke,
too, and Ellen. Remember, sin doesn't just separate us from
God and others—it separates us from our best selves. Luke de-
nied the self he was when he made a choice to target another
boy in order to protect himself. He sinned against the boy. He
sinned against the self God made him to be. And he sinned
against Ellen, who raised him to treat people respectfully.

The thing about sin is: It's something we do (or fail to do).
It's not who we are. We believe in a God of infinite second
chances, a God who is working on us to be people of courage
and character and who will keep working on us until the day
we die. Although Ellen started the conversation with guilt and

recrimination because of her own fear and shame, God entered the space with them, giving both Luke and Ellen the gift of tears, giving Luke the humility to come clean about his own fear and suffering, and giving them both a chance to respond differently next time.

Labeling our own or other people's children denies them the opportunity to take chances, to explore alternative identities, to try harder or differently next time. Our kids intuitively know this. They often try to tell us. Have you ever told your fifteen-year-old that you worry a particular friend of his might be a "bad influence"? And had him argue with you? It's not because he wants to go out and graffiti underpasses with his new friend (well, maybe that, too). It's because he knows that even if the friend is prone to bad decisions, he is able to see so much more in him.

If we claim to know who our kids and their friends are, it limits the possibilities of who they can become, by constructing the false reality that people can't change. And perhaps the greatest sin we can commit is the sin of certainty: more specifically, the certainty that people can't grow and learn. It puts us in the place of God, the only One who is really aware of every possibility and reality.

In the Bible, one of Jesus's followers starts a conversation by asking, "Good teacher, what must I do to deserve eternal life?" The asker, who happens to be young, rich, and powerful, is clearly trying to butter up Jesus. But Jesus turns the tables on the schmoozer and says, "Why do you call me good? No one is good but God alone."

No one is good but God alone. Jesus uses hyperbole to make his point: stop trying to be perfect. There's no such thing when it comes to human beings. Ironically, thinking we *can* be perfect leads us into the quicksand of hubris. And believing our children can be perfect sets them up for stress and anxiety, and even worse, for lying to us when they know they have failed to live up to our stringent expectations.

When Rafe was thirteen, he told Molly that there was a boy at his school who had poor hygiene. Rafe, because he sometimes mistakes Molly for a peer, tried to get a laugh out of her by sharing that he would mumble in a British accent, every time he walked by the boy, "Cheese, Gromit!"

Molly didn't laugh. She told Rafe in no uncertain terms that his behavior was unkind. His behavior was bullying and he should know better, because he'd been bullied himself. She reminded him that thirteen-year-old boys are among those most vulnerable to depression and suicidal thoughts, and who knows how Rafe may have fueled the boy's fragile mental health. (Molly may have overdone it just a tad.) Rafe began backtracking, moving back into "good guy" mode: "I didn't actually *say* 'Cheese, Gromit,' I just *thought* it."

He went to his room and lay down. Molly followed him in a few minutes later, and started in on him again: she was worried about this boy she didn't even know, and, to be totally honest, she was worshipping the golden calf of her own idea that her children would embody kindness perfectly, following their mother's lead (cue laughter).

Then Rafe surprised Molly: He said, "Mom, I've been lying here praying for that boy. I've been praying that he didn't hear me, that I didn't do him harm." Here was a kid who could admit when he was wrong even when his mother desperately needed him to be right.

We are so grateful that our kids give us second chances (and ninety-ninth chances) to be the kind of parents who, like God, (1) love (and see) them just as they are, (2) love them too much to let them stay that way, and (3) make it safe to mess up, admit the mess-up, and do better next time.

It matters to our kids that we think well of them. We can

dial down our own emotional response to their behavior (especially disappointment and anger) and make time and space for them to be wholly truthful and to work this stuff out with us. Or we can blame, shame, deny, or shut down. Anger and disappointment may be great short-term strategies for gaining your child's compliance, but they do not, in the long haul, build the kind of moral discernment, emotional intelligence, and sense of self that will grow them into healthy adults.

We parents would do well, too, to remember how good it feels, temporarily, to get the cheap laugh at someone else's expense. Or to gossip about someone to feel aligned with another, more powerful peer. Who among us hasn't done it? We may have been nerds and social pariahs ourselves in junior high. But if we'd been able to, if we'd known how to play the game, we probably would have gone the cheap route as much as the next mean girl. It's human nature, and also a key result of our kids' impulsivity and lack of frontal lobe development.

It's our job to remind our kids—gently, with curiosity and questions more than judgment and declarative sentences—what the consequences of their unkindness might be. To talk about the gray area of goodness and badness, about their responsibility to own and acknowledge their advantages and their mistakes. We can and should tell them that we know they won't always do the right thing. We can also remind them, and ourselves, that more often than not the right thing is not only harder but also infinitely complex. There is *so* much more gray than black or white in the world.

You, your children, and everybody else, including that kid who has been mean to your kid, are wildly imperfect. And God loves us all anyhow. God couldn't love us any better. We have already been approved, not for what we have done but just because we *are*.

But that doesn't mean we can't do better. Saint Maya Angelou said, "I did then what I knew how to do. Now that I know better, I do better." This is where the power of redemption enters in: a loaded concept often annexed by fundamentalists that progressive Christians can reclaim for ourselves. The word *repentance* is derived from the Greek word *metanoia*, which means a change of one's mind. Repentance literally means "to turn oneself around, to get a new perspective."

The Shadow Side of Projection and the Power of Amends

We want to take you on a scary carnival ride for a moment. Imagine you parent a sweet, mostly obedient eight-year-old. Now imagine a decade has gone by: your child is now eighteen and in the throes of a raging heroin addiction. How did this happen to your child? How did you not know?

Statistically speaking, it will happen to some of our children, unless there is a dramatic sea change in how we treat the public health crisis of addiction in our society. Maybe they began using drugs as a way of self-medicating against teenage depression. Or as a sanctioned way to treat a sports injury. Maybe it started as a fun thing in their peer group, and their particular biochemistry ran away with them. Now the illness of their addiction, which does not in itself make them bad kids, is making them do bad things: they are lying to you and stealing from you. Your child has become unrecognizable, both physically and spiritually.

They may get sober. With the right help, with tough love and good boundaries, with smart treatment and some luck and blessing, they will be restored to themselves, and to you. Yet, once again, the statistics are scary. Most addicts will relapse. It takes opioid addicts an average of four to five times to get clean. This means it takes some just once and others ten times. We can't know who is who, but we can hope and pray for the turning to happen.

Sometimes our kids come by their inability to see the world in shades of gray honestly: they learn it from us. Molly has worked with many families who have struggled with addiction. One of the most sinister agents at work against such a family's recovery is black-and-white thinking. It works in one of two ways. When parents are unwilling to see any ill in their child, when their child is a "good guy," parents feed the addiction by enabling it. They believe lies, cover up theft, give in, and give up. Because they have to project a pretty picture to the world, they can't openly talk about what they are going through and thereby call on resources outside themselves, which are absolutely necessary for their child's recovery. When parents get fed up with the cascade of bad behavior arising from the illness of addiction, they may commit the opposite mistake: cutting off their child, kicking them out of the house, and/or severing from them emotionally.

This kind of black-and-white thinking is not confined to addiction but to any way our kids disappoint us or fail to fulfill our expectations about academic success, sexual behavior, or social behavior. Whether we project "good kid" or "bad kid" onto our child, we are limiting our kids' ability to grow, change, make mistakes, genuinely apologize, and be changed.

Kids learn from personal experience; they also learn from our example. Are we ourselves victims of black-and-white thinking? Are we able to admit our own mistakes to or in front of our children; to exhibit remorse, make apologies, vow to do better—and then change?

Have you ever said to your child, "I'm sorry I yelled. That's not a kind or respectful way to speak to you. Can we get a redo?" It may be a blow to our egos to say this out loud. We may feel as if we are relinquishing authority when we do this. But what we are relinquishing is authoritarianism, which makes our kids only *more* rebellious, not less. Instead of painting us into the corner of "my way or the highway because I said so" parenting, our capacity to acknowledge our own mistakes demonstrates and models respect for our kids, the respect we ask them to give us and others. **They are not peers, but they are equals in the sight of God.**

Apologizing is a kind of superpower. It makes us vulnerable, but in its vulnerability there is a curious strength, as we own our humanness rather than go into denial and ego-protective mode. Asking for forgiveness and making amends to our kids when we mess up has the corollary benefit of helping us forgive ourselves for our parenting fails. No longer do we need to protect or defend our parenting ego, an exhausting and chronic chore. We can surrender to our own humanness, as we demonstrate both the reality of imperfection and the power in repenting, redeeming, and trying to change.

Enough about Badness. What about Goodness? The Cultivation of Empathy

We've been talking a lot about badness, but teaching our kids to be "good" is not just about teaching them how to avoid being "bad."

Jesus asked us not to judge and not to hate. But it's not enough not to hate. He asked us, in fact, to *love*—even our enemies. Martin Luther King, Jr., said the best way to destroy our enemies is to turn them into friends. For us grizzled old adults, this sounds near-miraculous. But we've all seen how quickly and easily young children perform this deft magic: yesterday's playground nemesis is today's bestie. This is a skill we can support and foster in them.

We do this not by encouraging them to sweep slights or differences under the rug or by trading away core values for acceptance, which is a cheap form of friendship, but by actively cultivating their capacity for kindness and their powers of empathy, which are learned.

Empathy is governed by the brain's frontal lobe, which is woefully underdeveloped in young humans, and doesn't fully mature until about age twenty-five. Until then, kids count on us to be their frontal lobes and to help them actively practice empathy even when it doesn't come naturally.

The good news, though, is that much earlier in childhood, around the time that kids start moving out of black-and-white thinking at age eight, they also start being able to notice and hear the stories of others: they begin to be able to be empathetic. In fact, as early as birth, those neural pathways start to form. Research psychologist Paul Bloom did a fun experiment: putting a toddler in a room with an adult who pretended to struggle to open the door. The toddler came to the stranger's aid.

By encouraging kids to widen their perspective, as Ellen did with Luke regarding the bus behaviors, or Molly with Carmen and the robber, or with Rafe and the "Cheese, Gromit" boy, we are cultivating baseline empathic thinking. We can engage in this kind of imaginative, empathic thinking about others when driving in traffic (beats cursing at other drivers!), or when reviewing the characters and events from school that day. We can wonder aloud about alternatives to the stories and judgments we automatically make when thinking about others.

Parenting guru and vulnerability diva Glennon Doyle gave us the simplest and best tool for raising kind kids: be kinder yourself. They are watching us, and listening to how we talk about our mother-in-law with our spouse, or other moms with our best friend on the phone.

A note: being kind and being "good" does not mean always being nice, or compliant, or a doormat. **Oftentimes, setting boundaries is the only way to preserve kindness in our relationships.** Being "good" in the way of Jesus can mean making waves against injustice, or doing some hard truth-telling.

Let's make sure our kids know what "being good" means to us, their parents, because we have a lot of competition when teaching our kids about goodness. Their coach might equate goodness with competition and winning. Incessant advertising will tell them buying things will make them better. And your grumpy great-uncle may ask your spirited and autonomous child every Christmas if they are good (read: silent and perfectly compliant) before attempting to plant on them a wet and unwelcome kiss.

If your child knows that what you mean by *goodness* is kindness, or patience, or peacefulness, or generosity, or self-respect, they have a head start on values clarification in a confusing culture, which will help them hold their own over the long haul.

There's guidance from the Bible here, too. The book of Galatians (5:22–23) cites the "fruit of the Spirit" as love, joy, peace, patience, kindness, goodness, faithfulness, gentleness, and self-control. For a fun song to help your kids internalize these values, listen to Rev. Bryan Sirchio's album *Bugs for Lunch*. Or check out this summary of the Ten Commandments, in kid-speak, from Godly Play, a Montessori-based religious education curriculum:

THE TEN BEST WAYS TO LIVE
Love God. Love people. God loves us.
1. Don't serve other gods.
2. Make no idols to worship.
3. Be serious when you say my name.
4. Keep the sabbath holy.

5. Honor your mother and father.
6. Don't kill.
7. Don't break your marriage (kids will love holding us accountable for this one).
8. Don't steal.
9. Don't lie.
10. Don't even want what others have.

Moral Reasoning by Ages and Stages

So what might these scaffolding conversations look like with kids at different ages and stages? How do you talk with your four-year-old about the bad guy on the news without scaring her, or with your middle schooler about the Holocaust in a way that empowers him instead of overwhelms him? What do you say without saying too much?

The Preschooler

Preschoolers are super concrete thinkers and are also about the most self-centered people on earth. On top of that, their vocabulary is probably pretty limited. Your job is to scaffold the skills of complex (gray-area) thinking, language, and empathy, but keep it pretty simple. **What might seem like platitudes or silly mantras now are setting them up for a moral worldview later.** Rafe and Carmen knew the phrases "We're all good and bad mixed together" and "God made everybody and everything good" from Molly well before they could fully understand them. But the words were there for them when the concept and meaning behind them became more clear.

Remind your preschooler that "People aren't good or bad, choices are." **Focus on actions: theirs and other people's.**

Point out the impact of their actions on others. "It is not nice to take Tommy's toy without asking because he was still playing with it." Focus on behaviors rather than concepts. A wise pre-school teacher taught Ellen to focus on encouraging toddlers to "take turns" rather than to "share." The first makes a lot more sense to a three-year-old because it tells her what to do. And it allows her to hold on to some of her developmentally ap-propriate selfishness, knowing she will get the toy back again.

You will want to shield preschool-age kids from news as much as possible, but they are going to know or hear about bad things happening in the world. **Follow their lead.** Don't answer questions they don't ask. Give them Mr. Rogers's advice to "look for the helpers" in any scary or uncertain situation. The reason so many preschoolers want to be police officers or firefighters is that the received wisdom they have from domi-nant culture is that those are the people in control, who know what to do and whose job it is to protect others. (For excellent writing about how to talk to kids about policing and institu-tional racism, see the resources section on our website, www .blessthismessparenting.com.)

The Grade Schooler

Grade schoolers are in what psychologists often refer to as the *latency period* of development. In general, this means grade-school-age kids are generally much easier to contend with than toddlers or adolescents with their intense mood swings and proclivity for being oppositional.

But when it comes to moral reasoning, grade schoolers may struggle the most. They can flip very quickly from concrete thinking based on fear of punishment or a desire to lock up all the bad guys, to the ability to reason more complexly, and back again. Remember, these are the kids who are beginning to understand just how big, wonderful, and scary the world is. They are also increasingly aware of other concepts, like the permanence of death, that can make even "bad decisions" terrifying in their potential consequences.

Some of the same concepts applied to preschoolers continue to apply to this age group, just expanded upon. Try to limit their exposure to news, but also use what news and events they are aware of to wonder together about the choices people make, and what might lead them to make "bad" decisions. **Wonder together about the alternatives people might have had and might even have chosen if given the chance.** Remind them that while bad things do happen all the time, many more good things happen in a day than bad. Point out the good and the helpers.

Answer only the questions they ask, and give them opportunities to talk. As much as you may be dying to get them to bed so you can watch a show or have a glass of wine or finally talk with your partner for more than five seconds at a stretch, lie down with them at bedtime when they ask. From a developmental perspective, grade schoolers' nighttime fears are totally justified. Allowing them to express what they are thinking opens up opportunities to scaffold their moral development.

While grade schoolers fear punishment, they are generally terrible liars. When you catch them in a "bad" behavior or choice, give them the chance to fess up and make amends. Help them think through how they might do things differently in the future, and **remind them that you love them unconditionally, even when you disapprove of their actions.** Remind them that the consequences will always be worse if they lie than if they come clean when asked or caught. And then follow through on consequences. When your child takes the tablet to play video games after bedtime *and* lies about it, they might lose screens for four days instead of two.

The Middle Schooler

By middle school, many tweens will move on from the fear and uncertainty of grade school morality and saddle right up on a high ethical horse. They may come home from school accusing a teacher of being racist, or accuse you of being sexist, narrow-minded, and "totally missing the point." While it can be awesome to see your child fired up about social justice, they probably still need you to help nuance their thinking.

Middle schoolers are very skilled at imagining another person's perspective or motives, but they aren't yet very good at getting them right. They may have difficulty coming up with more than one explanation for a person's behavior. Don't tell them they're wrong. **Try gently wondering with them if there might be another possible explanation for the offending person's behavior.** When they accuse a peer or adult of being racist, sexist, a druggie, and so on, help them talk instead about the person's choices and actions. Ask them to consider what might help the person change their behavior, and if there is anything they want to do to try to precipitate a change.

This is not to say at all that we should patronize tweens. They bring fresh eyes to age-old moral dilemmas, and there can be new wisdom in that. When discussing the unfairness of female athletes being paid less than male athletes in the same sport, Ellen's husband pointed out to middle schooler Luke that fewer people watch women's professional sports, so there is less money to pay. Luke swiftly pointed out that the fact that not as many people watch women's sports as men's is the result of sexist and gender-biased thinking. This led to a discussion of how he and his peers could increase attendance at girls' sporting events.

Our tweens, like all of our children, are also increasingly

facing the real possibility of encountering life- and soul-threatening situations in school shootings, sexual assault, hazing, and their friends' or their own mental health struggles, to name just a few. They need us to be talking about *all* of it. **Not talking about it is not going to protect them.** Talking about what might lead people, including them, to make bad decisions will help them prevent these situations from happening in the first place. At the very least, they will know they can come to us when they are facing their own moral dilemmas.

The High Schooler

For middle schoolers and even more so for high schoolers, go back to the SOLVE technique. Problem solving together in this way allows teens to feel a sense of autonomy in solving their own moral dilemmas. **Practice hypothetical scenarios so the "good" choices will be easier for them to make in the moment.** Remind them often of your stance on moral decision making. For example, we repeat to the point of literal groans in our households that "you will never be punished if you call for a ride home and are drunk; you will be picked up no questions asked."

By their teenage years, our kids can be capable of amazingly complex and insightful conversations about moral reasoning—from both historic and present-day stories. Try bringing up a news story you heard that day that got you thinking or wondering, and ask for their take or opinion on it. If they roll their eyes at you, offer your opinion and ask them to mount an opposing argument just for the sake of it. They'll love this.

BIG IDEAS

- Most of our stories are based on the myth of redemptive violence: a myth in which the world is separated into good guys and bad guys, and good guys are allowed to use violence against the bad guys. This is black-and-white thinking, and black-and-white thinking is immature thinking.

- We can influence our children's moral development and agency as "upstanders" through telling better and truer stories about people and the world and engaging in inquisitive unpacking of complex moral scenarios.

- One (or more) bad choices does not a bad kid make. God knows that every one of us can change. And, to decide how to be, our kids are watching *us* most of all: our capacity for kindness, our ability to admit we are wrong, be vulnerable, and apologize (even . . . no, *especially*, to them).

Prayer

God, we are all good and bad mixed together. I know You love me—and my child—exactly as we are. And You also love us too much to let us stay that way. Keep growing us up, in every way.

Amen.

CHAPTER 4

How to Fight—and Forgive

As we write this chapter, we both have teenage boys (and no food left in the house). Ellen's Luke is fourteen, and Molly's Rafe is sixteen. Apart from more serious fights, there are the daily battles over homework, chores, sleep, swearing, rudeness, hygiene, wet towels strewn everywhere . . . we could go on. Maybe this disqualifies us from being experts on conflict *resolution* in families, but between the two of us, we have logged well over the ten thousand hours of practicing conflict necessary to make us virtuosos.

Here's a typical fight between Molly and Rafe: He comes home from school. Molly asks him to get chores and homework done before screen time. He pretends to start his homework, but as soon as Molly is distracted, he falls down the rabbit hole of watching idiotic YouTube videos. Because so much of his homework is online, Molly can't just ban screens. So for the next two to five hours, she nudges him, with increasing impatience, to churn through his assignments. He sneaks off for a nap when she's not looking, and despite multiple attempts to wake him up (which may or may not include a spray bottle) involving multiple four-letter words (his and Molly's), he is so sound asleep that he doesn't surface for two hours.

He is so far behind on homework now that he has to skip

soccer practice (which means missing out on fresh air, exercise, and healthy socializing) to finish an essay. At nine, Molly gives up and goes to bed, knowing the Internet is shut off for the night and he can't get into too much trouble. Then, at eleven, the smell of fried eggs fills the house, because he hasn't eaten the family dinner, citing lack of hunger. At least he gets up on time to shower and get to school, but Molly knows the whole pattern will repeat tomorrow afternoon.

Molly knows and believes that Rafe is God's beloved, in whom God is well pleased. If only she could feel as pleased as God does with him all the time.

If we still lived in the same state and were carpooling our boys to high school the way we did to daycare, Molly would confide in and vent to Ellen at pickup. Ellen would (gently and with much compassion) notice multiple things about the parent-child dynamic. She would ask Molly some key questions, such as these:

> *"Where is Rafe's intrinsic motivation? Because without it, he's going to get and remain dependent on parental threats/bribes to do his work."*

> *"Why do you care so much how well Rafe does in school—are you overly attached to his academic performance as an extension of your own identity?"*

> *"Is there something you might be missing about why Rafe is struggling in school? Some skill he seems to be lacking and needs to be taught or supported in?"*

> *"Why do you start in on him as soon as he walks through the door—relating to him only as someone who has to work through a to-do list, rather than as a whole human being who is*

arriving home with his own thoughts, feelings, preoccupations, and stress?"

And finally:

"Why, Molly, are you swearing at him if you really want him to stop swearing?!"

Any child psychologist can tell you that we have to understand what is going on in a conflict before we can fix it. Before throwing a bunch of possible solutions at the problem—bribes and threats, reward systems and reverse psychology ("go ahead and fail English!")—we need to take the problem down to its constituent elements by asking ourselves questions like the ones just listed.

It's also critical to remember that there is actually such a thing as healthy conflict. Teaching our kids how to fight fairly, assert themselves (even with us), cultivate empathy for the opposing person or point of view, and practice both apologizing and forgiving will make them spiritually mature and emotionally resilient.

Before annoying patterns escalate into a drag-out fight on heavy rotation, it's our job to help our kids find their own reasons to do the things we believe are good for them. We want those habits and values to actually stick, so that they will behave the same way when we aren't around as they do when they know we are watching.

Honoring Our Father and Mother: Parent-Child Conflict

The commandment to honor our father and mother is as good a place as any to begin to understand how Christianity can support our parenting through conflict. For most of us, it's the most obvious and common point of tension: the everyday conflicts between us and our kids, no matter their age. Put simply: Why don't they listen to us?!

Parenting expert Wendy Mogel rightly said in *The Blessing of a Skinned Knee*, "if you don't teach your children to honor you, you'll have a very hard time teaching them anything else." But she added that God knew we were not naturally inclined to respect our parents, and that's why God made it a commandment. "The inclusion of the fifth commandment in the Big Ten is proof that rude children are nothing new."

Psychology gives us an evolutionary rationale for parent-child conflict: the need for independence. If cave children didn't learn to fend for themselves, they were unlikely to survive for very long. So, the little cave humans who were brave enough to venture just far enough away from their parents to learn to survive and thrive were the ones nature selected to continue the species.

This doesn't sound so different from our goals for our kids now, does it? Independence is, after all, the ultimate goal of parenting. We want our kids to be brave enough to venture out, develop skills, and support themselves someday. But we don't want them to be so reckless and defiant that they take risks they might not survive. We have evolved to protect them and keep them close. There's the conflict. We want to keep them safe, and they want to fly away—seemingly sometimes toward danger.

This is true of the toddler who tantrums because you won't let her wander away at the grocery store, and true of the teenager who tantrums because you won't let him stay out all night with his friends. It was also true of Mother Mary and teenage Jesus.

Jesus himself was not a very good role model for the fifth commandment. When he was twelve years old and on a family road trip to the Temple in Jerusalem, he went rogue and worried his parents mad. When they found him and asked him how he could have gone off like that, he shot back sarcastically, "Didn't you know I'd be in my Father's house?"—a dig at Joseph, who wasn't his *real* father. As an adult, he abandoned his adoptive father's profession. And though he was the firstborn, he took off and left his younger siblings to care for his widowed mother. One day while preaching to the adoring crowds, someone piped up, "Jesus, your mother and brothers are looking for you," and he answered breezily, "Who are my mother and brothers? Those who do the will of God."

So perhaps we shouldn't feel too bad about ourselves if our kids rebel. At least they are in good company. And, truly, they are *supposed* to rebel at least a little. They need to carve their own path to independence, just like Jesus did.

Here's the rub. **The commandment is to honor and respect our parents, but it doesn't dictate that we get to tell our children how to think and feel, or truly even what to do.** Luke at age nine reminded Ellen sharply of this while making his bed. "You told me to make my bed and I'm doing it. I don't have to be happy about it!"

When parents say, "Why don't they listen to us?!," we really mean: "Why don't they do what I want them to do?!" It's natural and right to want what's best for our kids. But how can we be sure that we really know what that is in every instance? Our children's full potential is still unfolding, unknowable to us.

When parents in Ellen's practice ask her, "Will he be OK?" or even, "Will she ever be able to live on her own?," she responds, "I don't know. I don't have a crystal ball." This is the secular version of her basic belief that if there is anyone who knows the future, it is One much greater than all of us—who has our highest good in mind.

For our children to *listen* to us does not necessarily mean to agree with us . . . nor even to do what we want, but it does mean hearing and respecting our opinions and our wishes. If we remember that our ultimate goal is to "train them in their *own* way," we will be better able to follow one of the absolute best pieces of parenting advice: pick your battles. Our children are *of* us but they are not us.

Often, our kids will remind us of this just as Jesus reminded Mary and Joseph. Jesus was gifted in the art of *self-differentiation*, a concept from family systems theory, which views the family as one emotional unit with complex interactions within that unit. Jesus knew who he was. He knew how he was different from his family of origin in his values and his vocation. He was able to break away from the natural, tribal stuck-togetherness of family and move out on his own, calling others to that same self-differentiation, all while staying calmly connected to his family of origin.

That's hard to do. **To be self-defined is to say "I love you. I respect you. I'm different from you. We can disagree and still love each other."** And encouraging self-differentiation is how we foster our children's full flowering into adulthood.

There are tender scenes, too, of Jesus giving his mother her due. At the wedding in Cana, before he's revealed his powers, his mother (who has had a front-row seat to his gifts for decades) notices that the hosts have run out of wine. She tells Jesus to do something about it. He shushes her, but when she ignores him and tells the servants, "Do whatever he tells you to do," he grudgingly performs the miracle that makes the merlot flow again. He listens to his mother. This time, he even does as she asks. But he isn't necessarily happy about it.

As he is dying on the cross, Jesus looks down at Mary. She has never abandoned him no matter what he has said or done to try to shake her. He looks also at his best friend, and he makes the two of them family: "Mother, behold thy son." He may have rebelled to the point of taking risks that eventually separated them by death, but he feels the love, tenderness, and responsibility to care for his mother that we want our children to have for us as we (and they) age. The takeaway is: do what Jesus does, not what he says. (He was always a little given to hyperbole, anyhow.)

Every day, our kids do things that remind us they are their own people who will make their own decisions. As long as they learn to truly hear and consider our opinions as they make those decisions, and as long as those decisions are driven by core beliefs and values internalized by being part of our families, we are parenting well enough.

It is not our job to raise automatons who do as we say every time. It is our job to raise kind, empathic, mature, self-differentiated adults who can function in polite society—people who make decisions only after considering others' perspectives and the impact of their actions on others, who know how to resolve their conflicts using nonviolent communication, and who know how to apologize and forgive in order to maintain relationships.

For all our griping about blowouts, Ellen's and Molly's households have achieved a basic level of fifth-commandment "honor your parents" success. What it looks like where we live: Our children have their own seats at the table, they help clear and often do the dishes, they respect their parents' privacy and belongings. Molly's kids pause on the steps to the third floor where their parents' bedroom is and ask permission to enter the "parental oasis." They don't borrow things or take money from wallets without asking. They fix or replace our (and each other's) things if they break them. They never leave without saying "goodbye/I love you" on the way out the door. At age sixteen, Molly's big boy still often wants a back rub or quiet talk before going to sleep. And, after coming back from earning his own money babysitting, Ellen's fourteen-year-old still asks to be tucked in to his own bed. For all our conflicts, we are grateful that we have warmth, a closeness that is not "fusion," and a mutual respect in our households that signals we are doing something right.

The Hills Worth Dying On: A Family Mission Statement

How exactly do we get our kids to honor and respect us, to have calmer homes and fewer power struggles? How do we manage disagreement and conflict without completely losing our cool (at least most of the time)? If the rod is not available to us, but we do not want to let our kids walk all over us, is there a third way? How do we work through and resolve conflicts with our kids in a way that helps them grow in independence while holding and internalizing our values?

First, we have to identify what our family values are. Take a few minutes, perhaps with pen and paper, to think about your values: what you hold most important. If you have a co-parent, do this individually and then share your responses. Now go beyond that and ask yourself *why* you hold those things important. Now go further still and ask yourself just how important it is to you that your children hold and adhere to those same values. What are the hills worth dying on?

These are the blood and bones of parenting. Values are shaped by experience, not genetics. Most likely, you hold these values important because they have led to positive outcomes in your life. Or you hold values based on negative experiences: old wounds or regrets. Your power to parent differently from your own family of origin derives from your ability to name, claim, and live out these values consistently—to self-differentiate.

Once you've done your own work, you can engage the family in crafting a family mission statement: a shared set of values that everyone, from the youngest to the oldest, agrees to. Imagine putting those values onto a homemade poster, stitching them into needlework, or painting them on your stairs in a non-Pinterest-worthy hail of nail polish. Corny, maybe, but effective at reinforcing those principles that hold your tribe together, giving you all a shared sense of identity.

The mission statement can be as basic or as elaborate as you want. Here is an example created by a friend of Ellen's and her wife for their family of four:

> *Be kind. Be generous. Be brave. Learn from mistakes. Be a problem-solver. Listen to other people's feelings and experiences. Be a voice for social justice. Challenge broken systems. Be inclusive. Be a helper. Show love. Show up.*
> —THE PERRY-MOFFIT FAMILY

A family mission statement makes tangible the values that will shape your children and family. When you or your children make decisions, you can point back to the mission statement and talk about how those decisions nest in or push against your family's values. Assuming that those values have been mutually agreed on, this in itself can reduce conflict. As your children grow in independence, allow them more input. Consider making yearly revisions. You may be surprised to find what changes and what stays the same at each phase and stage of conflict with your kids.

A Framework for a More Peaceful Home

Now that you've taken the time to hone your family's mission statement and know the values you want your children to hold, you may be wondering how to inject those values into their DNA. After all, if our kids just operated on *our* values all the time—problem solved! Alas, once again, we have no simple solution. But we do have science.

Psychologists know quite a lot about how people internalize values. After all, kids need more than a list of rules to follow. It is far better if they genuinely feel motivated to do things that are good and right for them, for our families, and for the world. To do that, let's revisit self-determination theory and authoritative parenting: autonomy support, structure, and involvement from Chapter 2.

A theory of self-determination called *organismic integration theory* (OIT) addresses motivation for prosocial behavior and the environments that foster it. Applied to parenting, OIT provides us with a framework for raising kids who more often than not behave in ways that are in line with our family values. The framework doesn't rely on rewards and punishments (extrinsic motivation) or guilt when they've disappointed us (introjected motivation). It works because they know and share our values and try to live by them (identification) and/or because our values have become fully in line with their own (integration). It also leaves room for our kids to make their own decisions, ones that may be different from what we suggest or expect but that are probably still in line with our family values.

You've already learned how to enable this framework. **The**

Holy Trinity of Parenting—autonomy support, involvement, and structure—provides the energies that aid our children in identifying with and integrating our values. These energies don't eliminate conflict, but they do decrease it. And they make parent-child conflict healthier and more productive.

Autonomy support and involvement give our kids a sense that their choices are their own *and* that they make decisions in relationship to others. When we allow our kids to wrestle with our ideas and expectations and give them the choice of what to do, how to behave, and whether to adopt or reject the values held by the people most important to them (that means you— seriously, even if you have a teenager), they are more likely to feel that their choices and actions come from them, because they do.

To meet their need for relatedness, our kids need us to be involved, to know what is important to them and what is happening in their lives. This isn't helicopter parenting. Involvement is dependent on autonomy support because without it we can easily trip into becoming controlling. This is the difference between knowing that your child has a project due, taking her to the store to get supplies, helping when you're asked . . . and doing the project for her.

We tend to become controlling in this way when we lack healthy self-differentiation ourselves: when our kids' needs become our needs and vice versa. Maybe you regret not having worked harder in high school to go to a better college, which might have led to a better job and more financial security, so you push just that much harder with regard to academics. Or you played a varsity sport and an injury cost you a chance to play longer, so you transfer those hopes and dreams to your children. Red flag alert: if you catch yourself saying things like "We are playing three sports this season" or "We are looking at colleges," your boundaries may be getting blurry.

But autonomy support and relatedness are not enough. Remember, the Holy Trinity of Parenting is a three-legged stool. Kids need consistent structure. Providing structure means offering information and following through on consequences. Children need to know that certain choices are simply too dangerous, either for themselves or for others, to even be an option. And they need to know *in advance* what the consequences of their choice may be, so that they can make informed decisions.

This goes for toddlers and teens: "If you choose the donut over the toast you may get a tummy ache." "If you choose five beers over one, you will probably get sick." Lest you fear we are promoting underage drinking, there is good evidence from research on teen suicide and abstinence-only education (regarding both sex and substances) that *not* talking about scary things and potentially bad decisions does little to protect kids. Talking about risky behaviors makes it less likely they will make impulsive mistakes.

Our kids also need to know how their choices connect to their values and to yours. "If you hit your sister, she will get hurt, and we don't intentionally hurt people in our family." "If you choose video games over studying, you will likely fail that test, and we value education." "If you skip practice, you may not make varsity in the sport you love so much." "If you choose to drink yourself into oblivion, you risk serious harm to the beautiful healthy body God has given you."

When parents establish their natural authority, *firmly and consistently*, children feel safer and family life goes more smoothly. Autonomy support without structure is permissive parenting and risks leaving our kids adrift and unsure of themselves. Knowing what you think and what the consequences of their actions and choices are likely to be *ahead of time* also makes it far less likely there will be a huge blowup after the fact. No matter their age, we can't and shouldn't assume that our kids intuitively know the likely outcome of their choices and actions. Even if Molly's Rafe has missed every day of soccer practice this week for failing to finish homework ahead of time, he needs reminding.

A Quick Word on Rewards and Consequences

You might be wondering: isn't structure the same thing as "rewards and consequences"? Sometimes, but not always. Part of structure is just providing information that Y will naturally happen if you choose to do X. Structure also requires an explanation of why we expect and value certain behaviors and choices and not others. **The key difference is that structure fosters a sense of autonomy, whereas rewards and consequences risk undermining it.** When providing structure does mean imposing a consequence or bestowing a reward, here is a guide to using both more wisely.

Let's reinterpret the saying "The punishment should fit the crime." That doesn't mean the punishment needs to have the same magnitude as the offense. It means that consequences should be logical—not arbitrary, and not delivered out of an intense emotion like anger. This is structure: "If you find a way to be on your phone in the middle of the night when you know it isn't allowed, you lose the privilege of having your phone in your room" or "If you break your sister's phone, you pay to replace it rather than simply losing yours" (restorative justice!).

For the punishment to fit the crime, you also need to be clear about exactly what "crime" was committed. This is usually much less clear at home than in a courtroom. When you have to dole out a consequence, explain why and exactly what the transgression was. Tie it back to the values you are hoping to instill. The problem with your kid being on the phone after bedtime is not about the phone; it's about disregarding the body's need for sleep, and the family value of honoring the body.

Remember, your children don't need to accept your rationale. We have each gone too often down the "But why?" well, even with our fourteen-year-olds, when we should have learned better. Resist the urge to keep justifying your response. Give a simple explanation and leave it at that. Sometimes we have to agree to disagree.

The biggest pitfall of punishment is that it does little to help our kids internalize our values. It may change their behavior, but not exactly in the ways we are hoping. They may follow our rules or meet our expectations because they fear the punishment (or us), but then revert back to bad behavior as soon as they are sure no one is looking, or when the chances of being caught are low.

Maybe you have a rule-following kid for whom the fear of punishment seems to work just fine. But ask yourself how they feel about following the rules all the time. Temperament plays a role. Dr. Kagan's research discussed in Chapter 2 shows us that high-reactive, more "intense" kids are more vulnerable to guilt when they violate family standards than are low-reactive kids. Catholics reading this book know how good guilt feels. And parental criticism seems to impact them more negatively— often showing up as unhealthy anxiety.

Lots of parenting books will teach you about "natural consequences." Fewer teach you that "natural rewards" are usually enough. Popular parenting culture, though, is finally catching up to what psychology already knew. **Rewarding our kids for everything, regardless of effort or achievement, is not making them happier or more successful. In fact, it often does the opposite.**

Things get tricky when looking at the effect of rewards and

positive reinforcement on feelings of autonomy and intrinsic motivation. As an example, take a classroom of fourth-graders at the end of the school year and assign them summer reading. For every book read, students get a star. The student with the most stars starting off the new school year gets an award and a gift certificate to Amazon.

Chances are, the avid reader is going to win. But when she gets that Amazon card, research shows, she will be less likely to spend it on more books than if she had been given the card as a gift before the summer reading assignment. We've taken a kid who loved to read for the sake of reading and made reading contingent on an external reward. Her sense of autonomy related to reading has been undermined, and her intrinsic motivation to read has been decreased. Even verbal praise has the potential to undermine autonomy and intrinsic motivation! There goes another one of our perennial parenting tools.

When we reward kids for things that are intrinsically rewarding, we actually undermine their motivation to do those things again in the future without promise of a reward. Rewards are not inherently bad. **The problems come from the "when and how" we use rewards, and who we use them for.** Here's where knowing your kids well is again the key to knowing how to parent them. If your struggling reader needs stickers to get him to do the required extra practice, use them. But if your kid loves to read, that is its own reward. He doesn't need points or stickers. Helping your little sister get dressed or your dad clear the table is often rewarding enough in offering a sense of agency and contribution to the family.

Rewards and consequences do work, and they definitely have their place. We often need or want our kids to do things that are not intrinsically motivating for them, and it helps if we offer them a healthy reason. Actions have consequences, and punishment is sometimes appropriate. The problem is, if not used carefully, rewards and punishment may be expedient but do little to convey or instill values. When we give kids token rewards for doing the right thing and arbitrarily punish them for doing the wrong thing, they will probably react in the way we want them to in the moment, but they may be no more likely to make a good or better decision in the future than if we had done nothing at all.

Jesus's Third Way: Walk alongside Your Child

What about those times when the natural consequences just don't seem to be enough? When the cavity makes it no more likely your ten-year-old will brush his teeth or the hangover no more likely your sixteen-year-old says no at the next party? Or you provided all the structure, autonomy support, and involvement you could muster and your kid still broke a rule, violated a family value, or is just plain picking a fight with you. How do we fight fair with our kids?

Conflict is nothing more than two different ideas sharing the same space, often aggravated by a power imbalance. **It's fair to remember that in every conflict with your child, however it *feels*, you as the parent have most of the power.** They know it, and it's why they act out as they do. But our worst battles with them leave both sides feeling overwhelmed and oppressed.

The theologian Walter Wink wrote that Jesus advises victims of oppression to "Stand up for yourselves, defy your masters, assert your humanity; but don't answer the oppressor in kind. Find a new, third way that is neither cowardly submission nor violent reprisal." He was talking about epic conflicts between the powers and principalities of governments, corporations, and massive religious structures, but the "new third way" can apply to parent-child relations as well.

Jesus was a master of this third way of conflict resolution, a way that rejects both passivity (giving in, giving up) and dominance (getting one's way without any regard for the other side's position). This way asserts the core human need of both sides and is very much in line with the Holy Trinity of authoritative parenting as well as nonviolent communication.

A common misconception about Jesus's advice to "turn the other cheek" is that he was asking us to be human doormats. What he was actually encouraging us to do was hold on to our human dignity while resisting returning violence with violence. Jesus's third way helps both parties live up to their best selves. His advice was offered to powerless people (prostitutes, fishermen) for encouragement against the Powers That Be (religious authorities, the Roman Empire).

So what does "third way" parenting look like? As parents, *we* are the Powers That Be (remember: our child's first "God"!). It behooves us to think about the ways in which we use our authority. If you feel powerless in relation to your three-year-old's tantrum or your sixteen-year-old's outright rebellion, remember that you do have, and can claim, your authority for their betterment.

The Holy Trinity of Parenting (autonomy support, structure, and involvement) does this for us. We can draw on it even in the midst of an all-out war with our kids. We can fight the urge, in the midst of conflict, to teach, advise, or lecture—all of which will most certainly fall on deaf ears, or be drowned out by screaming (your child's and/or yours). Marriage and family therapist Susan Stiffelman urges us to come up *alongside* our kids instead of *at* them. When we come at them, we leave them no choice but (1) to come at us with equal or greater force (to fight), (2) to check out (flight), or (3) to surrender in humiliated defeat.

Here's what "coming up alongside" might look like. When

you are in the midst of conflict with your child, at any age or stage, take a breath. Walk away if you need to. When you are ready, come back next to them—literally sit next to them instead of across from them.

Get down to their level and make it clear that you are not there to threaten or overpower them. Then **ask for and reflect back your child's thoughts and feelings** (involvement). Next, **offer them or remind them of the choice they have or had** (autonomy support), **and of the potential or actual consequences of that choice** (structure). Weave in a reflection on how the available choices do (or don't) fit in with your family values.

The Holy Trinity of Parenting gives us space to problem-solve with our kids in a way that will save us so much in the long run: time, energy, face, relationship. Communicating values and consequences helps our kids better understand their own perspective and feelings, other people's perspectives (ours included), and how to reconcile the two when they are at odds. Research suggests that when parents engage in this kind of constructive conflict resolution with their teens, those adolescents go on to be the most psychologically healthy and to have the strongest and healthiest relationships with others.

Make no mistake. This kind of conflict resolution is incredibly hard to do in the moment. It requires digging deep for patience and calm, neither of which you have when parent or child or both are heated. It's especially hard if you are temperamentally prone to intense, high-emotion conflict yourself. It requires making enough room to let your child have her big feelings while you are having yours simultaneously, and then making a little more room for a different direction to emerge. It also requires logical thinking and stick-to-itiveness. We have both regretted naming consequences we don't actually want to follow through on. Don't tell your child you will have to leave the party unless you are really prepared to leave.

Being in Control without Controlling

When he was four, Ellen's Luke was prone to nuclear tantrums: screaming, flailing, hitting, and kicking. When Ellen's father witnessed one of these tantrums he looked at her knowingly and said, "What goes around comes around." Temperament revisited. But anyone whose toddler has ever screamed at them, "I hate you!" in the middle of the grocery store, knows the usual reaction from onlookers is horror and concern. "If he talks this way to you now, what will he be like as a teenager?" The implication is that the parents have no control, and the disrespectful child needs discipline. Only part of this is true.

A parent's goal in the midst of a child's meltdown is to be in control even when their child isn't. When Luke imploded, he was out of control of his emotions, his frustration, and his body. This happens at four, at ten, and at forty. What helps you calm down when you are out of control? Someone screaming at you or threatening to smack you if you don't stop? How about threat after threat to take away your dinner, your car keys, or your plans to go to a movie? Of course not. What calms you down is knowing that someone else is capable in that moment of being your calm amid the storm.

When an adult is threatening to hurt or kill themselves, a psychologist or minister is often called in. Threats are not going to work to calm down a person who is out of control. The goal is to give the person the opportunity to take back control of their own emotions and actions without doing irreparable harm to themselves or others. The clinician or clergy does this by giving them choices. Choices with structure: clear explanations of the likely consequences of their actions. They do this with caring involvement: staying present, not leaving them alone, hearing them out to understand their perspective and the experiences that have driven them to such an extreme. The basic dynamic is the same with the tantruming toddler or the teen smoking pot every day, albeit with less serious consequences.

After some trial and error, Ellen and her husband came up with a strategy to deal with Luke's tantrums. They would *breathe*—deeply and frequently. They would let him know when his behavior was becoming unsafe and tell him what he should expect if it continued. "If you continue to kick and hit, we have to hold you so you don't hurt yourself or us." They would give him choices: "Do you want me to stay here with you and hold you or do you want to hit your bean bag on your own to calm down?" They would tag out when one needed a break, so there was always an adult who was in control. And, when Luke did calm down, they would work toward apologies (on both sides if needed) and reparations, asking, "How should we do this differently the next time?" They did this until there were fewer next times . . . and until they moved to the next developmental challenge. (Remember: we're not aiming for perfection but for progress!)

Nonviolent Communication

This is a good moment for a confession. We have both been called passionate people (aka hotheads). We have each, in our ways, had to learn and practice conflict resolution skills, and we practice those especially hard as parents. Remember temperament? How quickly we rise to anger is a part of temperament, and temperament is heritable. So chances are, if you are a hothead, one or more of your children will be, too.

Or maybe you abhor and avoid conflict, and your child's temperament matches yours (or doesn't!). We each clash with each of our kids (and our co-parents) in uniquely challenging ways. Take a moment to think about how you react emotionally to, and deal with, conflict. What about each of your children? Your partner? Your own parents?

Now that you have more or less identified how the members of your family deal with conflict, what next? The field of nonviolent communication (NVC) has a lot to teach us about the mechanics of de-escalating a high-conflict conversation. **NVC, briefly, invites us to observe how we are feeling, observe how the other person is feeling, identify needs based on those feelings, and make requests of the other person based on those needs.** The ideal will be to meet each person's needs at least partway. This approach leaves room for different styles of conflict engagement, too.

Take your typical four-year-old meltdown over eye-level candy in the supermarket checkout lane (it's a conspiracy!). Here's how NVC might apply:

· Observe our feelings (irritation, anger, shame, exhaustion).

· Imagine our child's feelings, and name them aloud. ("You are frustrated because I won't buy you that Teenage Mutant Ninja Turtle Pez dispenser." "I'm also guessing you are hungry because we haven't had dinner yet.")

· Identify our own needs based on our feelings. ("I need to get home as soon as possible and get this kid fed, in the tub, and to bed so I can have time to finish that work assignment.")

· Identify our child's needs. ("This kid needs to get home and in the tub ASAP.")

- Make a request. ("I'd like you to choose a healthier snack . . . maybe this or that. You can eat it now while we finish the shopping and get home.")

It is hard to take another person's perspective when you are flooded with emotion and feel that your own feelings and perspective are being ignored. This is as true for you, the parent, as it is for your child. But pausing, taking a deep breath, and simply saying, "I'm sorry I reacted so quickly," can do wonders for your relationships with your children.

And remember: you almost always have time to fight differently. Your eight-year-old is using that whine that completely unhinges you. You are flooded with emotion (more specifically: fury) and you can't remember a single thing you've learned from any of the dozens of reasonable parenting books you have read because you are a good-enough parent.

But you can take time to stop and breathe. Unless you are trying to save your child from the burning fuselage of an airplane crash and they are insisting on putting their own shoes on, you have more time than you think. Try a "Four-Five-Eight Breath," great for adults and kids alike: inhale for a count of four, hold for five, exhale for eight. No props or previous experience required.

Forgive Seventy-Seven Times

The disciples asked Jesus how many times they should forgive someone who had done them wrong—up to seven times? Could they be done after that? Jesus answered: not seven. Seventy-seven times. Some translations even say: 490 times.

Some of you are already doing the math on your fingers and know you have *well* passed 490 acts of individual forgiveness for all the times your kids have head-butted you, defied you, lied to you, called you a festering cancer on the butt of humanity (not a fictional example). Luckily, our love and affection for our kids make it easier to forgive them without having to deliberately set our minds to it.

But just in case: remember you can always pray for the capacity you need to forgive them. Stop what you're doing, give yourself a time-out (which, as your child grows, may last five minutes or two days, depending on the transgression), and ask God to put you back in touch with your affection, tenderness, the take-a-bullet-for-them love you often feel for them. Thank God for the privilege of raising and loving another human being, just as they are, and as they are becoming. The Bible says: "Perfect love casts out fear." **Remember how much of our anger is based in fear, the fear that they will not turn out OK, and let your love overwhelm your fear, again and again.**

We will never love our children perfectly, but we can relax, forgive them, forgive ourselves, and give each other second and 490th chances.

Sibling Brawls, Parent-Parent Conflict, and Other Hot Messes

When their second child was born, Molly and Peter realized that two kids is way more than double the energy, because there is each individual kid, and there is also the dynamic between them. Add more kids, and the emotional escalation increases exponentially! Partly, this is because siblings are competing, from the get-go, for resources: food, toys, friends, attention, approval, and affection.

The Bible is rife with sibling conflict, starting with Cain

and Abel, which is to say: if you can keep your kids from killing each other, you're doing better than the first humans God made. Many of us have our own old wounds of sibling rivalry, conflict, and parental favoritism that impact our parenting. This intergenerational family cycle needs breaking—or at least some adjusting.

One of the most heartbreaking sibling rivalry stories from scripture is about the twin brothers Jacob and Esau. They were different in everything, and ultracompetitive. To make matters worse, their parents unwittingly fostered the competition by playing favorites. Jacob was ready to strike out on his own, and passing himself off as Esau to his blind father, he took the blessing meant for his brother and ran away.

Why, do you ask, did Isaac have only one blessing if he had two children? Good question. Do you confer favor unevenly among your children? Do you have affinities for one child over the others? What would they answer? We might have favorites (or at least natural affinities), but we shouldn't *play* favorites.

That said, **fair doesn't always mean equal.** We can begin to teach our kids this valuable lesson in the context of their sibling relationships. We can explain to and show our children that different people often have different needs. "I spend more time with your brother on homework because he struggles with math. But I love reading and discussing books with you."

Our children will fight. It's basic human nature and evolution. But the fighting will be toxic and the hostility lasting only if we as the adults interfere, aid, and abet it (or show favoritism). Obviously, ensuring physical safety is important. But be careful what assumptions you make about conflict between your kids—especially if you didn't witness what happened. You might offer to mediate, but try as often as possible to encourage them to work it out between themselves—maybe after a cooling-off period of separation.

Possibly more so than in any other family dynamic, how we behave as parents and speak about sibling relationships and rivalry matters. Remember: temperament means our children—the children it will take a lifetime to fully know—are born fundamentally different from each other, perhaps very different. They have different needs and require different strategies. We should guard our hearts against even the merest whiff of comparison, especially unfavorable comparison, which can cause deep and lasting hurt.

You can find some great strategies for dealing with sibling conflict with a hands-off approach in the book *Siblings without Rivalry* by Adele Faber and Elaine Mazlish. They recommend ignoring sibling fights as much as possible, lest we unconsciously fuel rivalry by taking sides. We have a God who loves each of Her children equally. There is enough love. There is enough blessing to go around. Let's act like it.

Just because we are grown-ups doesn't mean we handle conflict well ourselves. Lots of the same dynamics apply to our interspousal disagreements. Conflict is natural; we are governed by temperament but not at the mercy of it; we can work harder to understand our partner's perspective; sometimes patterns need breaking and a third-party mediator (couples counselor) can help; and we can use nonviolent communication to identify our feelings and needs and make a request.

Many of us worry that when we fight in front of our kids we do lasting damage. But here is the encouraging thing from a lot of research on interparental conflict and its impact on kids: **the most important thing for our kids is not that we not fight in front of them—but that they see us resolve our conflicts.** Normalize fair fighting—and normalize the kissing and making up (even if we gross them out).

Conflict by Ages and Stages

So how does all this work in real life, with kids at different ages and stages? Here are some examples from our own experiences. Some names and details have been changed to protect the guilty parties.

The Preschooler

In conflict with younger kids, it's most important to be calm, consistent, authoritative—and playful. Preschoolers are (generally) easily redirected and love silly humor that matches their overly concrete way of seeing the world. Jesus was often playful in conflict—changing the subject, telling a story. You can add all these to your arsenal of distraction. Try singing your request, tickling them (if they like it), or engaging your own lightheartedness to shift the emotional energy in the room.

A common example: getting a preschooler to wear clothing in public. Attempting to convince a three- or four-year-old that they need to wear not only a jacket but more than underwear or pajamas on a twenty-degree day has driven plenty a parent to the edge or over it. What to do? We've both been there—often one after the other during those early days of carpooling to daycare!

First, what is your aim and what is driving you as the parent? Most likely you want to have easier, less hectic mornings and a child who doesn't freeze to death. Are you also concerned about what others will think? Your neighbors or the preschool teacher if your child leaves the house or shows up at school in pajamas and sparkly sandals? You have to toss that one out. The neighbors, and especially the preschool teachers: they get it. So, in a calmer moment, explain to your preschooler that you want to have easier mornings with less yelling and with more time for them to do something they want to do—play or watch a show. Acknowledge their perspective: "I know you like to stay in your PJs/underwear/naked as long as you can."

Autonomy support is relatively simple in this scenario. Give them a choice of outfit. Not options you would choose because they coordinate, but ones that they actually want to wear and that meet basic weather-related needs. But no more than two choices—structure. And if they still don't want to get dressed, give them the option of either putting the clothes on before they leave the house or bringing them with you. Many a grandmother will tell you that even the pickiest eater won't starve herself. Nor will the most ardently nudist four-year-old actually choose to freeze to death. Let him go outside for a few minutes and see how quickly he chooses the clothes. There were many times we would hand each other a bag of clothes—shoes, hat, jacket—at daycare pickup along with a half-dressed child.

The good news is that preschoolers thrive on structure. Set up a picture schedule of the steps for getting ready in the morning and have them check each step off as they finish it. Make sure you include their chosen fun activity at the end. Explain in simple terms such as if/then. "If you choose not to put your shoes on now, then I need to carry you so you don't hurt your feet." And then follow through.

The best involvement at this stage is playfulness: "Do we put this winter hat on your foot? What? No!?" You can freak out on them, or play with them, to gain compliance. But one of those two will be much more enjoyable for you, and more likely to meet your goal of a more peaceful, easy morning.

The Grade Schooler

When Carmen turned eight, Molly expected her to start help-ing with chores in a meaningful way. Carmen's size made this tricky. At forty-five pounds soaking wet and the shortest kid in her class, it was hard for her to reach the sink to do the dirty dishes or haul laundry around—a fact she fully exploited. As an anxious kid, she was also easily overwhelmed by the tasks set to her, and she wanted help. Molly found it easier just to do things for her rather than "help" her, in order to avoid tears and frustration.

Yet Molly also knew this was not going to foster Carmen's grit or growth. So they'd set a timer, put on some fun music, and do chores in adjacent rooms, with Molly coming in to help Carmen only when she *really* needed it (and always waiting an extra beat for Carmen to see if she might push through and figure it out herself).

One of the keys here was scaffolding, challenging Carmen without overwhelming her. Molly would give carefully crafted choices of chores (autonomy support), remind Carmen of the positive consequences of helping with chores like more time for family fun (structure), and dance and clean alongside her (involvement). Over time, this fostered Carmen's competence and self-esteem. And now Molly gets to relax and eat bonbons while the kids do all the housework (#aspirations).

The Middle Schooler

We will shock no one by telling you that both of us were uber nerds, good students who worked hard without anyone telling us to and who *always* did the extra credit work even though we rarely needed it. Our boys . . . not so much.

When Ellen's Luke started getting actual letter grades in the sixth grade, his first progress report was straight . . . C's. Ellen wasn't observing much effort at home, and the grades were simply proof that it wasn't enough. Ellen and her husband, Eric, calmly strategized a plan to talk to Luke, emphasizing the value of effort. Why effort? Because their family values education as a means of keeping all future options for a life path open. The plan was to come alongside, rather than at, Luke and figure out a strategy that would result in Luke working harder.

At dinner one night, Ellen took the approach she advises parents to take all the time: notice and comment on what you're seeing, without a lot of emotion or judgment, to begin the conversation. She started by taking Luke's perspective. "We know this is the first time you have ever gotten actual letter grades, so maybe you were surprised, too, like us, that you have all C's." Then Luke threw the first curveball. "Well, a little. But, Mom, a C is average." Ellen, who was the girl who always did the extra credit, even when she already had an A+, was speechless. Eric, who had spent more time in middle school meticulously editing report card grades than earning them, stepped in, communicating the family value of "effort in education" they had planned. Co-parenting often looks a lot like a relay. Remember it's OK to tag out when your kids leave you stumbling.

It turned out that that dinner conversation was just the first of many. Conflict that pokes at fundamental values rarely resolves with one talk. Ellen had fallen into the trap of thinking this argument could be resolved by simply explaining to Luke where he had gone wrong and how to make it right. But Luke is going to grow up with his own set of values. They are shaped by his parents but forged on his own so that they truly are *his*, not simply behavior that follows the rules or expectations when he's being graded (by his teachers or his parents).

There have been a lot of conversations since then, mostly, if not always, guided by the Holy Trinity of Parenting. First,

involvement. Ellen had assumed Luke would be the student she had been, whose parents didn't need to ask if homework was completed. She had been trying not to be a white-knuckled helicopter parent. The couple of times she had tried to "help" with writing, it was way too tempting to shape Luke's words into something that wasn't his voice but hers. But she had stepped back so far that she had no idea he wasn't doing assignments. A little digging revealed Luke was also struggling. Meanwhile, Eric had assumed Ellen would handle the school thing, since that was her strength. What they discovered, and renegotiated, was that Eric was actually the one better equipped to understand where Luke was coming from.

Second, **autonomy support.** Luke had the opportunity to retake a quiz he had not studied for and (surprise!) had done poorly on. When Ellen prompted him to study, the master of curveballs replied that he had no intention of retaking the quiz. He explained that it had been a "stupid" quiz on classroom policies. He had lost points for not knowing the teacher's email address, something he pointed out would autopopulate if he needed to email her anyway. Why did he need to know that? It had nothing to do with science or the "education" that was a family value. Good point. But for Ellen, this was *again* about the value of effort. Luke noted that he valued being able to have lunch with his friends over spending the period retaking the quiz. For him, this was about the value of time with people he cared about. While Ellen could see his point, she also knew Luke had sacrificed the time needed to study for the original quiz to watch YouTube videos.

So Ellen gave him a choice—and the **structure** of knowing what would happen depending upon what he chose. Luke could spend a half hour studying and retake the quiz the next day, or he could turn in his phone and all screens for the rest of that evening and the next for face time with his parents and little brother. Luke needed no time to think to make his choice and immediately handed over his phone.

At first, Ellen thought she had failed. Where had she gone wrong? She went back to Luke ten minutes later feeling she needed to be honest. "I just need you to know that I was hoping you would make a different choice." Luke responded, "I know, but you told me it was *my* choice." Right! The conflict was about the relative values between academics, time with friends or family, and time on screens. Luke had chosen family over YouTube, and friends over what to him was a meaningless grade. Not the choice Ellen was hoping for, but still one in line with her values, if in a different way.

Here's the hardest (and arguably the best) part. The conflict over education, hard work, earning grades, going to a good college, and getting a good job is a conflict of values. Allowing Luke the opportunity to consider, decide, and express his own values has forced Ellen and Eric to reexamine their own. The amazing thing is that Luke's decisions in many ways are a truer expression of the values they were claiming to hold than straight A's would be.

The High Schooler

High schoolers want and need more autonomy and independence. But **don't be fooled into thinking they don't need or want you to be involved anymore.** Parental involvement in adolescence is related to higher school achievement and positive social and emotional development and is a protective factor against suicide. Again, the key is balancing involvement with autonomy support and structure. A gradual release of responsibility works well for teens, as does taking the time to talk decisions out with them and let them feel their agency in the decision.

And, of course, middle school conflicts don't magically resolve by high school. The unholy trinity that causes most of
the fights between Molly and Rafe is phone, chores, and grades.
Rafe was diagnosed with attention deficit disorder (ADD) at
the end of middle school and is working on intrinsic motivation and time management skills. What helps him is knowing
what's coming: knowing ahead of time what is on his schedule
and what the consequences will be of not following through.
And regularly taking his phone away in "microbursts," not as
punishment but as a reset for his brain, helps him to get moving in the right direction.

Rafe has a new best friend in their new town. He wants to
go to the playground after dark to hang out on the swings
with his friend. Molly doesn't love the idea of him being out
unsupervised, at age sixteen, after dark. She first gives him a
curfew of nine on a Friday night. He negotiates for ten-thirty.
They compromise at ten, with the caveat that he will keep his
phone on, answer any texts from her, and be respectful communicating with any police or other adults who might engage
them in conversation. She says the same thing she always says
when he walks out the door: "Have fun, be kind, and be good
to yourself—not in that order."

Make no mistake, the conversations can get a lot harder at
this stage and the stakes seem that much higher. In high school
more than ever, kids need to be challenged to greater empathy
and perspective.

Take a recent example: Rafe's eleven-year-old sister Carmen
is sick. Molly has some errands she needs to do during the day.
Wanting to leave Carmen home but not without a phone to
reach her in an emergency, Molly asks Rafe to leave his phone
behind for the day for his sister. He resists and refuses, and no
threat would help. Molly takes a deep breath and decides **to get
curious instead of angry.** "Is there something on your phone

you don't want me to see? Why this resistance? Why would you rather lose your phone for a month than for six hours? You normally have more common sense than that. What is fueling this?"

He says, "You always give her more. She gets everything sooner than I do. This is the one thing that's mine." Ahhh. Molly expresses disappointment that he wouldn't help the family out, but understanding that he felt they were being unfair. Molly, a middle child, has felt that, too.

Fighting with high schoolers takes time, an enormous amount of empathy and understanding, and a willingness to share power with them. The relationships this investment of time and perspective will forge, not to mention the resiliency and values it will help them scaffold, will serve them, and the whole family, for a lifetime.

BIG IDEAS

- The fifth commandment compels us to "honor our father and mother," but our kids also have a biologically driven need to rebel as they grow. Good-enough parenting walks a third way of mutual respect, between the guideposts of autonomy support and structure.

- Nonviolent communication asks us to identify and name feelings, honor universal human needs, and make requests of the other. NVC can help us fight fair by recognizing the inherent dignity and humanity of every party to a conflict: adults and kids both.

- Fostering our kids' intrinsic motivation through autonomy support and involvement rather than relying

on short-term rewards or punishments guides them
in making good choices more of the time, because
their need for relatedness is met and they are driven by
internalized values.

· Breathe, and pray, when you are flooded with emotion.
Whatever the argument is about, it is usually not an
emergency. Remember that anger is based in fear,
and perfect love (which you have surely felt at some
point for your child) casts out fear. We win when love
outweighs our fear.

Prayer

God, my kids are driving me bonkers. I'm driving myself
bonkers. Help us to breathe. Help us to see each other,
really and truly, as You see us. Help us to love each other
better, and in loving, cast out all fear.

Amen.

CHAPTER 5

How Much Is Enough?

How to Talk to Kids about Money and Stuff

Let's talk about what is likely a tender subject for many of us: money. It's painful if you don't have it, and problematic even if you do, because no matter how much or little you have, it raises thorny moral questions about how you save it, spend it, and give it away.

Shortly after moving from the city to the 'burbs, Ellen was driving six-year-old Luke to a friend's house past one McMansion after another. As if he could read her envious mind, Luke asked, "Mom, are we rich?" Ellen laughed out loud, "No!" But she added: "Wait. I take that back. We may not have as much money or stuff as a lot of the people we live near now. But we have a *lot* more than most people in the world do."

Molly remembers filling out an online quiz to help her understand into which percentile she fell in the global economic system. Molly's husband is an IT director and she is a local church pastor. At the time they owned one car, used. Most of their furniture was hand-me-downs. They did not own a house and still had student loan debt in the heavy five figures. There was no family money in the picture: they were on their own financially.

Molly took a guess about where her family would land. She was wildly off. They were in the top 0.05 percent. It was a stark reminder: by global standards, and most certainly biblical ones, we are rich. (Take the test yourself at www.globalrichlist.com.)

The guiding question here is: **what is your family history with money, and what do you want your family story to *be*?** And just as important: **what do you want to communicate to your kids about how much is enough?**

It's important when talking about money and class to be as concrete as possible with our kids and avoid euphemisms. To do this, we have to face facts ourselves. The concept of wealth is relative and nuanced. But that does not mean kids can't understand it. Even babies have a rudimentary mathematical concept of more and less. Grade-school-age kids are always making comparisons, and teenagers are wont to establish their own autonomous ideas about money as in everything else—and may rebel against you, whether you are stingy or spendy!

By early grade school, children naturally compare their family with other families, especially if they spend any time in other people's homes. As concrete thinkers, they primarily use possessions as a barometer for wealth. When Rafe was six, he grilled Molly about their family income. He insisted that his buddy Michael's family was richer because they had an SUV and a big TV with an Xbox. But Michael also had five siblings and wore the same clothes to school every day.

Molly told him, "I don't know what Michael's family's situation is. But we don't have a big TV because that's not a priority for us. We don't have an Xbox because when you were born Daddy quit video games so Mommy wouldn't divorce him for failing to change diapers or do the dishes. Also: we'd rather you play Legos or read books than get sucked in to screens all the time and give us another battleground.

"But just because they have more stuff doesn't mean they have more money. We actually probably have more money than Michael's family but our rich doesn't 'show' because of how we choose to save and spend." From there Molly gave him a simple, age-appropriate lesson in income, interest rates, cravings, and debt. She has repeated this lesson regularly since then, as Rafe gets closer and closer to the magical age of eighteen, when his mailbox will start overflowing with empty promises from credit card companies.

Here is where Christianity parts ways with dominant culture, perhaps even progressive secular culture. **The Bible consistently—from beginning to end—puts a priority on challenging materialism and excess and ending poverty for every human being.** It's not enough to elect a Bernie Sanders–type socialist and hope the government does it for us. Our Christian faith demands that each of us make personal sacrifices in order to live lightly on the earth God gifted us, and ever more generously with one another.

In the Sermon on the Mount, Jesus warned us not to store up treasure on earth, where moth and rust consumes and thieves can destroy, but to store treasure in heaven, because "where your treasure is, there will your heart be also."

Does this mean not to save for retirement, or invest in our children's college savings plans? Are we supposed to live like virtuous Jesus, couch-surfing our lives away in the same threadbare cloak?

Jesus spoke philosophically and in parables, so it's hard to know exactly how generous we would have to be, and how simply we would have to live, to satisfy his standards. At the very least, it means this: however well we think we are doing, we can always buy less and give more. We are, in fact, called to give until it hurts—give in a way that hampers us from some pleasures and even some things we deem necessities—and to keep on giving until it starts to feel good again.

Apart from the good our generosity does in providing for those in need, it also accrues serious spiritual benefits to ourselves. When we make the radical decision to give away what we have—even when we're not certain our own needs will be met—it shifts our thinking (and feeling!) from a scarcity mindset and the instinct to hoard, toward an abundance mindset that changes our whole worldview. Wherever we put our treasure, our hearts catch up. And social science research backs this up: the "paradox of generosity" proves that people who are generous are healthier, happier, and more grateful.

This is counterintuitive, because we're also hardwired for survival and stockpiling resources. It's why we eat the whole bag of cheese puffs once it's open (what if there's a drought and all the cheese puffs dry up?), and why it is so easy to keep what we earn for ourselves rather than giving it away. It's easy to confuse our wants and our needs. It's easy to buy into the myth of personal financial scarcity when the buzz of advertising reinforces what we don't yet have. We measure our success by how well we are doing in comparison with (how we imagine) our immediate neighbors. H. L. Mencken purportedly said, "Happiness is making ten dollars a day more than your brother-in-law."

Even our biology works against us: the dopamine hit of retail therapy provides instant gratification, unlike the slow, lasting soul-satisfaction of giving that same $75 to a refugee camp or the local shelter.

And yet Christians follow a guy who owned nothing, who said to his disciples, "Take nothing for your journey: no staff, no bag, no bread, no money, not even a change of clothes." When a rich young boss-type asked him what he needed to do to gain God's approval, our teacher said, "Sell everything you have and give the money to the poor."

Maybe we could find an easier religion?

. . .

If you have suddenly developed a little indigestion and find yourself about to flip to a different chapter, stay with the uncomfortable feeling for just a little longer. If you are feeling guilty for what you have and how much your family keeps for yourself, there's a pretty straightforward solution: give more away.

But, you ask, how much is enough? How can I feel confident and good about my giving, instead of living with this constant, low-level, miasmic liberal guilt?

Lucky for us, the Bible has given us a clear answer to a murky question: **tithe.**

The biblical measure of faithfulness is to give a tithe, the ancient word for 10 percent of our earnings, off the top. We can give it to our religious communities, charitable endeavors, or a mix. We can assess the 10 percent on our gross income (as Molly's family does), on our net income, or on our after-student-loan net income (as Molly's family used to do, when they were more burdened by debt and less lucky in income).

If it sounds impossible, it's not. Lots of folks in our old church in Somerville, whom you would never suspect of giving sacrificially, in fact do: college undergraduates, debt-burdened twentysomethings working two jobs, retirees on a fixed income. And if it still sounds impossible, that's OK, too. This is a process. There is a concept in psychology called *gradual exposure*. It means slowly and gradually upping the ante to expose yourself to something anxiety-provoking. Start somewhere. Pick a smaller percentage, or start the family conversation about tithing.

If you think tithing is something for evangelicals, well, it is: right-wing fundamentalists (and Mormons) tend to be more generous than liberal Christians. But it doesn't mean we can't match their pace. Here's the beauty of tithing: every step we make toward that 10 percent makes us feel happier, healthier, spiritually tougher, clearer with God, and closer to Her. And, not coincidentally, the miasmic liberal guilt decreases to far more tolerable levels. Unburdening ourselves of excess creates a palpable shift from going to God with our fingers crossed behind our back to meeting God face-to-face and unashamed.

For the record, we categorically reject the idea of the prosperity gospel, which proclaims that God rewards the generous and faithful with in-kind blessings. While it may have helped mobilize and motivate many people to articulate their dreams and pursue them, it has also been used as a cudgel to beat the downtrodden. "Your business failed? You lost your home in the last recession? The cancer came back? You didn't have enough faith." That's junk theology. It is antithetical to everything we want to teach our kids—that all people are equal in the eyes of God and deserve to have their most basic needs met without question.

The Bible is full of contradictions, which makes it difficult for anyone who tries to take it literally. For example, alongside Jesus's dictum that "To whom much is given, much will be required" is a corollary scripture that goes "To those who have much, even more will be given—and those who have little, even that little will be taken away." What do we do with this? Common sense, held up against the sum total of Jesus's other words and deeds, gives us a clue as to which one hews more closely to the Way of Jesus. In this case: err on the side of sacrificial generosity.

From a very young age, **we can help our kids to distinguish between needs and wants and to choose their words carefully.** This might seem simple. "You *need* winter boots. You *want* a new Nerf gun." But it gets a lot stickier when we try to model this same principle applied to ourselves. "We *need* a roof over our heads. We *want* a new kitchen or a nicer car."

Repeat the "needs versus wants" concept enough in a

household with young kids and they will become the teachers. Somehow, it is always obvious to them. We should let them be our prophets in all things—especially when they call out our hypocrisy. Ellen's eight-year-old Jonah very honestly acknowledges when he is having a tantrum over a want. And he has been known to tell Ellen very pointedly that a lot of wants have been arriving in the mailbox from Amazon. For her. Grade-school-age kids are truth tellers.

Likewise, encourage your kids not to say "I'm starving to death" when they are in fact just very hungry. There are actual starving people in the world, many of whom are children. We disappear their suffering when we use their harsh reality as an everyday idiom. This may seem overly pedantic, but words matter, and they shape our prevailing worldview. Pausing to say "I'm sooooo hungry" gives our kids' brains a split second to think about those who won't be able to eat some applesauce or microwave popcorn the second they get home.

For better or worse, our kids are watching us all the time. They are picking up the vibe of abundance or scarcity. Ellen has noticed a distinct uptick in what we call "the gimmes" whenever the parents are visibly spending money on fixing up the house or buying new things. Consciously or not, when they see us spending on wants, kids sense that there is more money available to be spent and want it spent on *them*. Remember: survival of the fittest (and best-outfitted).

So, apart from teaching our kids to speak about needs, wants, and hungers differently, how do we structure our family financial life in a way that embodies a Christian ethic of having and giving?

Allowance, Chores, and Save-Spend-Share

There may be more debate in the popular parenting literature about chores and allowance than on any other topic—and, unfortunately, less research to guide us. There are, however, plenty of data telling us our kids will likely face even harder questions about money than many of us did or do now. As going to college increasingly becomes the norm, the cost of higher education creeps further toward six figures *per year*. Our kids have no guarantee of state- or employer-funded health insurance, pensions, or Social Security. Income inequality is on the rise, and middle-class wages have been stagnant for decades.

Thankfully, there is sound anecdotal evidence that allowances help children and teens to understand the power and necessity of money. If kids have their own money to manage while the stakes are low, it helps prepare them for the fiscal autonomy that comes with young adulthood and the uncertain financial future many, if not most, of them will face.

Earning their own money gives kids a chance to feel the impact of their generosity, in buying gifts for others or donating to charity. Likewise, kids who have a chance to squander their own money learn about regret when the cheap toy immediately breaks or they spot a better one they want even more. And learning how to save builds their capacity to defer gratification.

When it comes to allowance, there is no right amount per week or month, so figure out what works for your family. But **consider choosing a number easily divisible by three.** This allows you to divide each kid's allowance into thirds: a third for savings (for college or for a big-ticket healthful or educational item, like a personal computer or a bike), a third for charitable giving and gifts to family and friends, and a third for spending. There are loads of tools and websites out there to help you implement this system (check out www.threejars.com), and even kid-friendly debit cards with built-in tools for teaching money management (www.gohenry.com, www.greenlightcard .com, www.current.com), but you can also use an old-fashioned spreadsheet or an actual array of three piggy banks.

In our families, we don't yoke the allowance to chores. There are good arguments on both sides of this equation but surprisingly little actual research to guide us on what's best. We do know that doing chores is good for kids. Data collected by Marty Rossman of the University of Minnesota from 1967 to 1992 showed that children who were required to do chores beginning at age three or four were more empathetic, better adjusted, and more successful in their careers by their mid-twenties than those who weren't. And we know that learning to manage money is good for kids. But it isn't clear whether the two concepts should be tied together.

We want our children to get the message that they do chores because they are a part of the family, and families work together to get done what needs doing, not because they are being rewarded or paid for their participation. We also want them to leave the nest of our nuclear families with the skills they will need in whatever families they create next. Their spouses will thank us if they know how to clean a toilet and do laundry. Their children will appreciate any culinary skills they pick up along the way.

At the same time, paying kids for chores completed and withholding payment for incomplete chores teaches them a real-world work ethic. Even truer, giving kids an allowance just for the purpose of learning how to manage money is a privilege of families with enough extra income to do so. So if out of philosophy and/or need you choose to make an allowance contingent on chores or some sort of work, good on you. Arguably, what matters most is teaching them to manage the money once they have it.

Try keeping the weekly "spend" allowance amount relatively low. Give your kids opportunities to earn extra money by doing chores that are above and beyond the day-to-day expectations. The eight-year-old might decide she wants to wash the car for a few dollars. After completing his expected weekly mowing of the lawn, the thirteen-year-old might offer to rake leaves. Or pay him if he is asked to stay home to babysit his sibling for more than an hour.

On every birthday, Molly's family makes a little ritual around increasing each kid's allowance on their spreadsheet, and giving them, in a sealed envelope, one new responsibility (such as, for the ten-year-old, beginning to do her own laundry, or for the fourteen-year-old, taking his sister to kung fu on the city bus) and one new freedom (such as, for the ten-year-old, walking to school by herself, or for the fourteen-year-old, taking the subway to his grandmother's house across the city). As they grow up, they earn more responsibility and more income, because Jesus said, "To whom much is given, much will be required."

An additional benefit of keeping allowance amounts relatively low and untethered to chores is that, in our experience, it motivates the teenagers to get jobs. Working for non–family members not only earns them money but also teaches them an ethic of service and accountability. Working the kind of jobs available to teens will probably also force them at some point to consider how much and what kind of work they are willing to do, for what price. This is a great opportunity for discussions about what it means to have the privilege of choosing, and what it is like for those who don't have a choice. This will hit much closer to home for some families than others and is a good time to share family stories of strife, struggle, and privilege.

Giving kids the responsibility of sharing some of their money is a way of making spending money a spiritual practice—not just for them but for you, too. It can also give them a sense of control in an often frightening world. Money can't solve every problem, but as our kids hear about global climate change, poverty, war, addiction, and other stories that might make them feel helpless and sad, the ability to spend their own money to relieve suffering or shift the status quo lets them feel that God is using them in powerful ways.

It's a pretty awesome thing to have your eight-, ten-, thirteen-, or fifteen-year-old come to you and tell you about something they've read or heard about and propose they do something to help. Maybe they saw an image in the news of Syrian refugees washing ashore, children shivering, hungry, without clean water, sick or dead. It's still sad and scary, but they know they have some power to be part of the solution in a small way now, and someday in a bigger way.

Consider engaging in an end-of-year "Christmas blowout" of charitable giving. Sit down as a family, with your tithing budget (theirs and yours), do research about different local and global needs, and set giving priorities. Do this right after the holiday, on one of the twelve days of Christmas, to refocus the season on an ethic of generosity beyond your personal tribe.

Privacy versus Secrecy

Personal finance columnist for the *New York Times* Ron Lieber started an online column several years ago to help parents answer kids' questions about money. One question that seems to come up again and again, and that leaves parents stumbling, is this: how much money does our family have, exactly?

Many of us have no idea how much money our own parents

made. We could probably guess, but money was a verboten sub-ject in our families. The implicit message, amid the deafening silence on the subject, was likely "there's not enough." And if money did come up, it was often in the context of an argument between our parents. In New England, where we were both raised, we were told that money matters were private, when in fact, they were absolutely taboo and *secret*. Even these days, a shocking 43 percent of married people do not know how much money their spouse makes.

The question of how much money we have is really a differ-ent way of asking: Where do we stand? Are we rich? Poor? In between? *Where* in between? We don't need to tell our kids our salaries to answer these questions and foster a healthy relation-ship with money. **If we just talk transparently and nonanx-iously about money and giving, we will raise kids who as adults will have a better grip on their own finances.** Parents who actively cultivate a sense of abundance instead of scarcity in regard to money and things will communicate that mindset to their children, who will catch that joyful, generous spirit.

When we were trying to cultivate greater generosity and fi-nancial transparency at our church in Somerville, one of the questions we asked was this: what is the difference between pri-vacy and secrecy? A therapist in our midst said that something that is secret is something you don't tell anybody—most likely out of shame; something that is private is something you tell people when they need to know—because it is information they need.

Society has wrongfully taught us that how much or little money we have is a measure of our value (we even *call* it "net worth"!). Money is a deeply spiritual issue because it has tre-mendous power over our relationships, not to mention our psyche and well-being: how much or little we have, how we much we hoard, spend, save, or accumulate in debt. The Bible says the love of money is the root of all evil. But our fear, shame, and secrecy about money work just as much evil as our love of it.

Jesus heavily implied that money would not make us any happier, but generosity would, and now research has borne this out. It is true that household income is positively correlated with emotional well-being and quality of life. But the relationship between wealth and well-being seems to follow the law of diminishing returns. For families at the 20th income percentile, every extra dollar earned has a big impact. Studies that follow people over time have found that happiness rises as income increases to about $70,000, or at about the 80th percentile. After that, each additional dollar offers dwindling returns in well-being . . . all the way to zero, at about $200,000.

Positive psychology has given us hard data over the last ten years proving that habits of generosity make us happier. People who tithe have significantly lower rates of depression. Psychologists have also found that if we spend money on ourselves, it will give us a small dopamine hit of pleasure, but if we spend the same amount on someone else, it will give us a much bigger and longer-lasting hit. God has embedded a reward for generous living in our brain chemistry, if only we take advantage of it.

In *The Paradox of Generosity*, Christian Smith and Hilary Davidson draw on a survey of two thousand Americans and sixty in-depth interviews to show that there's a direct correlation between generosity and joy. Regularly giving of our time, money, and effort makes us less anxious, less afraid, and downright happier.

What if the reason Jesus was so severe with the rich young entrepreneur was not that there were so many poor people who needed a handout, but that Jesus knew that too much of the man's security and fulfillment was linked to his stuff? What if Jesus knew that, counterintuitively, the way to "come into eter-

nal life," or what we might call the juiciest kind of life, was to
have less, not more?

Downward Mobility and Digging Deep

We all want our kids to do better than we did. We want them
to have advantages we didn't have. We want them to build off
what we have accomplished and achieved. We couch it in terms
of them having every opportunity for a broad, fulfilling life.

But the "biggest life" may not be what you think it is. Tel-
evangelist Joel Osteen built an empire by branding Christianity
with the slogan "Your best life now!" as if God's deepest desire
is for us to fulfill our personal ambitions for money, power, and
public acclaim. Even the most casual read of the life and teachings of Jesus belies this.

Often the biggest parenting tension in households with
teenagers is their academic track record and motivation (or
lack thereof), and the worry and anger parents have for what
this means for their futures. This worry and anger stems from
fear for our children's adult livelihood and also from ego-
involvement. You may have been a straight-A student, but the
fact of the matter is, your child is not you. They have their own
temperament, interests, wishes, and dreams. He may not go to
the best college, or to any college at all. She may, either to dif-
ferentiate herself from you, or just to follow her own holy calling, become downwardly mobile. He may become a preschool
teacher, a relief worker, a farmer, a boxing coach to at-risk
youth (jobs our teens have actually considered). It is hard work
to quiet our fears, projections, and expectations of our children so we can really see who they are with their own strengths,
longings, and path.

Jesus called us again and again to reevaluate our personal

ambitions—especially when those ambitions are driven by or littered with stress, anxiety, and workaholism—and to live differently. The good news is: we don't have to wait until our kids show us how it's done. We can take the initiative to do it ourselves. Have you ever thought about taking unpaid leave from work or leaving your work entirely to volunteer with vulnerable people or stay home to raise your kids? Have you thought about downsizing your household so that more time is spent being with people than maintaining things?

We often ignore the research that tells us that it *is* possible to have too much, because the secular capitalist system relies on spending! We cannot look to advertisers, banks, our government, our neighbors, or even our financial advisors to tell us truly how much is enough, because the answer will almost always be: more than you have now.

The problem again is **fear.** It is fear for our children's long-term security and happiness that pushes us to push them. By now you know the problem with parenting out of fear: it too often leads us to be controlling and unable to step back and to see what our kids really want and need. If they want and need a PhD to do the work that feeds them (as Ellen did), then by all means encourage them. And while you're at it, have honest conversations ahead of time about how much you can financially support them to meet their goals, and how much you expect them to do for themselves.

But if you are pushing for an MD or a JD because being a doctor or a lawyer equals some protection for your kids against the uncertainty of life—be careful. The bottom can always fall out. Wouldn't it be better to focus on teaching our kids the value of faith, community, and interdependence? So that, God forbid, if the bottom falls out someday and we are not there to catch them, they'll have others to help them? Faith *can* answer the question: how much is enough?

In her private practice, Ellen does a lot of testing. Parents bring their kids in to better understand their learning styles, strengths, and weaknesses, and often to rule out (or in) learning disabilities or attention deficit/hyperactivity disorder (ADHD). They also get an IQ score. There is nothing magic about an IQ score. It is a summary score of how your child did on a few tests like verbal skills, attention, and processing speed relative to other children their age. If they fall between the 25th and 75th percentiles (the middle half of their age group), they are considered "average" on that skill; above the 75th is "above average," while below the 25th is "below average."

Ellen finds herself repeating the same conversations over and over: no person is "above average" in *every* skill area—not even Einstein. Everyone has strengths and weaknesses. "Average" in most things is good enough. And these tests by no means measure every skill. Arguably, they measure the least important skills—we have no percentile ranking for empathy, kindness, generosity of spirit. And what human do you know who is expected to be good at *everything*—math, science, writing, public speaking, athletics, social relationships? When did society's definition of "good parenting" shift from giving kids every opportunity to figure out what they are passionate about and good at to ensuring that they excel at every *single* opportunity we give them?

There is good evidence to suggest that this shift in expectations toward excellence in all things has contributed to increasing rates of anxiety, stress, and depression in our kids, as well as *less* ability to think creatively and to solve problems flexibly. Parents with the means to do so (and many without) pay for tutors, extra math classes, college consultants, and special sports teams with elite coaches. Our attempts to protect our kids from vocational, social, and financial insecurity risk leaving them insecure in themselves, wondering why they aren't good enough—either giving up in response or working themselves to the point of mental, emotional, and physical exhaustion.

It also needs to be said that the opportunities we are talking about here are not available to all kids. **When we pressure and privilege our own kids out of our inherent anxiety about their futures, we risk leaving other people's kids behind, perpetuating the same inequalities we are trying to teach our kids to change.**

In her documentary *The Race to Nowhere* and the follow-up book *Beyond Measure*, Vicki Abeles argues that change begins with conversations in wealthy, high-achieving school districts. It is up to privileged parents to create a cultural shift toward moderation and classwork that is meaningful and more than a means to an end (e.g., to get into the best possible college).

A good way to begin these conversations in our school communities is to start talking at home (and at church!) about abundance and scarcity, needs and wants, and to consider what our kids and our world empirically need. This shift in ambition and achievement is about much more than money. Frankly, it's a matter of life and death, for ourselves and the planet we inhabit.

After all, Christians worship a God who in Her human incarnation never got an advanced degree, didn't have a steady job, and died broke (and young!). And yet, this God was so "successful" in worldly terms that two thousand years later we are still talking about Her ideas, telling Her stories, and building monuments and communities to Her memory.

This is the God who can do so much more than we ask or imagine. This is the God who will give us everything we need—if not everything we want—and this is the God who can especially provide for us if we stop trying to provide every single thing for ourselves.

The Currency of Time: What Kids Really Need

In 2017, just over 70 percent of women with children under age eighteen were working. Numbers are higher still for fathers. Most parents need to work. Even those of us who work because we are passionate about our jobs, or because we like having extra money, often end up finding ourselves working more hours than we really want. One of the (arguably many) problems with money is that the more we have, the more we tend to buy, and the more money we need to maintain our lifestyle.

Beyond working to provide their basic needs, many parents work long hours hoping to give their kids more than they had—be it things or opportunities. If you have a teenager in the house, it may seem like all they want is your money. But when kids are surveyed and asked what they really want from their parents, the most common answer is not the one you might expect. They want time: quality time. They want time spent together as a family, meaningfully engaged in an activity. Even more, **they want you to be less stressed, more present, and focused.** Ellen's boys have a common refrain: "Mom, you can work on the book tomorrow. You have to come ice skating because it's family time."

Sometimes our kids ask for our time in a way that makes us feel just a teensy bit bad about being full-time working moms. Like, "I wish you didn't work so you could be home every day after school." If you hear this, guilty-feeling mamas especially, remind yourself to listen for the music behind the words. They are asking for quantity of time with us, yes. But more so, they are asking for our undivided attention, at least for a moment.

Maybe something is weighing on them, or we have been more distracted than usual recently. It's time to tap the brakes, slow down, and refocus on them. It probably means letting go of some expectations and forgiving ourselves our inability to do all things at all times for all people. To do this on a regular basis, we might need to work a little less, spend a little less, let some things go (because the laundry will never really be done anyway), and disappoint some people outside the family.

Glennon Doyle of Momastery launched to Internet fame years ago with her blog post on "Chronos vs. Kairos Time" in parenting, aptly titled "Don't Carpe Diem." It's worth a read if you aren't already familiar with it. Chronos time is earthly time, and it can be grinding. It's the baby blowing out three diapers in an hour Time; the carpool to and from school in traffic with road ragers and a bad back Time; it's leaving work to pick up a sick kid (again) Time. Kairos is God's Time. It's the baby's smile and giggle on the changing table, the sick teen who wants to cuddle and watch a movie with you, the moment when your jam comes on the radio and you stop screaming at the traffic long enough to rock out with the whole family in unison to "Bohemian Rhapsody." The thing is, you can't have Kairos without Chronos. And sometimes, you have to downshift the Chronos to find the Kairos.

Addictive Behavior

The downshift to Kairos time involves changing our patterns and confronting our addictions, because **addiction is a consequence of not knowing how much is enough.** It's a means of escape when Chronos time becomes too much for us. Whether it's a glass (or a bottle) of wine at the end of a hard day, or ignoring our kids or our partner to "read the news" or scroll Facebook endlessly on our phones, addiction is how we escape from life rather than face life on life's terms, confronting what's hard and letting God transform it for us into something richer, a life of meaning, purpose, and strength.

We live in a parenting culture that regularly sells escapism as a means of coping and makes a joke of addiction, on view in the ubiquitous "mommy juice" marketing campaigns, as the acceptable hour for that first glass of wine creeps ever earlier. One year for Christmas Rafe bought Molly a wineglass that holds a whole bottle of wine. It was supposed to be a joke—but was it? "Do you think I'm an alcoholic?," she asked him. "I think you're a *momaholic*—you get tipsy when you are with your mom friends," he answered. "You're right, I do." They talked about how that made him feel—and whether it worried him. He said it didn't. But this prompted Molly to seriously consider how she was modeling for him, especially as he reaches an age when a lot of his friends are binge drinking or smoking pot with their friends for fun, and also to mute their own feelings and stress.

Here in the United States, we're not good at teaching moderation and self-regulation. We're an all-or-nothing culture when it comes to our vices and addictions. Driving through Indiana last year, Molly listened to Christian right-wing radio for four hours straight, while driving past liquor stores and strip joints every few exits. We have legitimate desires and needs—for peacefulness, connection, intimacy, joy, laughter—and have created shortcuts to meet those needs by numbing ourselves with social media, substances, and even religion.

We need to model self-regulation to our kids if we want them to learn how to self-regulate. They need us to set limits, because they can't. They get the same hit of dopamine as adults from consuming alcohol, drugs, or screens, but their brains are less prepared to handle it. The "reward center" (the mesolimbic pathway) of the teenage brain is highly excitable, and the "control center" (the frontal lobe) is not yet fully mature. This leaves tweens and teens especially prone to impulsivity. They lack the foresight to see the longer-term downside of spending too much time on screens now or too much money on a pair of sneakers. It's our job to point out the longer-term outcome, give them choices, and know when to say no.

Molly has a dear friend who lives largely off the grid. Her family has no wifi and no TV. They live in a valley along a creek on acres of beautiful farmland. Her kids play music, make art, jump on the trampoline, and go skinny dipping. They eat kale without complaining. They were six years old before they ate their first M&Ms. And they are happy and well adjusted!

Mostly. Molly was visiting last summer, and she and her bestie were down by the river talking over the trials of mothering teenagers. "Elias is fourteen now, and he's stopped playing mandolin. All he wants to do is hole up in his room, with the transistor radio glued to his ear, listening to baseball games under the covers, eating apricots!"

Molly laughed out loud. What her friend was describing was the hippie-kid equivalent of watching screens and eating candy nonstop. Perhaps there is a deep biological instinct among early adolescent boys to cocoon, to hoard calories and hide emotion, before they emerge from the chrysalis into later adolescence with its greater maturity and deeper capacity to self-regulate appetites.

All our kids have these appetites to one degree or another, not just for screens or sugar, but for treats, toys, distraction, entertainment, status symbols—anything to feel better for a minute or two, to escape from uncomfortable feelings. Let's ourselves learn to practice **how to sit with discomfort,** how to let ourselves be a little hungry, to do without and see what happens next. Resist the initial outcry when they don't get what they want. Wait it out, breathe, remind yourself of the goal: a calmer, quieter, hopefully happier home, and kids who understand that their capacity to feel "enough" will most often come from within.

Talking about Money by Ages and Stages

The Preschooler

There is no age too young to begin conversations about money, or at least about the concepts that drive money: needs, wants, and the value of time and effort. Start making the distinction between needs and wants as soon as your child is old enough to talk. Teach them, too, **to look for cues that signal needs versus wants.**

Hunger is a good place to start. Suggest to your preschooler that they check in with their belly to decide when they have had enough to eat. Talk about healthy foods that people *need* for energy and less healthy foods that we eat in moderation as special treats when we *want* them. "Clean plate clubs" may be motivating, but not intrinsically so! Food should be its own reward. Try to stay away from forcing or rewarding eating. And be wary of using food as a reward or panacea.

Using hunger cues for healthy eating quite literally teaches your child to let hunger drive appetite rather than external or emotional reward. And this can translate to things other than food. Point out the difference between the needed new winter coat and the wanted sparkly jacket. Needs are obvious and pretty limited, while wants are seductive and abundant.

The Grade Schooler

In 2009, companies spent over $17 billion marketing to your grade-school-age kids. This was more than double the amount spent in 1992. Capitalizing on increased flexible spending and what they dub "pester power," advertisers know they can get to your pockets through your children. Now is the time to talk in more nuanced ways about wants and gimmes.

The Save-Spend-Share allowance system is a good way to do this. Saving can spark discussions of what kinds of things are worth saving for and of the challenges and power of delayed gratification. At the same time, go ahead and let your eight-year-old impulsively use all her Spend money on a flimsy plastic necklace, especially when it breaks a day later and she feels the regret of giving in to whim. Just be sure you know her temperament well enough to anticipate the reaction—it may be no more than a sigh, a full-blown sobfest, or even self-flagellation ("How could I have been so stupid?!").

When deciding to whom and where they will give their Share money, **help your child think about others' needs and wants**—whether it's their little brother's wish for a video game or another child's need for socks and a toothbrush. And go ahead and be honest with your ten-year-old about the motivations of those advertisers. If kids realize that their desires are being manipulated, they may be more amenable to pushing back and saving you a lot of aggravation (and money) in the process.

The Middle Schooler

Kids in middle school naturally begin to spend more time away from home and with friends, giving them a front-row seat to the greener grass in their buddy's yard. This, unsurprisingly, correlates with an increase in materialism in middle-school-age kids. Now is the time to decide how much detail you want to share with your children about your family's financial situation. **Use the "privacy versus secrecy" rule of thumb.** Most middle school kids can keep private information confidential, and it is OK to tell them what they need to know to reason through thorny questions about money.

Knowing how much you make in a month and how much you spend on rent or mortgage, bills, and utilities, and on *them*, allows your middle schooler a concrete sense of how much is left over for other wants. Again, **keep temperament in mind.** No need to have your worrywart fearing you may be homeless. But if you do need to move to a smaller, less expensive home because of a bad investment or an unexpected job loss, your kids deserve to know that.

Money is a place where kids often *do* learn from parents' mistakes. So be honest about yours. They can't take another person's perspective if they don't know it. Help them make lists for birthdays and Christmas that consider how much their givers actually have to give. It's OK for them to know that Grandma A gives bigger checks than Grandma B because she is lucky enough to have a bigger retirement fund.

The High Schooler

Many middle schoolers will take on extra chores or babysitting to make a little extra cash for spending on wants. In our opinion, **every kid should have a job before they graduate from high school**—regardless of whether they want one. Even if you have the means to pay for things like car insurance, gas money, or their cellphones—don't. You wouldn't throw your toddler into the deep end of the pool without first teaching them to swim in the shallow end. Don't send your teen to live on their own without first teaching them gradually to make and manage their own money.

Talk, too, about how the decisions that they (and you) make about spending money now can affect them well into their future. If they plan to go to college, start talking when they are high school sophomores about how much you can (and can't) afford. Help them think through the potential implications of taking on huge loans versus going to a state school. And above all, **listen.** Help them think about the financial implications of their dreams and goals—not only of your dreams and goals for them.

It is entirely possible that your teen will become an adult who is happy living with less than you think—and even with less than you have. Ultimately, our kids will need to decide how much is enough . . . for them.

BIG IDEAS

- Money is a deeply spiritual issue, because it has so much power over our feelings and relationships. Getting right with ourselves, our spouse, and our God about money (less secrecy and better habits of giving, spending, and saving) will help our kids adopt a healthy spirituality around money and stuff.

- Help your kids distinguish between wants and needs in the language they use and the cravings they have.

- Start your kids early in managing their own money by learning how to save, spend, and share. The Bible says that "those who are trustworthy in a little will be trustworthy with a lot" (Luke 16:10).

- Taking a cue from Jesus, downward mobility is a Christian value. Downsizing, taking a sabbatical, buying used, making do, not competing with neighbors or culture—all of these protect Creation and right-size our spirits.

· What our kids really want from us is not more or better stuff, but more time and shared experiences.

Prayer

Jesus, you once said, "Where your treasure is, there will your heart be also." Help me put my treasure where it belongs, and let my heart catch up. I want our family to live in a mindset of abundance, and not in the myth of scarcity.

Amen.

CHAPTER 6

Service and Community

How to Follow Jesus

The Way of Jesus is fundamentally a way of service to others, including, and even especially, those who are different from us. Perhaps no story sums up the Way of Jesus better than that of the Good Samaritan.

A lawyer, looking to catch Jesus on a technicality, asked him what he had to do to have eternal life. Jesus put it back to him: "What does the law say?" The lawyer mentioned the Great Commandment, which Jesus had earlier named as the most important: "Love God with your whole heart, soul, mind, and strength—and love your neighbor as yourself." (*Someone* was paying attention in class.)

Jesus said, "Right you are. Now go and do it, and you'll live." But the lawyer, going for the A+, wanted precise terms. "Who is my neighbor?" he asked. Jesus, by way of answer, told a story about a man traveling an isolated road when he was mugged, beaten, stripped naked, and left for dead by robbers (Luke 10:25–37). A priest saw the man lying there—and promptly crossed the street and kept going. A Levite, who outpriested the priests, followed suit. Finally, a Samaritan (foe to the Jews) spotted the man and stopped for him, feeling moved to help—without worrying about whether the robbers were still around waiting for a new victim. It was the Samaritan who administered first aid, brought him to an inn where he could recover from his wounds, and paid the bill. At this point, pausing for effect, Jesus asks the lawyer, "Who was the neighbor to the man who fell victim to the robbers?" The lawyer responded, "The one who showed him mercy." And Jesus said, "Now go and do likewise."

There's plenty of backup material in the Gospels to support Jesus's prevailing opinion that **our lives are fundamentally and primarily given to us in order that we may be a people for others.** He commanded us to "love one another as I have loved you" (John 13:34). He preached countless sermons about loving enemies, mercy, peacemaking, and generosity. He told us that whenever we feed the hungry, tend the sick, clothe the naked, or visit those in prison, we are in fact doing those things for him (Matthew 25:31–46).

Jesus himself spent most of his time, even when he was exhausted, detouring from the path in order to feed hungry people, heal chronically ill people, and in every way put his own needs or preferences aside to serve others.

And though he never traveled more than about a hundred miles from his hometown and spent most of his ministry tramping around a lake with fishermen, his world was huge. In an age of little social mobility and a lot of social taboos, Jesus made a point of reaching out to people who were different, invisible, or meant to be shunned. His best friends and closest compadres were lepers, prostitutes, folks suffering from mental illness, tax collectors, and kids. He considered women his equals (shocking!). No one was off-limits: he even healed the child of a Roman colonel, one of the hated occupiers.

Regardless of whether you believe that doing good works is the ticket to eternal life, it's hard to deny that Jesus asks us to regularly go out of our comfort zones to be of service to God's Creation and creatures. But if you are anything like us, you may struggle with just *how* to be a person for others when the people already in your life put so many demands on you that you fall exhausted into bed on top of clean laundry at the end of the day. You want your kids to have a sense of responsibility for making the world a better place, but there just don't seem to be enough hours in the day to be their example. **How can we be a people for others, and teach our kids to do the same, when life is already so full?**

When Peter and Molly were engaged, they spent a year volunteering at the Casa San José, an orphanage in Mexico. They were young, idealistic, and game for the idea of deferring their massive student loan debt. The year shaped them profoundly: from the challenges of bugs in the breakfast soup, homesickness, and depression when things didn't go their way, to victories in living more simply and gratefully, teaching kids how to read, working through cross-cultural conflicts, and discovering that failure is an excellent spiritual teacher. They traded a lot of ego for soul that year. God humbled and nourished them profoundly through the love and trust of the children in their care and the friendship and generosity of the self-sacrificing Mexican staff who remain in their lives to this day.

Molly spent the next twenty years being homesick for the Casa. The experience gave her and Peter a spiritual and financial plumb line against which they've measured their lives since.

Perhaps you, too, have had an experience of serving others that shaped you profoundly and broadsided you with joy, meaning, and purpose. Maybe it was a year abroad, a weeklong service trip, a once-a-month gig at the homeless shelter, or a day spent hammering nails at a Habitat worksite. After it was over, you couldn't shake the feeling of deeper purpose. Even when you went "back to everyday life," in moments of objective reflection or sentimental reminiscence you had to admit that life felt more real and rich during that time of sacrifice and service.

You probably yearn for your kids to experience that same feeling. But chances are that your transformative experience of being of service, like Molly and Peter's, happened before kids. In kid life, you are short on vacation days and can't figure out how to spend a week in sacrificial service while also making time to visit family and maybe, just maybe, even use vacation days to take an actual vacation. Is there a way to make service and other-centeredness a joyful and effortless part of family life amid all of life's other demands? Yes.

Kindness as a Family Value

What do you want most for your kids? When researchers ask this question, most parents say they want their children to be kind. It has become a mantra in many of our families. But interestingly, when those same researchers ask their kids what *they* think their parents want most for them, they answer, "To be happy." Why the disconnect? How come kids aren't getting the message?

Richard Weissbourd, architect of Harvard's Making Caring Common Project, argues that our kids think we most want them to be happy because modern parents spend an awful lot of time focusing on their kids' feelings. When we focus exclusively on their feelings, it forces them to do the same. The honest truth is that we really want our kids to be both kind *and* happy. How do we get that message across? We do it by asking them not only how *they* feel, but how they think their actions make *other* people feel.

Weissbourd argues that in order to have kind and happy kids, we need to make responsibility for others a priority throughout their development. We don't need to spend all of our vacation days and budget on a family service trip. We can make service and kindness a part of our family's every-day trip. Martin Luther King, Jr., said that the surest way to be happy was to seek happiness for others. Perhaps all of Jesus's modeling behavior, and imploring us to love and serve one another, was enlightened self-interest after all. He knew that we would do best by ourselves by doing good for others.

Think about that feeling when you are walking to the park and you decide to stop, look that unhoused man in the eye, give him a protein bar, and say "God bless you" instead of walking on by. Or when you take two hours of your Saturday to sort cans at the food bank. Or when you do a litter pickup together at the beach instead of zoning out with a magazine while your kid wave-jumps. Or when you deliver Meals on Wheels, mow your elderly neighbor's lawn together, write letters to prison in-mates, or sing Christmas carols at the homeless encampment under the underpass and bring along your *best* homemade cookies.

Apart from the hit for our own dopamine levels, there is an even more important reason to serve: because there is need. To live too well in a world where others lack basic necessities hol-lows out our claims to justice and makes us hypocrites.

Remember: our kids are watching us. They watch how we speak to the telemarketer who interrupts dinner. How we be-have on the sports field when we think the ref made a bad call. How we talk to the cashier who seems to be moving at a snail's pace. Or to our elderly mother who is driving us just a teensy bit crazy. Weissbourd asks his wife and friends, "If I'm ever model-ing behavior that you think is not good, tell me." We need to be willing to be called out so we can be aware of the messages we are sending about what it means to be kind, to serve, and to be in community with others in daily life.

We can continue to live in a me-first way that sucks all the best juices from the planet and depends on the machinery of capitalism to whir ever faster in order to satisfy our appetites. We can teach our kids, actively or passively, to do the same. And we and they will continue to be afraid, feel alone, circle the wagons, buy more locks, and raise walls higher against the outside world. We will always need the next fix in order to forget our fear.

Or we can tear down the walls that separate us from the naked, the sick, the hungry, those in prison. We can enter their world, ask them what they most need (instead of assuming! Which, you know, makes an *ass* out of *u* and *me*), and answer that need. We'll likely find that in serving others we ourselves are served, because we belong to one another, and our best joy lies not in pursuing our own happiness (which will always elude pursuit) but in trying to make life a little easier for another child of God.

And if we actually teach our kids to be kind and give them opportunities to practice ninja-level kindness skills, we will make them happier and the world a little better.

In his book *The Secrets of Happy Families*, Bruce Feiler talks about the power of creating a family mission statement as a way of surfacing (or setting!) the core values that guide your family. He invites us to ask four questions when the family is all together:

What words best describe our family?
What is most important to our family?
What are our strengths as a family?
What sayings best capture our family?

When we can articulate what makes our family tick, and what our aspirations are, it gives us an everyday shorthand for motivating ourselves to live up to our high ideals. When we can say, "We are the kind of family who [strives each day to be kind, looks out for the underdog, lives simply, gives to others because God has given to us, fill-in-the-blank]," it sets us in a virtuous cycle where deed follows word.

But the exercise in surfacing our core values is not without peril: **are we spending our time, as a family, in ways that are consistent with our highest ideals?** Remember, Jesus said: "Where your treasure is, there will your heart be also." Time is an even more precious commodity than money in many of our families! We may find, when we look hard at how we allocate ourselves, that we have gotten off track and not lived up to our ideals. But that's why we call this spiritual *practice,* not spiritual perfect. We can always reset, and begin again.

Faith and Works

In the olden days, church nerds got pretty heated up about what was more important: faith (what we believe) or works (what we do). Protestants like Martin Luther, railing against corruption in the Church, like the payment of indulgences in exchange for absolution, said that there was nothing we could do to earn God's favor or love.

On the other hand, it can't be right that our actions don't matter. What we do is as important as what we say, if we are sincere in our beliefs. In the New Testament letter of James, the purported brother of Jesus writes to the early Christian churches about religious hypocrisy: "Be doers of the word, and not just hearers who deceive themselves. . . . Religion that is pure and undefiled before God is this: to care for orphans and widows in their distress. . . . What good is it, my brothers and sisters, if you say you have faith but do not have works? If a brother or sister is naked and lacks daily food, and one of you says to them, 'Go in peace; keep warm and eat your fill,' yet you do not supply their bodily needs, what is the good of that? So faith, by itself, if it has no works, is dead."

Raising moral and kind kids demands that we do good together as a family, in service to the community. But service also begins at home. We've talked in earlier chapters about some of the ways you can do this. Give your kids chores and responsibilities for which they don't get paid but are expected because they are a part of the micro "community" of the household. Have big kids watch littles without expectation of payment. Ask younger children to clear the dinner table, or fetch things you need from another room. Broaden ideals for respectful service to the extended family: setting expectations that kids will carry on a polite conversation with the adults in their family, ask them questions about themselves, and look for ways to serve and support the eldest.

You've probably heard the advice from psychologists to praise effort rather than results. Don't tell your straight-A student she's smart—tell her you're proud of her for working hard to learn. That's all well and good for résumé-building skills, but when it comes to raising a moral kid, this strategy works a little differently. Do try to notice them being kind, and affirm that: "It was really nice of you to spend some time talking with your great-grandma today." But Weissbourd argues that you should go a few steps further. **Point out the impact that their kindness had on someone else, even if it cost them something.** "I could see it made her really happy, even though you had to take time out of playing with your cousins." Go ahead and label the character trait that their actions suggest, too. "You are a really kind kid, and you're good with old people." They are more likely to identify themselves as kind, and to continue to behave in ways that are consistent with that identity, if you name it explicitly.

Low-Bar, High-Impact Service Opportunity Ideas

- Buy high-quality protein bars and keep them in the glove box of the car to hand out at intersections where people are panhandling.

- Make bag lunches with PB&J sandwiches to bring to warming centers in the winter.

- Many major cities now have spiritual communities where you can worship al fresco with unhoused people. Meet them there or at a shelter and bring small toiletries, hand warmers, flashlights, beef jerky, and $5 gift cards to places they can rest and wash up.

- Take your kids to a lobby day for trans rights, affordable housing, or the environment; there are organizations that will teach you how to talk to your representative. Let your bigger kids skip school so they can practice what they're learning in social studies class!

- Volunteer at a place like Cradles to Crayons, where they have figured out how to create meaningful and age-appropriate service opportunities for the whole family.

- Do administrative work/cleaning/organizing/client holiday gift wrapping for the local homeless coalition or domestic violence agency.

- Set up a gift tree at the local public school at the holidays for men in the local shelters, who are often overlooked at Christmastime.

- Start a food pantry in your church, school, scout troop, or neighborhood.

- Use the kids' Share money to buy ingredients for a smoothie stand and donate the proceeds to disaster relief.

- Stuff Christmas stockings with things unhoused people most need and pass them out on Christmas Eve.

- Decide your end-of-year charitable giving as a family, allowing even the youngest to make decisions about where your dollars will go.

And Some Bigger Ideas for Service

- Adopt a family through a refugee resettlement program, helping them navigate their new hometown, learn the language, and find the resources they need to make life work.

- Instead of a family vacation, go on a work trip or service-learning trip with an outfit like BorderLinks.

- Take a year to pare down your belongings by half. Sell the higher-ticket items and give the money away to the poorest of the poor.

- Buy a used car instead of a new one and donate the difference, or donate your still-reliable older car to a new refugee family to help them get to work and school.

- Buy no new clothes or small appliances for a whole year! Put the money into a college scholarship fund for low-income students.

- Decide to tithe, just for one year, as a family. Take stock at the beginning, middle, and end, to see what your happiness barometer is.

- Encourage your high school senior to take a gap year before college to gain valuable skills and perspective on life (not to mention getting another year of maturing under their belt before they spend your hard-earned money on college tuition while sleeping the day away).

All of these things can be done without volunteering outside the home. Volunteering just helps you magnify the lesson. And don't forget the other tool you have: stories. Make responsibility for others a family value by presenting your kids with stories of ethical dilemmas (remember Chapter 3 on goodness and badness). Use stories from the news, the Bible, and your own daily life where people acted unkindly, or put others' feelings and needs before their own, and ask your kids what they think they would do in that situation. How easy would it be to actually do what they think they would do? Give your own input. Acknowledge that being kind is not always easy. But it *is* always a choice.

The "Kin-dom" of God: Beyond Teaching Tolerance

For many years, *tolerance* was our cultural buzzword to urge people to be more sensitive toward and accepting of differences in color, class, sexual orientation, and gender identity and expression.

But let's be real. No one wants to be merely tolerated. People want to be wholeheartedly accepted, loved, and embraced. God made us good—not perfect, but good. *Every* one of us. How do we move ourselves and our children, practically speaking, toward a theology of embrace not in spite of but *because* of our differences?

Weissbourd talks about **the importance of teaching our kids to see invisible people.** They should know the names of people who help make their daily lives run more smoothly, like bus drivers and cafeteria workers. We model this for them by getting to know the people who make *our* lives easier—the parking lot attendant, security guard, and cleaning person at work. We do this even when our kids aren't watching. They will know if kindness is an act you put on only when you are with them.

In order to train our kids in seeing others, which includes

seeing themselves and their place (and privilege) in the world accurately, **we have to be willing to have specific, explicit, and often uncomfortable conversations about race and class.** It's not enough to hand them bromides like "God loves everyone."

Po Bronson, in his book *NurtureShock: New Thinking about Children*, alerted us to groundbreaking research on how unconscious attitudes about race develop in, particularly, white children and teens when parents refuse to talk plainly about skin color with their children.

Think of all those Facebook memes of little blond girls and black boys playing in the sandbox together, claiming, "They don't see color." We call bullshit. Kids are not color-blind. Beginning around about age three, kids start to zoom in on physical differences wherever they see them. Until they are capable of more abstract, nuanced thinking, they also tend to generalize what they know about one person to a whole group, as they find themselves in the early stages of attempting to make sense of their world.

Take this benign example. Ellen has type 1 diabetes. When Luke was about four years old, after Ellen had picked up insulin at the pharmacy, Luke piped up from the backseat with a logical question from his perspective: "Do all mommies have diabetes?" His question was an easy opening into a conversation about what it means to have diabetes, how anyone can have it, and how yes, he might get it someday (hopefully not) and Ellen would know how to take care of him if he did.

If white kids are going to be raised to be antiracist, adults must first acknowledge color differences and teach children the ways racism has suppressed and oppressed large groups of people based on the propagation of racial caste. We can and need to explain institutional racism to them in age-appropriate ways. Promoting color blindness erases a history of discrimination and oppression that is still very much alive in our present.

Of course, the problem is that when our kids ask questions about race, white parents tend to fumble. If the question sounds racist, we freak out, thinking we have done something horribly wrong, and worry we are raising mini-fascists. It happens to the best of us. It was Ellen's first reaction when Jonah, at age four, was sitting in the grocery cart attracting the warm and silly attention of an elderly black man bagging their groceries. Jonah commented on the way out, "That man looked like Big Papi." For sports dummies, Big Papi was the then-slugger for the Boston Red Sox, originally from the Dominican Republic, a big guy in his thirties. The slender and graying man bagging groceries looked nothing like him, except for the color of his skin. Ellen reminded herself that Jonah had also asked just a week before, "Why are all doctors women?" OK. So she was only halfway failing.

We start by understanding that kids do not necessarily ascribe value to differences or, for that matter, to similarities. They just notice them, and begin to generalize from specifics. Take this example from a white four-year-old who asked her mom a question on Martin Luther King Day after the grocery delivery guy left:

ALICE: "Why is that person not in jail?"

ALICE'S MOM: "What do you mean?"

ALICE: "He had dark skin and Martin Luther King was in jail because he had dark skin."

ALICE'S MOM: (After a pause) "Martin Luther King did a lot of hard work to try to make sure that wouldn't happen anymore. That work isn't finished. But it happens less than it used to. . . . Our delivery guy isn't in jail because he hasn't done anything that people go to jail for."

But Alice's mom was worried she had only succeeded in confusing Alice more. She worried that she and Alice's dad, for all their previous conversations about racism, were fumbling and failing. So she asked for suggestions from the Facebook hive mind and got some good ones:

> *"We live in a country where people with brown skin are not as supported and cared for by the people who run our country as people with whiter skin. Mommy and Daddy vote to try to change that."*

> *"Sometimes people like MLK are put in jail not just because of the color of their skin or even because they did something wrong. They get put in jail because they did something right that people with power don't like and are scared of."*

> *"People with brown skin are often treated unfairly just because of what they look like."*

> *"MLK and Jesus were both treated unfairly and punished because they talked about loving and accepting everyone, and some other people didn't like that idea. They worried that things they had would be taken away and given to other people. They were being greedy."*

One wise mama of an older white child noted that he had shifted from a place of overgeneralization about race and difference to greater awareness because she asked him questions like: "Who is in jail, and why are they there? Who decides why they have to go? Who doesn't end up in jail even if they commit crimes?"

Another mom commented that she feels like she "messes

up" conversations about race more often than not, but that she keeps trying—an attempt to move past her white fragility and demonstrate that even if white people say embarrassing or ignorant things about race as we awaken to the pervasiveness of structural racism, we will not let ourselves (or other white people) stop learning and growing.

Molly's family used to live just across the river from a middle-class African American neighborhood that formed as a result of Boston's redlining housing practices throughout the twentieth-century that forced black families into concentrated enclaves. Whenever seven-year-old Carmen came with Molly to pick up the dry cleaning across the river, she would ask Molly to lock the car doors while she ran in. This moment became an opportunity to examine the basis of Carmen's fear, to talk about racial stereotyping, to push back on a bigotry inherited from the white supremacist cultural ether with a big dose of reality and exposure therapy, as Molly challenged Carmen's fears.

We need to talk to kids, in age-appropriate ways starting when they are very young, about such things as the history of slavery, the rise of the Ku Klux Klan (KKK), and little Ruby Bridges walking into school in her bobby socks that first day with grown white men spitting on her. Most important, we need to own how racial oppression is still manifest today: in the systemic underfunding of schools, the economic incentives to building and maintaining a large prison population, the uneven and grossly unfair application of drug sentencing laws, immigration policy, family separation and detention on the southern border, and the killing of many, many unarmed young black people by law enforcement. And perhaps one of the most personally painful examples of structural racism: white Christianity's role in building and maintaining it.

If these examples are too high-concept for your young children, look for everyday examples. Of what race was the person pulled over by the police in your mostly white neighborhood? Is that store clerk treating the Latina customer differently from the Anglo one? How does the teacher treat the kids of different colors or abilities in the classroom?

Don't worry so much about whether the conversations are going over your kids' heads. Some of it probably is. But the goal here is a long-term one: to raise antiracist kids who will operate differently in the world. Remember that being aware is merely a beginning, not an end. Our job is to give our kids the information and tools they need to come to their own conclusions about tough topics like racism and to have the knowledge, wisdom, and courage to act on it. Don't worry about getting it "right." Keep trying.

Arguably the best thing we can do to help our kids navigate an increasingly diverse and pluralistic world is to make the world they inhabit *now* more diverse. How do our own families work to embrace, love, and encourage diversity, rather than reinforcing monoculture? If we are white, do we have friends of different skin tones, or family members who are people of color? Do we unconsciously consider the ways of white culture better than others? If we are middle-class or wealthy, do we ever socialize with people from a different class? When we do engage them, is it as "helper to helpee," or as siblings and equals in God's great family? How do we need to train ourselves out of the social stratification and de facto segregation that modern society has imposed on us?

Not everybody has this asset in their geographic community, but for us, our church is the way a lot of families have been able to take steps to embrace diversity. Church is where our kids regularly mingle, as equals, with people who are different from them in every way. They visit nursing homes and hear the stories of old people. They share the pew with unhoused mentally ill people talking out loud to themselves and learn not to be afraid of them, even learning their stories. They take as their confirmation mentor that cool (trans, black, wheelchair-using, atheist, fill-in-the-blank) young adult with the amazing hairdo and the photographic memory of the Bible. They visit a friend in chemo, or in the eating disorder unit of the psych hospital, to bring homemade cards and to pray together. They sit on the floor in front of the first pew on Drag Gospel Sunday and stare in wonder at the glory of a flock of drag queens in full regalia, singing their hearts out under the cross, and all they are thinking is "They are so *beautiful*."

Difference isn't scary when kids regularly get to meet the people underneath the differences and discover their love for one another and their common humanity. Progressive Christianity calls this, in shorthand, the Kin-dom of God. No longer is there a top-down kingdom with a ringleader who is necessarily white, male, bearded, able-bodied, and old. God's goals have been finally revealed not on a vertical axis but on a horizontal one: the way all God's people gather in dignity, peace, and mutual respect.

The Perils of Voluntourism and the White Savior

For white, educated, middle-class people like Molly and Ellen, there is always the danger that we'll take on service projects in a way that reinforces privilege or otherwise sets up the servee as the "poor one" whom we are helping, in our largesse. Then again, many of us often overthink things, and that can paralyze us from serving at all!

After Peter and Molly came home from the orphanage in Mexico, they still went back every couple of years on "work camp" trips with Molly's churches, first bringing teenagers from Molly's mostly white wealthy suburban church for an immersive experience of another culture, and later family trips with diverse folks of all ages from her new church in Somerville. As Molly grew to understand just how perniciously classist the trips were in practice, she became a little horrified with the trip dynamic, such as the "down day" the group would take to a beach resort midweek, or how close the attendees would get to the kids during their time there, only to have the Casa kids sobbing at week's end while the volunteers went back to their daily lives with nary an emotional hitch.

But rather than abandoning the Casa or the loving relationships formed there, the American volunteers learned to adapt and hopefully to evolve. They started bringing the Casa teens with them when they went on their offsite beach day. They employed local workers to help paint classrooms and build a shed and spent time making the kids a special meal, deep cleaning, and reading to and playing with the kids—bonding in a lighthearted way that wouldn't leave them (or the volunteers) heartbroken and retraumatized when the trip was over. They started fundraising to bring some of the older Casa kids to visit them in the States—why should the volunteers always get to be the travelers?

And Molly brought her kids to the Casa. Rafe was six months old on his first trip. He is now sixteen, has visited five times, and has a well-developed sense of how the Casa kids live and work and eat, the trials and challenges they face, and the opportunities they have—or don't. It's given him enormous perspective on his own privilege and comforts. And best of all, when one of Molly's kids complains about something trivial, the other is often quick to shut them down with a "What would a Casa kid do?"

Teaching Kindness by Ages and Stages

The Preschooler

The important thing to remember about preschoolers is that they are inherently selfish, but this doesn't mean that they are completely incapable of perspective taking. They need to literally *see* how another person is feeling in order to grasp it. Adults adapt to this without even realizing it: if your co-worker accidentally steps on your toe you're unlikely to exclaim "Owweeee!" But if your three-year-old does it, you might even add some hopping around on one foot for emphasis.

Find ways to show your preschooler how their actions impact others—through real-life experiences, stories, and books. Go ahead and use those high school theater skills on occasion. Encourage them to act in ways that affect others' emotions—kissing their baby sister's boo-boo or sharing a cookie with their great-grandpa.

Frame kindness in ways that are acceptable to them, that don't threaten their sense of safety and security. It is natural for our youngest kids to instinctively hoard and sometimes even to pillage out of self-protection and lack of power or resources. **Be concrete about the behaviors you are looking for:** ask them to take turns rather than share. Be careful not to ask them to do anything you wouldn't do the adult equivalent of yourself. How would you feel if you were asked to share your new car with your best friend anytime she asked to use it, for however long she wanted it?

Remember that being *kind* is the goal, not being nice. Kids need us to help them start setting boundaries right out of the gate. For the preschooler who temperamentally doesn't like big hugs and kisses, help her find a more acceptable and still-kind way to treat aunts and uncles.

The Grade Schooler

By the time they are in grade school, kids tend to settle in somewhere along a continuum of empathic awareness. While not quite as easy to measure as height or math ability, empathy is a measurable trait. Some kids seem to be naturally more empathic. Unlike height, but like math skills, empathy can also be taught.

First, if you have a kid who temperamentally tends toward the lower end of the empathy scale, you may need to check your own anxiety over their becoming an antisocial hermit—or worse. Less empathic kids may just need more prompts and structure to practice compassion. Model for them. Tip well in restaurants and cabs. Say *thank you* and *may I*.

Go ahead and remind your kids to say *please* and *thank you* until it (hopefully) becomes routine. When you ask them to do something around the house, add *for me*, as in "Would you please help out by emptying the dishwasher *for me*." It's a reminder that often we do things we don't want to do because we are doing them for others.

The Middle Schooler

Middle school is a perfect time to engage kids in a wider community of giving. Encourage them to make and sell bracelets, baked goods, magnets, or anything they are into to raise money for a charity. Run (or walk) a charity 5K as a family. Volunteer at a soup kitchen or sorting donations for the holidays.

Don't just do—discuss. Talk about why the needs you are attempting to meet are there in the first place. Go beyond talking about individual decisions and misfortunes to talk about systemic racism and injustice. Use stories from the news to encourage your middle schooler to take the different perspectives of everyone involved. Why is the shelter or methadone clinic needed? For whom? Why don't people want it in their neighborhood? What might be another solution?

The High Schooler

High school is an ideal time to encourage kids to go beyond doing *for* and encourage doing *with*. Many high schools require community service hours for graduation. This is great but often not enough. Too many service projects are well intentioned but a "fly in and fly out" experience, a drop in a bucket, or sometimes a bucket that is already full.

By the time they are in high school, set the goal of teaching your child to listen first (especially to impacted people) and respond second. Encourage them to go further, on a bigger service trip, or to take on a deeper experience closer to home, one that requires them to work in community with people who are different from them but who, even more important, have needs different from theirs. This allows them the ultimate chance to practice perspective taking, which will shape them into becoming people of service rather than people who do charity.

BIG IDEAS

- The Way of Jesus is fundamentally a way of service to others and community building across difference.

- We say we want our kids to be kind, above all. They think we want them to be happy, above all. How are we prioritizing responsibility to others as a family value—thus scaffolding their development as empathic creatures?

- What are your family's core values? Who do you say that you are? Surface and reinforce your family's values in everyday life, in conversations, in praise and practice, and on a poster taped to the fridge.

- Children learn about race and racism only if adults talk with them about it explicitly. Children learn not to fear or judge difference when they are exposed to people who are different and get to know them beyond surface differences like skin tone, gender identity, and disability. This is the "Kin-dom of God."

Prayer

God, gift us the community that our kids—and I—need to live in Your Kin-dom, a wild mix of people to love us and be loved by us. Send us a spirit of service—to make time and space in a busy life for being people for others, so that we can know our best joy.

Amen.

CHAPTER 7

Sabbath

How to Make Every Day Holy

It's Sunday night. Everyone is exhausted from all the "fun" they had over the weekend. Homework remains untouched. There seems to be a single dirty sock somewhere on the floor in every room of the house. The refrigerator is empty even though you spent $200 on groceries yesterday. Someone is sobbing softly in a corner because you were cruel and denied them ice cream for dinner. Someone has gone into their room and slammed the door, vowing to run away as soon as they get the cash together.

Where is the restful Sunday sabbath you long for? Where is the three-course family meal, the relaxed and jokey vibe around the table, the endless, exciting rounds of Apples to Apples?

In Christianity, Sunday is the ordained day of rest, but in modern life, it's anything but. Even (or especially) when you are a pastor and a lot of your family's Sunday is oriented around church activities, Sunday afternoons often find us depleted and out of sorts. We have to take our sabbaths where we can find them.

This chapter offers suggestions for building rhythms of rest and play, as well as gentle religious and spiritual observance, into your home life so that you can take a little of the sucky out of Sunday—and every day.

The Case for Parents as "Pastors"

A Pew research study on religion in America proves beyond a shadow of a doubt that the best thing you can do to raise kids for whom faith is important is to attend to your own spiritual practices and religious observances. This doesn't *just* mean going to church (more on church later). It primarily means finding ways to integrate spirituality and religious instruction into *your* daily life.

Many of us have left church altogether, feeling it was too controlling of and too limiting to our own spiritual growth, or too at odds with our core values and beliefs—exactly the opposite of what faith is meant to be. But by leaving, we have also left the structure of church as a strong container for raising our children with faith and spirituality. Our own experiences of feeling controlled, defined, or judged by rigid or even abusive religious communities have left many of us squeamish about talking with our kids about what we *do* believe. So we throw the baby out with the baptism water.

This is in many ways especially true for parents who are scientists or clinicians. A psychiatrist colleague of Ellen's, himself a devout Muslim, wondered aloud why it seems so much easier for progressive religious parents to talk to their kids about sex, money, drugs, and alcohol than about, say, God and prayer. This had come home to him when someone asked his son what prayer is, and his son answered, "Prayer is when you stare up at the ceiling."

Like lots of parents, you might feel like you don't have enough knowledge to credibly teach your child about Christianity. But here's the thing: you have an experience of sex, so you can talk to your child about sex. You have an experience of money, so you can talk about money. You *also* have an experience of God, so you can talk about God. It will just require a little courage, conviction, and intention. It will probably also require you to spend some time reflecting on your own faith story and brushing up on the Bible's faith stories.

Get a good children's Bible and read it to yourself before you read it to your kids. Or get a couple different ones! Leave them in the bathroom: Bible as bathroom book. You'll find several suggestions for good versions on our website, www .blessthismessparenting.com. If you've had any Christian formation at all, it will all come back to you. And if you haven't, Christianity isn't rocket science. We have a story-based tradition, which lends itself easily to both learning it and wondering about it aloud together. What does it mean that God made humans "in the image and likeness of God"? Did Jesus cry as a baby? Did the animals fight on Noah's ark—or eat one another?

If you go to church, your Sunday school program may use the Godly Play curriculum, which uses story boxes to teach the Bible. See if you can borrow a story box to bring home—and let your child tell *you* the story. Talk with your child about what they learned in Sunday school that day. Or ask your pastor or Sunday school teacher to write up a simple question or two to guide a family discussion. Talk about it on the ride home, while folding laundry together, or at bedtime. You may not get a perfect Sunday dinner experience, but don't let *perfect* be the enemy of the good in bringing faith home.

You are your child's first and best minister. The Protestant reformer Martin Luther called us the "priesthood of all believers." Amend that to: a priesthood of all believers who often have massive doubts, which are, in the words of author Frederick Buechner, "the ants in the pants of faith."

The slogan for the UCC, our denomination, is "God Is Still Speaking." God speaks through ancient Bible stories but also through everyday encounters. The stories we are living right now are also holy. Tell your children about your own mystical encounters, times when you've felt what scripture calls "the peace that passes all understanding" (Philippians 4:7) even when common sense was telling you to freak out. Tell your kids how you pray. This is very different from telling them how *they* should pray. Talk with them about your experiences with church and why you don't currently have one, if you don't go. Use the tips later in this chapter to build prayer practices into your daily routine.

And listen to them. Take their spiritual questions seriously. Even if you feel like you're beyond your pay grade, be curious with them in looking for answers or calling them forth from deep within yourself. They need and deserve this effort from you.

Learning the Rhythms of Rest and Play

When Ellen was growing up very Catholic, Sundays were sacred and sabbath was kept. She and her cousins would be gathered from sleepovers or dragged out of bed to mass, followed by brunch at Grandma and Grandpa's for a day of homemade pasta, play, cable TV, and rest that set the rhythm for the week. Now, even when Ellen and her family get to church on Sundays, it's usually followed by a mad dash to a sports game or to Costco to be ready for the week.

How can busy families make time for sabbath and still make sure there's food in the fridge for a week of lunches? Here is another place where we shouldn't let the perfect Sunday sabbath be the enemy of the good-enough.

In Molly's old neighborhood, a group of her neighbors hosted an impromptu happy hour every Friday night. Families would gather around sundown at one house or another.

Someone would bring wine or apple cider, someone else hummus or too many tomatoes from their farm share. It was never a formal meal, but nobody was hungry when they left. The kids, ranging in age from seven to fourteen, would bomb through, polish off three bags of chips, and then disappear for the rest of the evening, playing kick the can in the street or sardines in the basement. The grown-ups would talk about everything: politics, religion, family tensions and joys. There was no formal prayer, no mass, no acknowledgment that what they were doing was mirroring an ancient biblical practice, but one of Molly's friends, when he ran into a Jewish acquaintance on the way to their house for happy hour, said he was on his way to "well, I guess it's like Shabbat."

Rabbi Abraham Joshua Heschel, who wrote the amazing little tome "The Sabbath," said, "The one who wants to enter the holiness of the day must first lay down the profanity of clattering commerce, of being yoked to toil." *Shabbat*, the Hebrew word for *sabbath*, means, quite literally, "stop."

Molly has often been envious of Judaism because so many of its observances are based in the home. They don't require special training or lots of props. They are holy and yet embodied, real, and simple to execute. Here are the basics of a Jewish Friday night Shabbat observance: As the day ends, stop working. That means everybody, including (and especially) moms, on whom the burden of housework disproportionately falls in heterosexual families. Anticipate the coming of Shabbat as you would a treasured friend. Within eighteen minutes of the sun's setting, light a candle. Wave the light toward your face. Bless the bread. Bless the wine. Sit for a meal. Voilà!

A full Jewish Shabbat lasts a little over twenty-four hours: until three stars are visible in the sky the following day. What would it be like to have a full twenty-four hours of family "stopping"? Christian pastor MaryAnn McKibben Dana did a year-long sabbath experiment on her family in *Sabbath in the Suburbs*. If you get serious about doing this in your own family, see her book for some pro tips and a road map.

We can learn a lot from observant Jews (or Catholic families in the 1970s and 1980s) about the rhythms of work, rest, and play that are intuitive to our bodies and spirits. We ignore, to our peril, our body's daily and weekly need to stop. How many of us have made ourselves sick because we thought we'd "just push through," and then gotten everybody in the house sick?

Sabbath—*stopping*—is not a guilty pleasure. It is a gift from God, and if that doesn't help, it's a commandment, one of the ten. The commandment to observe the sabbath has the longest word count among the ten, as if God is speaking over our protests that we can't possibly slow down (we might never get going again!), let that go (who will do it if I don't?), eat on paper plates (the environment!), and stop martyring ourselves to our endless to-dos.

Here is a question to stop you in your tracks: do you think you're better than God, who Herself had to rest, and then for eternity enshrined all Creation's need for regular rest?

Whatever we do—or stop doing—we are modeling for our children. We show them by our deeds what we think is most important. It is no wonder so many of our children are anxious and driven and feel like they are always falling short. They come by those feelings honestly. Stopping also allows us to watch our children and to see what they value as most important— and observe their "grain." Given a day to do nothing, what does your child choose to do? Read, sleep, fish, talk, play pretend, build something? Watch and find out.

When we commit to a real sabbath, we become radically countercultural, resisting the dominant paradigm in a way that moves us toward a tipping point. It affects first our families, then a whole city block. Next: world domination!

We hear your protests already. "But football/soccer/ballet/ cheerleading happens every Friday night/Saturday morning at five a.m. and then Sunday at eleven. . . . There's no way we can have a real sabbath and keep up with our commitments." Exactly. Sports and other structured activities have encroached on our sabbaths because individually we have not resisted them. It is OK to say no to the ubiquitous six-year-old birthday parties that seem to happen *every* weekend, unless it is a best friend's birthday. It is OK for our children to play one sport instead of three, to be a little more mediocre, boring, and bored, in the interests of sabbath.

Sabbath is not just a "palace in time," as Rabbi Heschel called it; it's also a palace in space. There are little fixes you can make not just to your family schedule but to your family spaces to make sabbaths natural.

Moving from their old house to a new house, Molly committed to creating intentional space for sabbath—including for herself, since she realized with chagrin that she spent more time in the kitchen than in any other room. They bought a giant couch, with room for all four (and more!) of them to nap, read, and snuggle on. The kitchen has an entire drawer dedicated to tea, and an electric tea kettle on the counter—ingredients for a "tea with honey and love" ceremony that has become a hallmark of winding-down time. Children's rooms are right off the common areas, easy for parents to check in while they are waking up or going to bed and physically connecting them to the hearth of the house. The parents' room is on the next level, and kids have to shout upstairs to ask permission before they can enter that sacred space, setting a clear boundary. The practice has supported Molly's bond with her husband—the acknowledgment that the kids will not always be with them, and the need to maintain friendship and intimacy during the (hopefully) many years that they will be empty nesters.

On a women's retreat she once ran, Molly met a single mom and her daughter. Mom had had her daughter at age eighteen. Now her daughter was almost grown and ready to leave the house. They seemed emotionally close, without being fused. "Tell me how it was, for you, as a single mom—was it hard?" Molly asked her. "It was hard, but it's also been the best life I could imagine. One thing I have always done to make our life together holy is set out cloth napkins every night and light a candle, even if we were eating ramen noodles because we were so broke."

Having a life together that supports sabbath doesn't have to cost more money. It doesn't require more props. It is simply a matter of paring down the life you already have, to reach the life in God that remains at our core.

The Importance of Play

As a young doctor, Stuart Brown was doing research into the character of murderers who otherwise had no criminal history. He discovered something amazing, a common thread in 90 percent of their stories: as children, their play was severely restricted.

Brown, a workaholic, spent many more decades studying play. He learned that children grow empathy through the rough-and-tumble of play, that play lowers stress, and that play makes us more innovative and helps us adapt to change. Child psychologists took play and turned it into *play therapy*—a safe space and way for kids to work through their feelings in their own language. Brown finally got the message and started to play more.

Play, Brown said, is any activity that is purposeless, dissolves ego boundaries, and ultimately brings joy. It's also an activity that delights God, who, after all, was the first one to play. What was the Creation, after all?

It's easy to buy into this concept of play—but then how do we enact it in our busy, overscheduled lives? You already know the answer: **We do less.** We allow our kids to have more un-structured time, to get bored. We allow some messes, keep cardboard boxes around, art carts, costume boxes. We give ourselves permission to stop what we are doing to kick the ball around, doodle and color, make robot noises. If your eight-year-old is melting down because she is flying from swim team to karate to harp lessons, cut one (or all three) of those things out. Yes, you might be killing her chances of getting into Har-vard. But you'll also be giving her a bigger life *right now*.

Molly and Ellen met up one summer at the beach in Maine to work on this book, and we took our primary research sub-jects with us. Luke (then thirteen) and Rafe (fifteen) started digging a hole in the sand, burying each other, and then build-ing a fort for the littler kids (but really for themselves). In those two gangly growing bodies, one at least a foot taller than the other now, we saw the reflection of the two-year-old and four-year-old who used to tumble together at daycare. They were playing: safely retreating to the comfort of each other and into the simple joy of digging in the sand. It was prayer for everyone.

There's another benefit to play. It gives us a window into our kids' temperaments, personalities, feelings, joys, and strug-gles. **How do we know what God's plan is for our kid? We *pay attention* to our kid.** This in itself is a spiritual practice. The skeptical mystic Simone Weil called prayer "absolutely un-mixed attention." In play therapy, the therapist does not join in or direct the child's play in any way other than to provide the safe space and materials to explore. They simply observe and occasionally comment on the play. What if the next time your kids are playing, you use it as an opportunity for your own sabbath instead of for chores? What if you put down your book or device and simply watch them, fully absorbed in their play? What might you see? *Who* might you see?

Better yet, what if you joined them playing on the floor? Christian author Madeleine L'Engle said, "Far too many people misunderstand what *putting away childish things* [1 Corinthians 13:11] means, and think that forgetting what it is like to think and feel and touch and smell and taste and see and hear like a three-year-old or a thirteen-year-old or a twenty-three-year-old means being grownup. . . . [I]f this is what it means to be a grownup, then I don't ever want to be one. . . . [I]f I can retain a child's awareness and joy, and *be* fifty-one, then I will really learn what it means to be grownup."

Easy Prayer Practices with Children

Prayer is so much more than staring at the ceiling. Or asking God as a sort of full-time Santa to deliver things we want. Even children know that. A casual poll among Molly's Facebook friends revealed these answers from their brilliant progeny (who admittedly skew heavily toward being preachers' kids) to the question "What is prayer?" (All responses are from children ages three to nine, of different races and religious identities.)

> *"Prayer is talking to God and praying for people we love. It's not asking for mean things."*

> *"Prayer is opening your spirit and heart to God. It is not just saying, 'Blah, blah, blah.'"*

> *"Prayer is something that is necessary for human beings to do, owed because there is a lot of bad people and too much hunger*

and even worse many sick people. My prayers are always for these."

"It's when you talk to God and God tells you to help people."

"What's not a prayer is 'God, give me toys,' or telling God that you're better than someone else because you're not. What is a prayer is 'God, thank you for this life I am in, and thank you for creating me. You are my spirit and soul.' I prayed to God to take my nightmares away last week, and it's been a good week. I feel like God is always beside me in everything."

"Praying isn't begging."

"You wouldn't pray about poop." (Long discussion ensues regarding the Jewish prayer thanking the Source of Life for our ducts and tubes, and for keeping open the ones that should stay open, and keeping closed the ones that should stay closed.)

Here are some easy, tried-and-true ways you and your kids can pray together. They work for all developmental levels (including adults with beginners' minds).

Help, Thanks, Wow

A gift from the funny, fabulous Christian writer Anne Lamott, this is a prayer prompt that works for table grace, bedtime, or anytime. Lamott once said that the two best prayers she knows are "Help Me Help Me Help Me" and "Thank You Thank You Thank You." She's since added a third prayer: "Wow."

Help me prayers are prayers of petition: they normalize that it's OK, in fact, to ask God for stuff. (Try not to edit your kids' prayers! If they pray for a new Xbox, they'll learn in their own time that God is not Santa. You can model the kind of prayer requests God really might be able to grant with your own prayers, though.)

Thank you prayers are prayers of gratitude: they remind us that prayer is a two-way relationship, and that God has actually been at work in our lives all along. Gratitude prayers also have the empirical ability to improve our mood and happiness levels!

Wow prayers are prayers of awe and wonder, of acknowledging where God has been present with us in our day. It makes God a guest at our dinner table, and a partner in our living. According to psychologists, people who regularly feel awe are more likely to be generous, helpful, altruistic, ethical, and relaxed. And awe doesn't cost a thing!

Molly has a centerpiece on the dining room table, a wire frame with durable cards with the words *Help*, *Thanks*, and *Wow* printed on them. Anyone at the table, during prayer time, can take whichever card they have a prayer for—or pray a hybrid prayer.

The prayer conversation might go like this:

"God, help me focus on my homework after dinner so I can get it done fast and have time to play Sleeping Queens."

"God, help me sleep through the night tonight without any waking up or bad dreams."

"God, thank you for fresh corn on the cob grown right near our town! And please help those who have no supper tonight."

"Wow, God, that sunset was a doozy tonight. You sure know how to show off."

*"Wow, God! I asked for your help last night in talking to my best
friend today—and we had a really good talk. Thanks for being
there with me and giving me the courage to raise my voice."*

It's good for our kids to see and hear us praying—it demonstrates that even parents don't have it all figured out, and
that we ourselves *need* a parent. It humanizes us and gives us
dimension—which, as our kids grow up, is an important piece
in helping them outgrow their natural narcissism.

Ten-Finger Prayers

Ten-finger prayers are ten-word prayers that are easy to remember because when you've used up your fingers, you're done
with the prayer. They have a cadence and an almost talismanic
power.

Here are three adapted Bible verses that can be used as nighttime prayers. You can feel free (with your kids!) to look through
the Bible for more, or to make up your own from scratch.

> I can do all things through Christ, who strengthens me.
> (Philippians 4:13)
> If God is for us, who can be against us? (Romans 8:31)
> Nothing can separate us from the love of Jesus Christ.
> (Romans 8:38–39)

Metta Prayer

When kids are going through a hard time emotionally, are full
of fear and anxiety, or are doubting the existence of God/not
wanting to speak to God personally, you might try this prayer

adapted from Buddhism. They can tape it to their wall and pray it every night before bedtime. They can also pray this prayer with five fingers or with prayer beads or any beaded necklace or bracelet, one line per bead.

> *May all beings be peaceful.*
> *May all beings be happy.*
> *May all beings be safe.*
> *May all beings become the person God intends them to be.*
> *May all beings be free.*

Molly's Rafe once amended it with this line:

> *May God challenge me in the right ways.*

You might ask your child, when they have become familiar with the prayer, what *they* would add to it.

Mobile Blessings to Cultivate Empathy and Power

From early on we have practiced praying in the car and on public transportation with our kids. When a fire truck goes by, Molly and her kids pray for the people at its destination. Whenever an ambulance would pass by the window of Ellen's beloved grandmother's house, they would pray for the EMTs to have focus and wisdom, and for the person on the gurney to feel that God was near.

Ninja-level prayer: When someone cuts Molly off in traffic, she blesses them—asking God to bring them safely where they are going and to keep them and other drivers near them from all harm, because Jesus asked us to bless, and not curse, our enemies. At red lights, Molly and Carmen notice pedestrians and the drivers in other cars and enter their situations imaginatively and prayerfully.

Try praying by raising your hands in the ancient symbol of blessing: palm out toward the blessed, two smallest fingers slightly bent. Praying in this way gives our kids agency: the understanding that God's power, to some degree, depends on our engagement and is literally "in our hands." Our hands, according to a quote misattributed to Teresa of Ávila, are the only hands Jesus has left on earth. Our hands are not just for doing good works. They are one of the ways that God's supernatural power actually gains mystical entry into the world.

Praying in this way also ignites our kids' empathy. Some of our kids are naturally very empathetic—they are able to read the emotional expressions of people from a very young age, they love to care for animals, they are deeply affected by bad news on the radio or TV. Other kids, not so much. Praying for strangers or people in faraway places is a way that kids begin to regularly practice empathy—because it is something they *can* practice.

And parents, beware! Now when drivers cut her off in traffic, if Molly chooses to curse instead of bless, her empathetic kids start in on her with a half-dozen reasons why the other driver might have done it: "But Mom! What if they are old and have trouble turning their necks? What if they are on their way to the hospital to see someone they love? What if . . . ?"

ACTS Prayers

A little more involved, but a powerful way for upper-grade school-age kids and older to pray, this acronymic prayer hits all the highlights.

Adoration (naming God: "Hello, Beautiful!" *or* "Dearest Father and Mother in Heaven . . .")

Confession (the Big Feelings you are feeling, the thing you are sad about or feel ashamed about)

Thanksgiving ("Thank you, God, for what I can see that is good *right now*.")

Supplication ("Can you help me with this thing I am worried about?")

The Lord's Prayer

The Lord's Prayer is the classic, the eternal, the one prayed in solidarity with Christians all over the world. When the disciples (who you'd think would already be prayer experts) asked Jesus, "How should we pray?," this is the answer he gave (Luke 11). To inclusivize it, because God is neither exclusively male nor female, try adding to the beginning: We pray to God who loves us like a Mother, saying,

> *Our Father, who art in heaven, hallowed be thy name. Thy kingdom come, thy will be done, on earth as it is in heaven. Give us this day our daily bread, and forgive us our trespasses, as we forgive those who trespass against us. Lead us not into temptation, but deliver us from evil. For thine is the kingdom, and the power, and the glory, forever and ever. Amen.*

The Baskette Blue Plate Special

Carmen and Molly prayed the same bedtime prayers every night from age three through ten. First they prayed the ten-finger prayers (shown earlier). Then they continued:

God, please bless and protect [full name of everyone in family including middle names, and anyone staying with us]. Give us good sleeping all through the night, and no waking up in the night, and no bad dreams, only good dreams about [fill in the dream theme]. We pray a prayer of the heart about [name particular joys, worries, and petitions from the day or the day ahead].

And they always ended with this line:

We pray in the strong name of Jesus. Amen.

After this they sang a simple spiritual song, or even "Twinkle, Twinkle, Little Star." After approximately 2,423 iterations of this version, they got a little bored. So they migrated to this simpler but still rich practice: the Serenity Prayer, attributed to Reinhold Niebuhr:

God, grant me the serenity to accept the things I cannot change,
The courage to change the things I can,
And the wisdom to know the difference.

From there, they moved to a free-form "prayer of the heart," ending with the magical formula "in the strong name of Jesus. Amen," before singing a short spiritual song. And now that Carmen is twelve, she sometimes puts *Molly* to bed.

Bedtimes, Mealtimes, Church, and Other Routines

Bedtime

Bedtime is a scary time: it's the time of day when all the monsters come out of the closet—and not just for our kids! How many times have you gotten into bed and turned off the lights, and your anxiety went into overdrive as you perseverated about the dumb thing you said earlier or worried about how a meeting was going to go the next day.

Anticipate that stuff will also come up at bedtime for your kids. Put them to bed early enough that you have a little energy left for them (take a disco nap if you need to as your kids get bigger and their natural circadian rhythms keep them up later than you!).

The conversations that happen when the lights go low and the distractions of the day ebb away can be immensely valuable for your bond. Your preschooler will ask you big God questions. Your grade schooler will reveal his deepest fears. Don't be startled when your eight-year-old suddenly makes the connection from "all things eventually die" to "you will eventually die" to "I will eventually die." This is a normal developmental part of gaining the wider perspective of growing up. Your teenager who thinks you are an idiot by daylight will suddenly want to confide in you, and may even ask for advice.

And again, a short and simple prayer practice, done daily at bedtime, will go far to provide the comfort of ritual and make your job of settling down your kids easier in the long run.

Bedtime is also a time when power issues come out, coupled with exhaustion. This seems to be particularly true for toddlers and teens. From a biological standpoint this makes some sense. Our kids' brains are developing synapses at about the same rate when they are teens as when they are toddlers. This means that our big kids need nearly as much sleep as our littles do. Yet it seems also to be human nature to fight what we most need.

If you find yourself in the middle of bedtime battles, try Susan Stiffelman's approach (described in her book *Parenting without Power Struggles*): coming alongside your toddler or teen to help with sleep. Usually, something is going on emotionally that interferes with the overwhelming natural impulse to sleep. Often, and somewhat counterintuitively, it is exactly the overtired state that is the obstacle. Help your child to identify the obstacle and come up with a solution together to address it. Maybe your teen feels she has no free time between school, sports, job, and homework and so nighttime is her only downtime. Maybe your toddler simply cannot settle his body for sleep.

Coincidentally, or not, many of the techniques psychologists recommend for sleep are very much like prayer. Progressive muscle relaxation is a way of focusing on the body in a mindful way to release tension and energy. Try guided imagery with it. Take the opportunity to practice an embodied spirituality: God loved bodies so much that She insisted we rest and restore them each and every day.

If sleep problems persist, consider that there may be an underlying medical issue. Some regions have pediatric sleep disorder clinics that can help identify medical problems like sleep apnea or help exhausted parents build a strategy for changing the energy around bedtime.

Mealtimes

". . . they broke bread at home and ate their food with glad and generous hearts, praising God and having the goodwill of all the people."

—ACTS 2:46-47

Meals are when and how Jesus demonstrated God's power and love: when he fed the five thousand disciples (plus women and children), when he broke bread and drank wine at the Last

Supper, and when he cooked his disciples breakfast on the beach the day after he rose from the dead.

This doesn't mean every family dinner will be the picture of domestic bliss. But that's not why we eat together. When Jesus sat down with his disciples and fed them what turned out to be the first Communion meal, he also fed Judas, who was about to hand him over to be executed, and Peter, who would deny him in public after his arrest. This bears remembering next time you or your partner cooks a lovely dinner at which ungrateful kids bicker, complain, or pick. But Jesus sat down with his chosen family anyhow, warts and all, for love's sake—and to make memories: "Do this," he said, "to remember me."

We assume it is peak experiences—the road trip to Yosemite, the graduations, the birthday parties—that will resonate most in our children's memories as they become adults, and we work hard to accumulate happy memories for them. **But at the end of the day, what matters most are our daily habits of simple connection, gratitude, and shared attention.**

There are practical reasons to sit down to eat together, too. A lot of research has been done into the emotional benefits of families regularly having a meal together. Some studies have shown that eating together on a regular basis can make your teenager less anxious or prone to risky behaviors. Children of any age may be less likely to engage in disordered eating. Regular family meals are linked to higher GPAs and self-esteem.

A device-free family meal is also the perfect opportunity to engage in the kind of storytelling and sharing that allows parents to be involved meaningfully in their kids' lives and facilitates ethical and spiritual discussion. This does not mean you all need to sit down together at five-thirty every evening for a home-cooked meal. It just means making time to routinely break bread together.

An easy way to start making meals a spiritual practice is to begin them with a prayer whenever you happen to find yourself eating together as a family. Most kids love to say grace. Ellen's seven-year-old Jonah knew grace as the thing that happens most often when grandparents are at the table. He would patiently hold his hands out until everyone was seated, no matter how hungry he was. (And lest you think he is a highly spiritual being, this is the same kid who detests church.)

Grace is said at every meal in Molly's house. If people have been snappish before dinner, they're less snappish after praying. If they haven't given God a thought all day, they can't help but think of God when talking to God.

Furthermore, saying grace is good for us. The secular world has caught on to this with "mindful eating." Saying words of thanks actually makes us feel more thankful. Pausing before digging in helps us enjoy the meal more. Mindful, grateful eating also slows us down so that we eat only as much as we need.

If you're not sure how to say grace, steal a mealtime prayer from another tradition. Or start by asking each person at the table to share a high and a low from their day (a rose and a thorn, a popsicle and a poopsicle, add your argot here) and then pray for one another. And decide to officially end your meal *together*. This can be as simple as requiring each person to ask to be excused before leaving the table—parents included.

Here are two graces Ellen grew up with. One is from Catholicism, said every night, and the other was said anytime her Episcopalian uncle was at the table:

Bless us, O Lord, and these, Thy gifts, which we are about to receive from Thy bounty. Through Christ, our Lord. Amen.

Bless this meat that we shall eat, this bread that we shall break. Make all our actions kind and sweet. We pray in Jesus's name.

Or sing "Johnny Appleseed" off-key:

Oh, the Lord is good to me, and so I thank the Lord, for giving me the things I need, the sun and rain and the apple seed. The Lord is good to me. Alleluia. Amen.

For a wealth of more fabulous ideas on how to get started or make your family meals better, including discussion starters and recipes, check out the Family Dinner Project (thefamily dinnerproject.org), a nonprofit co-founded by psychologist Anne Fishel, Ellen's mentor in family therapy.

What about Church?

There are a lot of compelling reasons *not* to go to church. Families are already overscheduled. We work, have sports, and attend those endless grade school birthday parties. We need more unstructured time.

And, let's face it: a lot of churches are Not Good. They are boring, sexist, homophobic, judgy. Church can make us feel socially anxious or lonely when we have trouble connecting with others there. We might worry we will be judged for being too broke, too divorced, too agnostic, or too gay, or for having kids who are loud or have unexpected behaviors.

But Christianity is a communal religion. The summary of Jesus's message is *love your neighbor as yourself*, and church gives us neighbors with whom we can put that teaching to the test. Church provides us with opportunities to give generously, serve the vulnerable, and love people who can be difficult—as well as inviting people to love us when *we* are difficult. The Church is often called the "body of Christ." Taking ourselves out of that body might make it easier to be a Christian, but that would be a Christianity without much depth.

Also, spirituality without church generally lacks structure. While it is certainly possible to have a spiritual practice as a family without church, it's a lot harder. Remember, kids need structure. They thrive on routine. And, if we are being honest, most of us parents need structure for our own spiritual practice, too, whether it means a commitment to our weekly yoga class or to Sunday morning service. We need ongoing spiritual guidance and good teachers so we have a well to draw from for our children.

Because **remember: you are your children's first and best spiritual guide.** Even if you do it imperfectly, own this role. We are spiritual ancestors for the next generation. We can't expect our children to magically adopt spiritual practices or have language and concepts for spirituality and religion if we don't bring some intention and formal instruction to our childrearing.

Molly often hears parents say, "I don't want to indoctrinate my child into religion the way I was indoctrinated." Don't be rigid, or judgmental, or exclusive. But you can still expose them, be transparent about what you believe and what moves you, makes you doubt or hope. If you had a bad math teacher in childhood, you wouldn't decide not to let your child take algebra. Heal your own spiritual wounds, and reclaim (or adopt for the first time) a Christianity that is generous, just, loving, and expansive. If your children are exposed to nothing in the realm of religion, that is exactly what they will learn.

Whatever your value is about church, stick to it and keep it consistent. This is what Molly tells her teen, who seems afflicted with a kind of temporary sleeping sickness on weekends:

> *Going to church is something we do as a family, and we are going to go to church together as long as you are living in our house.*

You don't have to believe in God to go to church—atheists have reported higher levels of happiness if they go to church. You can go to church for community or for the cookies at coffee hour—but you have to show up and be respectful and engaged.

You don't have to go every week—you can miss church once in a while for a social event that seems particularly important to you, because Jesus said, "The sabbath was made for humans, and not humans for the sabbath." But generally speaking, this is something important that we do all together.

When we commit in this way, we show our kids that church is not just something we do because of our personal preferences. Our commitment matters more than our feelings on any given Sunday.

Dads, take note: whether our kids will stick with church as adults correlates to whether Dad went to church. So in straight families, even if Mom wrestles the kids into the car every Sunday morning while Dad works more, goes fishing, or kicks back at home, it will tell, eventually.

If you don't have a good church, look for one. And keep looking. Look for code words to a church's theology. "Open and Affirming" or "More Light" are signals for queer-friendly in the United Church of Christ and the Presbyterian Church. Look at the staff page to see if they have people of color and women in top positions of leadership. There are a *lot* of good churches out there. Many of them are small and below the radar: you can make them a little stronger and more viable numerically. They will adore you just for being a family with kids. If you don't find a church you love, join a good-enough church and make it better. If you go to a church that claims to want kids but you find yourself shooshed when your kids make a little noise, shake the dust off your sandals and find a church that's ready for your whole family, just as you are.

Because there are churches that *love* kids: where kids play tag in the sanctuary after worship and nobody complains; where kids get first dibs at the coffee-hour feast. A church can provide lots of positive associations that aren't directly about faith: intergenerational community for families who live far from home; whole-life education about sexuality, ethics, and opportunities for service to others; other adults who can provide counsel and support for your kids as they naturally separate from you emotionally. Art, music, and singing; shared food and beauty. A place to lay down burdens in hard times and amplify your joy in good times. A place to experience, and participate in, transcendence. It's wonderful to observe the divine in nature. But in key moments in church, when the magic happens, we understand the Divine not as something we get to witness, but as something we *are*.

Finding Sabbath by Ages and Stages

The Preschooler

As our kids move out of toddlerhood, it can be so tempting to pick up an increasingly busy schedule. They probably don't need a nap anymore, or if they do, it's a short one that can easily be skipped. Three-to-five-year-olds are capable of doing so much more—eating in a restaurant without throwing food (sometimes), staying up past bedtime without an immediate meltdown, wiping their own bottoms (and the angels sang!)—that parents often start taking on more and more activities without even realizing it. Maybe a parent who stayed home when they were little has returned to work, and there is just less time in the day to cram it all in—so you resort to takeout and loose bedtimes more nights than you would like.

It's a good idea to take stock of your family's sched-

ule when moving from one stage of your child's life to the next. Preschoolers still thrive on rest, rhythms, and routines. Kids ages three to five still need ten to thirteen hours of sleep a night. You may need to schedule a "rest time" in place of a nap on weekends. You may need to cut some things out or plan ahead so you can all sit down to eat together at a reasonable hour most (or at least more) nights of the week. Be wary of scheduling so many playdates and activities that your preschooler never has time to be bored, to come up with her own entertainment and play. And at least once a week, put down the laundry or close the laptop and get down on the floor and play with her. This will be your best chance to really get to know her.

If you feel the tug to look for a church now that your preschooler is asking bigger questions about God and the universe—great! Just be ready to church-shop until you find one that not only encourages preschoolers to be present but also welcomes their presence, where even the youngest kids are involved in worship and children and adults are all encouraged to play.

The Grade Schooler

Many middle- to upper-middle-class U.S. households spend a huge amount of time and money on our kids' activities. Parents of grade-school-age kids spend an average of $500 a year on extracurricular activities, while parents of middle schoolers spend an average of about $650. By high school it's an average of $1,000, and plenty of families are spending upward of $10,000 per kid on activities. Much of this is sports activities fees, sometimes to compensate for school budget shortfalls but often to pay for elite coaching and training.

Grade school is the time to begin to take stock of your family's priorities for rest and play, but even more so for

your definition of success. We all want our kids to try different things, to find their passions and talents. But when this comes at the expense of sleep (up to age twelve, kids still need nine to twelve hours a night), family time, well-being, and happiness, we need more sabbath. If that doesn't convince you, maybe this will: plenty of evidence suggests that overspecializing in one sport or activity in grade school is associated with both psychological and physical burnout. Why? In part, because the reason for playing the sport or the instrument or for getting the grades becomes about external rewards rather than internal drive. Intrinsic motivation is undermined and sometimes snuffed out altogether.

Consider setting a one-sport-per-season rule for each kid, or a limit on how many evenings a week they can have an activity. Keep each child's interests, temperament, and abilities in mind when helping them choose what they will and won't participate in. Ask them *why* they want to join the elite soccer club. Is it because they genuinely like soccer and hope to keep playing for a long time, or because all the other kids seem to be doing it? Talk honestly, as a family, about the budget for extracurricular activities. Keep a family calendar both to track activities and to schedule downtime and family time—meals, bike rides, walks, church. Keep those events just as sacred as the piano lesson or lacrosse practice.

Remember that your grade schooler is still a child. Be a little wary of that term *tweenager*. An eleven-year-old is not in her teens, even though she may be as moody as a fifteen-year-old sometimes. Just because our kids are physically maturing at earlier ages over time, they aren't intellectually, emotionally, or spiritually maturing at a faster rate. Your grade schooler is probably very capable of doing many things for herself. This should be encouraged. Have her pack her own lunch and do her own laundry. But remember, too, that she sometimes needs and wants you to do things not so much for but *with* her. She can read on her own and say her bedtime prayers on her own, but lying down together to pray or to alternate reading pages of a beloved book aloud—that's sabbath.

The Middle and High Schooler

Many of the same principles for finding sabbath in grade school will continue to apply until your child leaves home. They just may become harder to follow. As our kids spend less time at home, the culture of our schools and communities tends to dictate family rhythms of rest and play more than we would like. At this age and stage, you may find that you need to advocate for changes outside your family to make room for sabbath. (You know, in all that free time you have.)

Fear not. You don't have to become an activist to fight for more sabbath in your community. Though if you want to—more power to you. Parents in Ellen's town have started a nonprofit encouraging a pact to save smartphones for high school. And there are smaller and simpler ways to promote change. If practices are scheduled for ten a.m. on Sundays, let the coach know at the start of the season that your daughter and a few others you know have church and either will miss or would be happy to shift practice time to later in the day. There's strength in numbers. Show up at a school board meeting or parent-teacher group and ask what your child's middle or high school is doing to keep homework to reasonable levels, or to help kids manage the increasing stress and pressure that is contributing to rising rates of anxiety and mental health problems.

Talk to your kids and to other parents. We often assume that everyone else is in the rat race because they want to be rats, when the truth is that most parents are feeling the same stress and yearning for sabbath that we are. Even better, it may be enough for our kids to know even one other family who chooses church camp over the summer soccer intensives or a mix of classes rather than every AP course that's offered.

Don't be afraid to set firm limits for your middle and high schooler on screen time and bedtime, and even on activities and opportunities. Kids still need eight to ten hours of sleep a night until age eighteen, but 40 percent of them are sleep deprived. Their brains are developing at the same rate they were in the first five years of life and they need nearly as much rest. This is why having a teenager in the house often feels like having a toddler again.

When it comes to limiting opportunities, this is going to be hard. Even that phrase "limiting opportunities" seems wrong in a parenting book. None of us wants to be the parent who stifled their child's talent or chance at their biggest, best life. Yet we can't possibly give them every opportunity. And sometimes we get so focused on what they might be missing out on, either now or in the future, that **we actually keep them from having their biggest, best life right now: one that includes time for rest, play, and a God who reminds them it's not all about them.**

BIG IDEAS

- Sabbath is not a guilty pleasure. It is a commandment, one of the ten. It is radically counterculture and deeply nourishing. Observe sabbath by having unplugged time—twenty-four hours each week—and making restful space.

- Play is fundamental to healthy child development and human well-being. Stopping yourself to observe your children in play helps you see their "grain."

- You are your child's first and best spiritual teacher. Pray as you are able, in different ways and throughout the day, together: mealtimes, drive times, bedtimes.

- If you've written off church, reconsider. Good church provides a strong container for your child's spiritual development, other loving adults to supplement you, and access to participatory transcendence, art, music, cathartic ritual, antidotes to loneliness, empirical joy, and homemade pie.

Prayer

God, we're too busy. We crave sabbath, and yet find it so hard to grasp the rest You are always offering us. Give us the courage to scale back, slow down, and tune in, so we don't flame out.

Amen.

CHAPTER 8

The Beauty of Bodies

Sex, Drugs, and Going beyond "The Talk"

You might not guess from some of its press, but Christianity is a shoo-in for body-positive theology. After all, one of the core stories of our sacred texts is that God loved bodies so much, God decided to get one. The Nativity is a story about God with skin on, God not as an anatomically incomplete Barbie or Ken, but a fully fleshed human being.

The other core story is Easter, which teaches us that even though bodies are vulnerable and die, God doesn't give up on them, and life continues to find a way.

In between Christmas and Easter, Jesus's life is rife with the juicy joy of being a human being: from weddings where the wine flows like the water it once was (John 2:1–12), to impromptu picnics with new and old friends (Matthew 14:13–21), to letting himself get a vaguely erotic foot massage from a female friend of his (John 12:3), Jesus reveled in having a body and living life to the fullest in it. So much so, in fact, that his enemies branded him "a glutton and a drunkard" (Matthew 11:9). What a friend we have in *this* Jesus . . .

Unfortunately, somewhere along the way conventional wisdom grew up around and choked out these body-loving lessons like so many weeds in a garden. This weedy theology, rooted in both ancient Greek philosophy and fundamentalist mores, is at best indifferent to the body and at worst loathing of it. Most of this perspective can be summed up in three words: "Just say no." No to anything outside a married, monogamous heterosexual relationship, and no to the natural appetites and delights of the body.

The problem with much of current Christian morality is that it follows false binaries—good/bad, yes/no, boy/girl—when reality is much more nuanced. Tattoos are satanic. Masturbation is sinful. Sex before marriage is flat-out wrong, and with a person of the same gender? An abomination. The immaturity of black-and-white thinking rears its head again.

The next generation has a shot at practicing a much more mature level of moral reasoning about their bodies. We can help this evolution by giving our kids room to figure out what is right for them, even to make mistakes, and not to fear coming to us when they do. **We want them to revel in their bodies in the same way Jesus did, and by doing so to care for their physical selves as part of their spiritual practice. Physicality *is* spirituality.**

To do this, you might need to get a teensy bit uncomfortable. We are going to challenge you to move beyond binaries in ways you may not have considered, and then talk about tricky stuff with your kids. Not once. Not twice. But over and over as part of regular family conversation—because when it comes to bodies, binaries don't serve us well.

Take "Just say no" as a simple example. It was the 1980s when Nancy Reagan first uttered the phrase that would become a ubiquitous byword in antidrug programs like Drug Abuse Resistance Education (D.A.R.E.), which thirty years later is still going strong despite evidence that it just doesn't work. These programs have an emotional appeal, but the data don't bear out their effectiveness. A 2009 meta-analysis of twenty studies looking at the effects of D.A.R.E. on kids showed that teens enrolled in the program were *just* as likely to use drugs as those who received no intervention at all. A 2002 study showed that teens who went through D.A.R.E. were actually somewhat *more* likely to drink and smoke cigarettes than those who never went through the program.

Abstinence-only or abstinence-until-marriage sex ed may be even more problematic. Teens with abstinence as the only option for preventing sexually transmitted diseases (STDs) and pregnancy, who don't have access to health information about how to protect themselves if they *do* decide to have sex, are (1) no more likely to choose abstinence than teens who have had more comprehensive sex ed and (2) at higher risk for STDs and unintended pregnancy.

The research suggests that when we give kids abstinence as their *only* choice, we are actually putting them at risk. To boot, there is zero scientific research suggesting that consensual, protected sex between older adolescents is emotionally or physically harmful.

If "Just say no" doesn't work, what does? As in all things, giving our kids choices and information (autonomy support and structure), knowing what they are up to, and being willing to have frank conversations about the tough stuff (involvement) is the best approach to helping our kids make healthy choices for their bodies.

The most effective drug and alcohol and sex education programs give kids options to choose from: abstinence, delay, moderation, protected sex. They provide information on the relatively low incidence of serious drug use and sexual intercourse among younger adolescents, so kids don't operate under the false assumption that they are the only ones not doing it (whichever "it" we are referring to). These programs teach kids the skills they need to say no if they don't want to drink or use drugs or have sex, and they give kids the chance to practice through role play. They give kids an out for when they make mistakes or change their minds. They also move away from false binaries and dichotomies. One drink is not the same as four. Smoking marijuana is not the same as smoking crack. Oral sex is not the same as intercourse.

So what can we learn from effective programs and from a progressive Christian morality that can guide us through these sometimes difficult, often highly embarrassing conversations with our kids?

Sex and the Christian

Perhaps the only topic harder to tackle with your kids than God talk is sex talk. As a parent, you might have a clear idea in your mind for how it will go: You will be upbeat, confident, and knowledgeable. Your relaxed and easygoing disposition will be contagious, and they will find you so approachable that they will open up to you about every last curiosity, worry, and fear. Your conversation will end with your arm casually slung around your five-, ten-, or fifteen-year-old as you walk along, laughing uproariously at some mutually hilarious (but not in any way embarrassing or shaming) joke, because let's face it: bodies are strange, wonderful, and a cause for mirth much of the time. (Cue a fart joke. Or even a fart.)

Unfortunately, that's not the way things usually unfold. It certainly wasn't in our families.

Ellen grew up in a Catholic family and attended Catholic schools from kindergarten through college. There seemed to be a lot of rules, spoken and unspoken, about sex. But she rarely saw people following those rules. Those who seemed to be—the families with six or more kids whom she babysat for, and who often seemed to be under a lot of stress—didn't seem like they were operating by their own free choice or even moral standards. It seemed like they were just following the rules set by a bunch of old guys who had never had sex. And at least some of them didn't seem very happy about it.

But for those who broke the rules in a visible way, guilt and shame ensued. Ellen's high school allowed pregnant girls to continue attending—until the skirts of their uniforms could no longer accommodate their growing bellies. No more fabric to hide your sin, no more school for you. This was about the sum of Ellen's sex ed.

When sex is defined as a set of rules, it doesn't leave a lot of room for discernment. Without any discussion of *why* the rules are there, kids make up alternative rules to accommodate their natural desires and to fit in with secular peer culture. Rules like "I'm not going to wait until I'm *married*, but I *have* to be in love" (whatever that means). Or "Oral sex isn't *really* sex." Worse yet, in confusion and consternation, a teen might just decide to acquiesce to someone else's needs and rules, because they are too confused about their own values to make a truly autonomous choice. Instead of talking to parents or another trusted adult, they look to peers who are just as confused as they are (though they might talk a good game).

When parents of Ellen's generation did talk about sex, it was usually pretty vague. They made statements like "We raised you to make good decisions." What did that mean? To be fair to Ellen's Catholic parents, it's clear from those vague statements that they didn't really want to give her a set of rules to follow or break. They wanted to give her values that would guide her in making good decisions. But nobody was giving her parents *or* her the information they really needed to have meaty and meaningful conversations.

Molly, on the other hand, was raised by parents who came of age in the free-love ethos of the 1960s. They themselves were

both raised by intellectuals who didn't hold much with organized religion and who gave them a lot of freedom. In theory,
they should have been great at talking about sex. But even
though her parents were at one time pretty wild themselves,
they had mellowed into fairly conventional serial monoga-
mists. By the time Molly came of age, here is how her conversations about sex went with her parents.

On a drive to the subway that took all of three minutes, her
father broached the subject. "So . . . ," he started optimistically,
"do you know everything you need to know about, ah, eh, you
know? [Awkward pause] The birds and the bees?" Molly, field-
ing poor Dad's waves of anxiety, rescued him by saying, "Yep."
The talk was done in one minute, with time to spare.

Molly's conversation with her mother was even more
oblique, and also a bit terrifying, as her mom shared, in detail,
her entire sexual history, including illegal abortions, affairs,
and heartbreaking failed relationships. This sharing was probably as much about her mother unburdening herself as it was
to impart wisdom. It's a cautionary tale against telling our kids
more than they are actually asking to know. When her mother
had finished talking, she summed up her story with the bro-
mide, "Cherish yourself." After the specific sadness and pain of
the earlier admissions, it was so vague as to be entirely unhelpful. Was she saying don't have sex? Or only do it with someone
who really loves you and whom you really love? Or be sure to
use birth control? Or thank goodness abortion is (mostly) legal
now? The main upshot of the cautionary tale seemed to be "Do
as I say, not as I did." But what child ever learned from their
parents' mistakes? Most of us reserve the right to make our
own mistakes. It seems to be the way of humans.

And many of us *have* made mistakes. Lots of us have complicated sexual histories, which have had a deep physical or
emotional impact in the form of STDs, unwanted pregnancies

and/or abortions, emotional residue, or trauma and abuse. If we are not going to project our own histories onto our children, we might have some work to do to continue healing *our* sexual selves. We do this to raise children who understand their own sexual power, autonomy, and dignity, and who intuitively claim sexuality as a positive aspect of their spiritual being and becoming.

The good news is, you *can* heal. The fact that you have kids provides a strong impetus to get to work. Remember that our God is the God of second and seventy-seventh chances. No matter what you have done or what has been done to you, you are beloved, whole, and forgiven. You have a sexual future as well as a past, a future in which you can choose healthy, consensual, loving sex (and of course let's not overlook the joy of sex with ourselves, by ourselves).

Then again, since you are a parent, you may have pretty much stopped having sex except on Valentine's Day. Maybe you are partnered and both of you are too exhausted and frazzled to manage having sexy times very often. We want to remind you that sex is an important part of maintaining a healthy bond marked by closeness, affection, and vulnerability. Maybe you are a single parent and sex is even more elusive and complicated, as you navigate relationships amid the difficulty of childrearing. As you guide your child through the stormy seas of sexuality, you may find that you are parenting yourself through new learnings about your own needs, desires, boundaries, fantasies, morality, and spirituality regarding sex. Which brings us to discernment.

Discernment is the hard work of figuring out our values—or more to the point, God's desire for us—on a case-by-case basis. It is messy. It is arduous. It involves being ruthlessly honest with ourselves and the people we are intimate with, being logical as well as emotional, and emotional as well as logical. Because you can never be *quite* sure that it is God's voice you are hearing. There is none of the delicious certainty that comes with following the rules, including the dopamine hit we get from judging others who themselves fail to follow them or fall outside the "norm."

Good Sex

As parents, you are going to have to discern your own values about sex, ideally before you start having in-depth conversations with your kids. Because, trust us, this is going to sneak up on you really fast, assuming it hasn't already.

For millennia, human culture has been oscillating back and forth between no boundaries and lots of boundaries about sex, trying to figure out what the sweet spot is. Here's a stab at a definition of healthy and good sex: **good sex is sex that is good for everybody involved.** Progressive Christians understand that everything we do has consequences beyond what we can see. We are linked in invisible spiritual and physical networks, and we know that our decisions matter. We consider this in how we drive, eat, work, buy. Why not consider this in how we sex?

One evening at a Bible study at our church, we crowdsourced a working definition of healthy sexuality. Two of the men in our group took things in a beautiful direction. "Why is it," one of them wondered aloud, "that in our culture we tend to talk about purity only in terms of virginity? It's either/or. Once you lose your virginity, we say that that 'pure' is gone. I'd like to see us develop a concept for purity that goes along with growing up as sexual people—the idea that we get more pure as we get older, as we learn what our partners want, as we become more generous lovers, as we learn to communicate clearly our needs and boundaries, as we commit to radical honesty and tenderness, as we make peace with our bodies, though they are imperfect, and learn to love them as they are." The other man at our table burst in, "We could call it the Sex: It Gets Better campaign!"

Paul, who wrote many of the letters in the New Testament, including the so-called texts of terror about homosexuality, also gave us this gem: "or do you not know that your body is a temple of the Holy Spirit within you, which you have from God, and that you are not your own?" (I Corinthians 6:19).

Progressive Christianity teaches that your body is uniquely yours, but not *exactly* your own. Molly tells her son: "I *made* your body, so you better be good to it." But it is in fact God who "knitted him together in his mother's womb" (Psalm 139). Adoptive parents know this even more poignantly: that they are stewards, caregivers, of these bodies they welcomed into their lives and the souls that inhabit them.

Reading this book, there are doubtless people who delayed sexual activity until marriage, and there are people who have been around the block, and there are people who have been around the whole city. There are people who have never really enjoyed the gift of sexuality, and there are people who have violated boundaries—hurt themselves and others—and repented, and there are people with little to no sexual desire. Every one of you is precious to God, and deeply OK.

If you don't *feel* OK about sex, you may have some work to do. Many of us do. Start by examining the messages you were given about sex and the messages you never heard and wish you had. Where are you now? What do you want and need to be a sexually healthy person? Think about how your sexual experiences to date either fit, or don't, with the values you have now and with the values you hope your children will hold. And if, after this, you are still struggling, talk with a partner, a friend, a pastor, or a therapist. Especially if you are co-parenting, be sure you are comfortable talking with each other about sex before diving into conversations with your kids. A common misconception about sex therapy is that it teaches you to have better sex. While that may be a nice by-product, sex therapy really teaches you to talk openly with your partner about sex. Consider it.

Let's Talk about Sex, Baby

Because kids lack a functioning prefrontal cortex to help them delay gratification and think through consequences, they need to discern alongside their parents about sex and sexual activity: not in "The Talk" but in many talks, over many years, starting as soon as they can name their own body parts.

What follows is not an exhaustive tutorial on how to talk to your kids about bodies and sex. There are plenty of really good books out there that do that. The way you talk about sex is going to depend on your child's developmental age, stage, and temperament. Here are a few guideposts, along with Molly's messy execution of one talk—because these conversations never go the way we plan.

Guideposts for the Sex Talks

· **Call it what it is.** Starting when your children are very young, use accurate scientific names for body parts, including the most intimate and "private" parts. Yes, grandparents may be a little shocked to hear two-year-olds talking ad nauseam about their penises and vulvas. Too bad! That's what they are called.

That is the first step toward showing your kids you are open to conversations about potentially embarrassing things that a lot of people can't or won't talk about—at least not in respectful ways. Using silly names for body parts suggests that our parts and what we do with them is "silly business" and not worthy of respect or serious discussion.

This also allows for conversations about privacy, safety, and consent. Teach your kids that their parts are theirs, and theirs alone. Part of respecting their bodies is to treat them with care. If you have a good pediatrician, follow their language around this. They will often say things like, "I'm going to look at/touch your penis because it is part of your checkup to make sure you are growing healthy. That's my job. Is that OK?"

· **Talk about and model consent.** When our kids were just toddlers, we told them that if someone makes them feel uncomfortable or unsafe for *any* reason, get out, no matter who it is. They can worry about being polite later. This is not the time to "respect adults." Be wary of teaching kids only to fear strangers. It is much more likely they will be hurt by someone they know. Instead, teach them to trust their gut. "You have permission to say no loudly to adults and other children when you feel unsafe. Then go and talk to an adult you trust about what happened, right away—even if the person who made you uncomfortable told you to keep it a secret or told you something bad would happen if you talked."

We also work hard to model consent in our families. This is not always easy. Ellen repeats about a hundred times a day to one boy or the other, "Your brother said stop. That means you stop. Now. Not after he says it

three more times." If we are horsing around, enjoying a
tickle fight, and someone says they have had enough, we
stop. "No" is a complete sentence. And no means *no*.

· **Teach kids that sex is fun. And it's special.** Sex is
supposed to be an expression of love, and it is supposed
to feel good. Nowhere did Jesus tell us that sex is only
for making babies. In the best-case scenario, it is a way
of getting and feeling as close to someone you love
as possible. There is no human physical closeness as
powerful as sex, excepting childbirth and nursing. Sex
was one of the first things God invented, in the book of
Genesis, and along with it nakedness, as a good thing.

· **Remember, this isn't "The Talk." This is an
ongoing conversation.** As with all tricky topics, don't
tell kids more than they are ready to hear. Yours would
not be the first ten-year-old to cover their ears and
yell "Stop!" Or "That sounds awful!" Or one of Ellen's
favorites from a friend of Luke's (really, seriously a
friend), who said "What?! Mom, why would you let Dad
do that to you?!"

It's OK for you to bring it up, but **follow their
lead.** Answer their questions honestly, but try not to
answer questions they aren't asking yet. It also helps
to have these talks in situations where you can avoid
the intensity of eye contact: in the car, riding bikes,
playing catch. Follow up later to check on whether they
understood what you were saying, after they've digested
it. Ellen's husband started a conversation with Luke at
age ten, throwing the football around. A few days later,
while folding laundry, Ellen asked him what his dad
had told him. He explained that he understood there

was "a difference between sex and sexual intersection."
Hmmm . . . getting there.

· **Don't forget about gender.** An estimated 1.7 percent
of babies are born intersex. Even more children and
adults than that come to understand themselves as
transgender, and even self-identified cis people have a
range of gender identities and personalities. Genitalia
don't always correspond to how we understand our
gender. Be careful of the assumptions you make about
your child as they grow. Again, pay attention to who
God made them to be—and believe and support them
when they tell you who they are. We are coming into
a new psychological understanding of gender as fluid,
one that lines up with the Bible's assertion that "There
is no longer . . . male nor female, but we are One in
Christ" (Galatians 3:28).

Additionally, schools often still fall into the trap of
separate/gender-binary sex education, as though girls
don't need to know what is happening to boys' bodies,
and vice versa. All young people need to know how to
give and get consent. All young people have legitimate
physical needs and desires. There is no remaining
biological or evolutionary value to boys being the
aggressors and girls the gatekeepers. In fact, that binary
hurts us all. Talk to your kids about what they are
learning in school, or find them supplemental human
sexuality education like the Our Whole Lives (OWL)
curriculum offered in UCC and Unitarian Universalist
churches.

· **And don't forget about same-gender relationships.**
There are only a handful of scriptures that mention

homosexuality: a few in the Hebrew scriptures (when the Jews and their ancestors were trying to survive as a tribe through exile and war and landlessness— and procreation mattered), and a couple in Paul's letters (when early Christianity was trying to define itself against the mores of the much more sexually liberal Greeks and Romans). Jesus never mentioned homosexuality, and he was not afraid to talk about sex, or about money, politics, or any other difficult and intensely personal topic. God made the world and called it good, along with penguins, giraffes, humans, and other creatures that are attracted to or form pair bonds with same-gender partners. We are just as God made us.

Molly's Tween Talk #17

I was determined, when it came time to talk with my kids about sex, that I would do better than my own parents. Because I know that sex is a beautiful and important part of being human, created and affirmed by God, I would not be embarrassed. I would not overshare but only answer what my kids were asking. I would keep the focus on them, and not on me.

I did all right when the talking was about body parts and basic functions. But one day in the car when my children were about six and ten, the ten-year-old started asking higher-level questions, and the six-year-old listened *very* closely. Questions like: What is a blowjob? Where do the legs go when people are having sex? How often do you and Dad have sex? How do gay people have sex if they don't have a penis/vagina situation?

I felt myself blushing and sweating. I felt the urge to euphemize, or change the subject. Darn it! Shame, you will not win this time!

Brené Brown, who has done groundbreaking research into emotions, teaches us that shame is the most powerful master emotion. Shame is highly correlated with addiction, depression, violence, aggression, bullying, suicide, and eating disorders. And, of course, shame and sex are inextricably linked. Shame shrouds a lot of our earliest sexual thoughts and our later sexual behaviors; it is both the source of some of our sexual acting-out and an aftereffect of it. Brown says that "shame, in a petri dish, needs these three things to grow: Secrecy, silence and judgment." It's also a huge source of confusion, and the last thing I wanted to do was confuse my kids!

Back in the car, I took a deep breath. I told myself that if I didn't give the kids good information and clear direction, they would make up their own rules. And that might mean getting hurt, or hurting someone else. I couldn't save them from every hurt or mistake—but I could help them start from a wiser, better-informed place.

So I pushed through my shame and spoke from heart, soul, mind, and experience. Here is the gist of our talk:

Feelings get deeply tangled up in sex—for people of every gender, not just girls, as the media teaches us—you might think you are ready or think you are in love and feel safe with this other person, but you find out the hard way after having sex that you really weren't ready—and you can't take it back. It is always there between you, and when you are young, it can put distance between you and the other person more often than it brings you closer together.

There is a range of sexual behaviors: fantasizing, kissing, touching, oral sex, anal sex, and sexual intercourse—and it is all sex, not just vaginal penetration—and it all comes with complicated feelings.

The longer you wait, the more likely it is you will be truly emotionally ready to have sex. Like, by the time you are thirty, I suspect. Just kidding. Sort of.

One gauge of readiness is: Can you talk about what you are about to do with your partner, face-to-face, without embarrassment? Can you see each other naked, be vulnerable with each other, and feel OK? Can you walk into the drugstore unashamed and buy condoms? Anything you have to get drunk to be ready to do, or have to do in the dark, or have to do furtively, or without any conversation before or afterward, is probably something you are not ready for. And drugs and alcohol will lower your inhibitions, leading you to make a choice you might not make sober.

It is important to get and give consent with every partner. And go further than that: sexual intimacy is an opportunity to be generous and selfless with another human being. Pay close attention to nonverbal cues, and to what your partner really wants—it's especially important for boys and men to do this, as it's not what the culture supports.

Then we role-played what to say if they should ever find themselves in a scary situation. When sexual abuse happens, the perpetrator is most often not a stranger but a trusted family friend, coach, teacher, camp counselor, or other authority figure who has groomed the victim over a period of time, gradually going further and further over the line. Fighting back requires a specific line of defense and a strong sense of self.

In my line of work, I have heard many disclosures from teenage and adult sexual abuse survivors, and I have also pastored pedophiles. I understand both how horrifyingly common abuse is and how well versed my kids need to be in finding their voice if someone is violating their boundaries. I told my kids that under no circumstances is it their fault if something happens, even if they feel ashamed, and how they *must* tell a safe adult who can help it stop, even if they have been warned to keep silent.

Kids who know the names for the body parts, who understand what consent is, who are comfortable speaking up for themselves with adults (which includes refusing to hug or kiss a family member who makes them uncomfortable), and kids who know their parents are open to nonjudgmental conversation about bodies and sex are more likely to speak up and speak out about sexual assault and abuse.

Our conversation continued, talking about the sexual double standard for girls, about slut-shaming, how it works, and why it's sexist and wrong. We talked about how teenagers lie All The Time about what they have and haven't done—and about how they should *never* have sex (or oral sex, or make out, or *anything*) because they think they are the only ones left who haven't done it. Because then they might just find out they are the only ones who *have* done it.

We talked about orgasms, and how amazing they are, and how God invented them, and how they happen during sex whether or not people plan to make a baby, so God must have meant for sex to be there just for fun sometimes. We get to talking so seriously and earnestly and academically about sex sometimes that we forget to tell our kids that it's not just about flaps and slots, but sex is darn *fun* when it's right and good—one of the very best things. Even better than Häagen-Dazs chocolate peanut butter ice cream, though that's a close second.

We talked about how masturbation is one of the very best kinds of sex because you can't get pregnant; it's totally safe, physically and emotionally speaking; and it's fun, relaxing, and exciting. You can do it as often as you like, in private, because it's a deeply personal activity (but *please* don't hog the shower).

Some kids start when they're very young, and that's OK and not weird. The majority start when they are entering puberty, or later. It's totally natural, and a gift from God.

We talked about fantasies: how they're pictures your brain dreams up and not necessarily things you want to do in real life. We talked about how sometimes our brains in sleep dream really weird things that make us feel a little oogy when we wake up. But you know what? That is also OK and perfectly normal and acceptable. The brain police will not come and secretly tape your dreams or fantasies and project them onto the TV next time you are hanging out with your parents and sibs having family movie night.

We talked about same-sex attraction: how it's normal, healthy, and how even people who do not ultimately identify as LGBT are sometimes attracted to individuals of their gender, or think boobs are amazing even if they otherwise identify as straight girls (let's face it: boobs *are* amazing).

We talked about pornography: about how, first of all, it resembles real sex the way that Martha Stewart's seven-layer perfectly frosted rainbow cake resembles the lumpen mystery I made for my daughter's last birthday. It's heavily photoshopped and, frankly, fiction. We talked about how pornography often reinforces gender stereotypes or power differentials (with women mostly focused on pleasing men, or being pleased sexually in ways that are not what many women actually enjoy). We talked about the fact that there is nothing inherently wrong with viewing pornography ethically made, but that the industry is rife with sex trafficking, including exploitation of vulnerable women and even children.

We talked about the fact that God made all bodies beautiful, including theirs: fat and skinny, big boobs/small boobs (boobs!), big penises/small penises, hairy and smooth, dark skin and light skin and everything in between. I told them that it is rumored that the angels are in fact jealous of us because we get to have bodies: bodies that can eat and sleep, play soccer and run marathons, dance and make love, and hug it out.

And finally we talked about the Bible's sex stories, complicated messy stories with people making bad choices, often in ways that hurt women. And how Jesus had, in fact, in thirty-three years and a zillion sermons, said nothing at all about masturbation, gay sex, or premarital sex. He apparently just didn't find it important enough. On the other hand, he said quite a lot about loving our enemies, not judging people, and looking to our own failings rather than pointing out what we believe to be broken or wrong or misbehaving about someone else.

There ended that talk—followed by a nap!

Further Resources

If you are still feeling intimidated at the idea of having The Many Talks with your children, there is plenty of help to get you started or complement your conversations.

Two of the best resources we can recommend are *Talk to Me First* by Deborah Roffman, and the series of books (*It's Not the Stork!*, *It's So Amazing!*, *It's Perfectly Normal*) by Robie Harris and Michael Emberley, pitched perfectly by age. We keep ours in the bathroom and our children have read them literally dozens of times. And now their friends like to come to our house to play, so they can secretly educate themselves while in the powder room.

Especially for preteens and teenagers who may be reluctant and embarrassed to have you start the conversation, using books can be an entryway. Ask them to read it and write down any questions they have. You read it, too, and then decide on a time to talk about it, maybe on a car ride. Or if the idea of a face-to-face is just too embarrassing, write your responses back to them.

Another excellent resource is the Our Whole Lives curriculum, developed jointly by the United Church of Christ and the Unitarian Universalist Association. Classes cover subjects like puberty concerns, body image, social media and the Internet, bullying and bystander responsibilities, porn, sexual decision making, and redefining abstinence. It gives kids a chance to be with peers talking about a titillating subject in a safe, fun, and often humorous way, and helps kids build relationships with safe and wise adults that they can ask any questions of anonymously.

Some of the most important choices our children will make in life relate to their sexuality. We owe it to them to give them all the tools they need to navigate this perilous, wonderful terrain.

If Your Child Is Queer

Your child comes out to you as gay, bi, trans, or genderqueer. You say: "You are beautiful and good, just as God made you, and I love you exactly the same as I did five minutes ago! There is nothing you could say or do or be that would make me not love you!" If you need more words than that, run, don't walk, to your nearest device and read Glennon Doyle's viral blog post on the letter she wrote to her son when he was a tween, "A Mountain I'm Willing to Die On" (http://momastery.com/blog/2013/03/26/a-mountain-im-willing-to-die-on-4/).

You are likely to have your own feelings of grief, worry, or loss when your child comes out. Worry for their safety, since queer kids are still at a high risk for bullying, self-harm, and suicidal ideation; grief at losing the gender you thought they were versus the gender they are discerning; sadness that, if they someday choose to have children, those children may not arrive into your family the way you had imagined.

Grieve privately. Support publicly. Get them and yourself *all* the resources you need, loads of community and affirmation. Help them find a gay-straight alliance (GSA) in their school. Get yourself to PFLAG. Get all of you to an Open and Affirming (queer-friendly) church that will not just tolerate, or gossip behind closed doors, but extravagantly welcome and embrace all of you, especially your kids, just as they are, and as they are becoming.

Body Image

When Molly was an exchange student in Russia, she went to a Russian bathhouse one day and saw women of every age and body type unselfconsciously walking around starkers. It was the first time she realized there are not two kinds of bodies: perfect and imperfect. There are umpteen kinds of bodies along all kinds of gradients, and each really is unique.

Parents have a lot of power to shape their kids' body image. All bodies are different, even within families. Perhaps more than in any other area of parenting, how we talk about and treat our own bodies directly impacts how our kids see themselves. We also have power over their body image by the permission and feedback we give them regarding what they choose to wear and eat, how they wear their hair, whether they paint their nails, and so on.

There is good research showing that moms are the most important influencers of their girls' body image—not by what moms say to their daughters about their bodies, but by what they say about their *own*. Moms, have you ever said something "innocent" like "I remember back when I was as skinny as you are now! I miss it."

You think you are complimenting your daughter, and you are, but you are also denigrating yourself in front of her. Until you say it, your kids don't think you're fat. Or ugly, or wrinkly, or short, or turkey-necked. They think you're Mom. Eating-disorder experts advise zero talk about your child's weight, or yours, and zero talk of dieting or exercising to lose a few pounds. Focus on eating healthy and exercising regularly to-gether as a family as a way of feeling good and strong in our bodies. Show confidence when you are wearing something that makes you feel good about how you look. Families that eat to-gether regularly have lower rates of obesity and heart disease. Cooking together is good for our kids' mental and physical health and gives us a natural opportunity to talk about serv-ing sizes, ingredients, and healthy eating without tying it to weight.

Boys are not exempt from body image challenges: rates of eating disorders are on the rise among them, too. Excessive ex-ercise and focus on weight loss and gain for sports is pervasive. In our hometown of Boston, sports radio spends hours dis-secting quarterback Tom Brady's strange and highly restrictive diet—questioning whether avoiding mushrooms really helped him bring home all those Super Bowl rings. Our boys wonder, too (with joy over an excuse to refuse mushrooms). They worry about being tall enough, thin enough, muscular enough. They also look to us moms to set standards of beauty for them, to provide a counterpoint to the waxed, airbrushed, and photo-shopped models of the ideal woman they are confronted with every day.

Neither of us is a perfect parent on this one, for sure. We have complained about our jeans not fitting in front of our kids, or mocked our mummy tummies. But we try really hard to remember that our bellies are what they are because they grew the kids we love.

The core issue is that our kids need to hear from us that their bodies are beautiful. They need to believe that their bodies are gifts, "fearfully and wonderfully made," just as they are. We model this for them in our words, our reactions, and our actions. We can do this by bringing them into communities where all kinds of beauty are on display: gay pride parades, all-ages drag shows, and dances at senior citizens' centers!

We also do this by letting them choose their own clothes, makeup, bodily adornments, and standards of beauty. Molly said yes when Rafe at age five, on a shopping trip to Target, picked out a T-shirt with a giant sequined heart on it. Ellen painted eight-year-old Jonah's fingernails whatever color he requested for family Christmas. We have held our breath hoping peers and family members wouldn't say anything to shame our kids and undermine our message: be proud of your body and do with it as you please; it truly is a gift from God and uniquely yours.

Alcohol and Other Drugs

Molly and her husband both grew up in alcoholic families, families where people used drugs and alcohol to self-medicate mental health conditions, and both grandparents and parents died of smoking-related illnesses or heart attacks tragically young. Ellen's boys, too, have an extended family history of alcoholism. We know that because of our family histories our kids may be at greater risk for abusing alcohol and drugs, and so we began talking to them very young about the impact of drinking, drugs, and cigarettes on health and mental health.

Psalm 139:13 says, "For it was you who formed my inward parts. You knit me together in my mother's womb." God has known our children since before birth and is responsible for shaping their miraculous physical forms. Whether you are a bio parent or an adoptive one, you have a lot invested in keeping those sweet bodies and souls safe and healthy.

Molly is not above bribery to prevent, or at least delay, her kids' experimentation with substances. She and her husband made their children a deal: if they made it to age twenty-six (when the prefrontal cortex is fully formed) without taking a single drag off of a nicotine-delivering device, they would each get $2,000.

We also need a more nuanced approach about alcohol and drugs than "Just say no" if we are going to help our kids navigate the experimentation years. When Ellen's Luke went through the D.A.R.E. program, she had him rip up the contract he had signed to never use drugs, never drink alcohol before age twenty-one, and never hang out with people doing such things. He had learned some good skills from the program, but the contract seemed like a setup for failure. There was no talk of what to do or what might happen if he broke it. There was no real distinction made between trying pot and trying heroin, or between drinking a bottle of wine by yourself and having a beer at a party. If we tell our kids that all drugs are equally bad, and therefore should be equally avoided, what happens when they try a less lethal one and are essentially fine? We've lied to them. Why should they trust or listen to us again?

If you are not allergic to alcohol the way someone predisposed to alcoholism is, drinking is an enjoyable part of life. The Bible supports us on this point! Jesus's first miracle in the Gospel of John is to turn water into wine, so that the guests might really celebrate. And the Psalms laud God, "You . . . bring forth food from the earth, and wine to gladden the human heart."

To have a healthy (and respectful) relationship with alcohol, Molly and Peter started allowing their children, at about age eight, to drink a small bit of wine with them at the family dinner table on special occasions. It is exciting and makes them feel grown-up. This makes alcohol not an all-or-nothing proposition but a normal part of life—not something to be binged on in secret, but sipped on in public.

When you talk to your kids about drugs and alcohol, don't just talk at them. Ask them questions: What do you think alcohol does? How do you think it helps or hurts? Do any of your peers drink? Try to get a sense of what is going on in their community and culture (involvement!). Talk about choices (autonomy support!), and be clear about what the likely and less likely consequences of their decisions may be (structure!). Make sure they know that they can always, *always* call you for a ride, no questions asked, at any hour of the day or night.

About other drugs: Talk from your own firsthand experience and scientific knowledge, although we'd suggest keeping your communications about your personal experiences general until your kids are older adolescents, lest they take it to mean they can't come to you if they try something you haven't, or as tacit permission to experiment. But do tell your kids (if this is true) that you know people who have tried lots of things and had different experiences, without naming names.

And rather than forbid some or all substances, you might tell them, in the words of Jesus, that "the tree will be known by its fruit." Not all people who smoke pot become potheads, but some do, and it has affected their education, jobs, and relationships in fundamentally harmful ways. Getting high might also seem like a welcome relief for depression, ADD, or anxiety, but while it is a short-term solution, it can create serious long-term problems. Tell them that some drugs can kill you with just one use, and are therefore on a *never*-try list.

Doing role plays with your kids about what to say if their friends offer them drugs or alcohol will help them resist in the moment without losing face. If they create those neural pathways and learn those scripts with you, they will be more likely to use them when they find themselves in difficult situations. Likewise, the drug and alcohol use prevention programs that actually work give kids social skills they need to set limits with others.

When it comes to alcohol and drugs, we need to treat our kids as people with brains and teach them how to do discernment. Remind them that their bodies are "temples of God, and not their own" (I Corinthians 6), that their bodies are in fact part of a greater "body" of human community, and that their decisions don't just affect themselves but also parents, siblings, girlfriends, boyfriends, and every single person on the road when they get behind the wheel after having a couple of beers.

If Your Child Becomes an Addict

Addiction is a disease, not a personal moral failing. If your child is addicted to alcohol or drugs, it does not mean they are bad (though the addiction may cause them to do bad things, like stealing from you or lying to you). It does not mean you are a bad parent.

Know that there is help. There is the amazing, ubiquitous, affirming, and life-changing resource of Alcoholics Anonymous and the Twelve Steps, which can be, incidentally, a gateway to a profound and meaningful relationship with God. There are also excellent child and adolescent therapists who know how to ask your kids about their alcohol and drug use in ways that not only encourage but allow for honesty. Know that this may require you to trust them to judge what is safe (and not) for your child. Ellen has conversations every day with teens facing difficult decisions about sex, alcohol, and drugs, conversations that allow for discernment without the burden of parental worry or judgment. Sometimes she has to convince kids that their substance use has gotten out of control, that their parents need to know and they need more help. But just because your kid has a beer at a party, don't assume they are on a one-way road to addiction. How you react and respond matters a lot.

Take an example: You come home from work and shockingly smell booze on your tween's breath. It's a Tuesday, for God's sake! Turns out they took a sip from an open wine bottle on the kitchen counter "to take the edge off" before doing homework. Before you freak out on them, consider the specifics of this decision. It's different from having a beer at a party. Be clear about why their choice worries you. Talk about the perils of drinking alone, or of drinking as a way of handling stress. Talk about escalation: how once you've done something once, it's easy to do it again. And about how when you lie to your parents, it puts distance between you and them, and they can't help you as effectively. Let them know that if this happens again (or if it wasn't actually the first time) you all might need more help.

If your child is an addict, Al-Anon is available to you, as you learn how to be in a loving relationship with your child without enabling them. See Jamie's beautiful story in Chapter 10 about parenting his alcoholic son. Make sure you get the resources and support you need to raise your child in the way they should go, or learn how to let go and let others shepherd your child in the ways of sober living and spiritual solutions to the disease of addiction.

Family Map Activity

In our therapy practice and pastoral counseling work, we sometimes use *genograms*, a kind of family tree with succulent details, as a way of getting people to see generational patterns of not only addiction but also abuse, divorce, migrations, cutoff, close or fused relationships, adoption, abortion, and all manner of tragedies and triumphs in families. If you are curious enough to create your own, a quick Google search will give you some templates.

Drawing family maps with our children (without giving them more information than they can handle for their age and temperament) can be a powerful way of teaching our kids family stories, helping them (literally) to *see* themselves as part of that unfolding story, and as part of a wider web of support and a community to whom they are responsible—because if something dangerous or detrimental is happening in one part of the web, it affects the whole system. Again, the Christian community is often described as "the body of Christ." And the New Testament writer Paul said, poignantly, "If one member of the body suffers, all suffer together with it."

Talking about S-E-X by Ages and Stages

First, a caveat: these conversations are not meant to be exhaustive. We also cannot possibly anticipate every question about sex, sexuality, bodies, drugs, and addiction that your kids will ask. These are some key points we encourage you to cover at each age and stage. Remember that it's always OK to respond to any question with "I need to think a little and get back to you on that."

The Preschooler

If your three-to-five-year-old doesn't already know and use the correct terms for their body parts, start now. Make sure they also know some other basic vocabulary. Grab a picture book to talk about how sex is the thing people do to make babies, but also sometimes just because they love each other and it feels good. Talk about privacy and private parts. They are private because they are special and shared with people we trust. Respect their temperament about privacy. Even the youngest kids vary widely in their comfort with nakedness, and it's all OK.

Gender identity begins to emerge around age three. This makes the preschool years the ideal time to talk about what it means to be a girl or a boy (and what it doesn't). It also means your preschooler may have some surprising questions or be prone to making seemingly highly inappropriate remarks. They may incorrectly assume gender based on a person's short or long hair (or in Luke's case once, based on an elderly woman's chin hairs. Awkward!), so it's also prime time to share your family values about sex and gender identity.

For us, this meant conversations about how sex is defined by whether a person is born with a penis or a vagina (or some combination in the case of intersex). Sex has nothing to do with what you like or the clothes you wear. But gender identity, being a girl or a boy, cisgender or transgender, is one piece of the beautiful puzzle of identity that our kids develop from the moment of birth to the end of their time on this earth. Most people are happiest when how they feel on the inside matches how they look on the outside—whatever that means for them. And it meant letting our preschool boys live that out in sparkly T-shirts or nail polish or a buzz cut, depending on how they felt at the time.

The Grade Schooler

Grade school is a perfect time to move on from teaching our kids the correct names for body parts and sex to acknowledging that we know all the incorrect ones. Chances are they are learning about *all* the different kinds of balls on the playground. When we acknowledge that we know that bodies and sex get talked about in ways that make them seem dirty or bad, we make it clear we think they are anything but. Bringing sex out into the open and brushing the dirt of popular culture off it turns it into the gift God intends it to be.

Forcing our grade schoolers to talk about this stuff with us may be hard, but we encourage you to work to fake an air of breezy calm. Point out that people use slang because they are uncomfortable with something that shouldn't be embarrassing at all. Let your kids know that it makes sense they would feel a little funny hearing and talking about sex because they are still too young to have it or really understand what it might be like. And what they see online or in the movies or hear about in music and from their friends is definitely *not* what it's really like. Sex makes babies and brings them into the world. Focus on the mechanics, since that is likely what they are most curious about. And most of all, make it clear this is a subject you are willing and able to talk about anytime.

The Middle Schooler

Let's spend a few minutes talking about social media. The ability of our kids to have access to information and images in the palm of their hand and to communicate with others in a split second has changed many things about parenting, but probably none more than sex. Internet porn, Snapchat, and Tinder may not all pose equal risks to our kids' sexual development, but all hold pitfalls we need to be aware of and talk about.

Starting in middle school, kids need to understand that the risks of Internet pornography are twofold. First, there's looking at it. They need to know that most of it is completely unrealistic. But we also need to acknowledge that we have a generation of visual learners. They rely on YouTube videos to teach them to make slime or repair a computer. They are naturally going to be curious about what sex looks like and how it works. If you find out your middle schooler (or even grade schooler) has googled "Miley Cyrus totally naked boobs," don't freak out.

The second risk of Internet porn is much bigger. The middle schooler passing on a copy of *Playboy* in 1985 didn't face the potential of criminal prosecution. Starting early in middle school, our kids need to know that sending explicit images or material to a peer is illegal and could get them into big trouble. Legal, life-changing trouble. There are plenty of examples from the news of entire middle and high schools wrapped up in Internet pornography distribution scandals. Use these to talk about the risks. Show kids how a simple Google search can bring up all kinds of things about a person, including information they would not want a potential college or employer to know about them.

Most of all, give them a pause button. They don't have one yet, and won't until their brains are fully cooked at about age twenty-five. Make sure they know you can and might screen their social media accounts and devices at any time. Remind them that other parents are doing that, too. Better yet, make a pact with the parents of your kids' friends that you *all* will. If your kid knows that the naked picture they are about to snap of themselves could be seen by you or someone else's mom or dad, they may just hesitate long enough not to hit send.

The High Schooler

The conversations about sex and social media will most definitely continue into high school. But now you are going to have to start talking about the very real possibility that your kid is actually having sex, or will soon. On average, teens in the United States have sexual intercourse for the first time around age seventeen, though many kids have sex earlier and many more become sexually active without having intercourse.

Now is the time to talk about values and boundaries. If you have a co-parent, it would be wise for the two of you to sit down first for a serious conversation about what you are and are not OK with. If your teen is dating someone, where and when are they allowed to spend time in your house, parents present or absent, doors open or closed? Get clear, so you can be clear with them. Don't assume they remember everything you have told them before. They may need reminders when faced with a real partner that, for example, birth control is a must every single time.

Be aware that these conversations can go south very quickly, or never even get started, if you come at your teen in a lecturing or shaming way. Instead, try taking what Ellen calls a "wondering stance." Use open-ended questions and comments to gauge their thoughts and to share your values. Try, "I've noticed that it seems like not a lot of kids in your class are paired off or dating the way they did when I was in high school. . . . I wonder why." Use this as a jumping-off point to talk about the pros and cons of dating versus hooking up, and how one or the other may or may not fit with your family's values. The "wondering stance" can work miracles. Just be careful not to overuse it, and risk your kids thinking you're a dunce. A nine-year-old boy Ellen worked with early in her career looked up at her one day and said, "You sure do wonder about a lot of things."

BIG IDEAS

- Christianity is body-positive: God made bodies, in all their strangeness, distinctness, and glory, and called them *all* good. Then God decided to take on a body Himself! Jesus is God with skin on. Sex is a gift from God when it respects all bodies and the people who inhabit them. If you need proof of its divinity, God invented the orgasm! Nicely done, God.

- "Just say no" abstinence policies (about sex or substances) have poor outcomes. When our kids feel safe enough to come to us with questions they have, bad choices they've made, or pressures they are facing, without fearing our anger or judgment, we can help them figure out what is right for them and learn from their mistakes. Remember the Holy Trinity of Parenting—autonomy support, structure, and involvement—and that "The Talk" is actually a series of conversations that unfold at different ages and stages.

- God made your child, trans or cis, queer or straight, just as they are, and as you are discovering.

- Your kids are listening to everything you say about your own body. Mirror to them what God thinks: that you are beautiful and beloved, just as God (and life, including that emergency C-section) has made you.

Prayer

God, when it's time for the next talk, banish shame and embarrassment and help me embody grace, ease, trust in my child, and confidence that You are also guiding them.

Amen.

CHAPTER 9

Routines and Rituals

How to Turn Holidays Back into Holy Days

Kids, from infants to teens, thrive on routine and ritual. *Routines* provide children with soothing structure and foster a sense of self-efficacy and security. Whether kids are struggling at bedtime or coping with a parent's serious illness, one of the first lines of advice is to try to stick to a routine as much as possible. Routines make us feel safe.

Rituals are different from routines. They help us define our core values or family culture, process big feelings, and make meaning of life in all its fullness. In a study summarizing the impact of rituals and routines on children's development, the authors describe the difference between the two this way: "When routines are disrupted, it may be a hassle; when rituals are disrupted, family cohesion is threatened." Family routines and rituals also relate to children's language development, academic achievement, and social skills.

Of course, rituals and routines are not mutually exclusive. Routines can be rituals. Take dinnertime and bedtime as prime examples. A dinnertime routine might include the ritual of eating together at the table, saying grace, and talking about the highs and lows of the day. A bedtime routine-ritual might include story time, the same songs sung night after night, and prayers.

Rituals also include holidays, birthdays, and the particular ways that families observe them. Rituals are sacramental—outward, embodied signs of internal, eternal spiritual truths and values: the way a family birthday celebration says "We are so glad you were born!" or a two-hour Christmas-stocking-opening experience says "Even little gifts have a big impact, because they are our love language."

The longing for ritual and routine is in part what brought Ellen into Molly's church all those years ago when now-fourteen-year-old Luke was just a five-month-old baby in a sling. Ellen knew there was no way she could teach Luke a faith that would sustain him outside of a communal spiritual tradition and the ways that collective ritual and routine would support his need for structure and a secure base.

When it comes to the construction of a child's faith—whether it evolves into Christianity, agnosticism, or a different set of beliefs altogether—kids need two things: play and participation.

Consider the philosophy that guides Montessori teaching. In this method, teachers provide students with the space and materials to independently explore new concepts and ideas in a hands-on way. In essence, they learn by doing. In these classrooms, you'll often see younger children trying on adult roles and responsibilities.

Nearly every preschool (Montessori or not) has a "house" area where kids can pretend to care for babies, cook dinner, and clean up. Kids love and need to have a safe structured space to try on roles, habits, and ideas. Little kids will do this through play (Godly Play and storytelling in our church). Older kids might do it through age-appropriate participation (being a part of the worship service or going to church camp).

Think of holy days and holidays, of sabbaths and Sundays, as ways of scaffolding kids' spiritual learning and growth. This is your chance to allow kids to physically "try on" faith and to grow into their own version of the role of believer—or nonbeliever. Rituals and routines help kids develop their own unique spirituality the same way they grow and develop in any skills, first through play and later through practice.

Ellen's faith had first been shaped by routines of weekly mass and yearly holy days, midnight mass at Christmas, ashes on the forehead and fish (yuck) on Fridays in Lent, and ribboned hats and clickety-clack shoes worn for Easter. She had pretended to be a priest in the front hall of her grandmother's house, feeding her cousins Necco-wafer Communion and taking their confession in the coat closet. Later, she read in church and sang in the choir. Her faith had been scaffolded first in play, and later in compelling philosophical discussions of heaven and hell at the kitchen table with her grandma. Finding First Church Somerville was a part of her searching for the same opportunity for a natural spiritual growth for Luke. But what about ways of bringing it home?

They Will Do as You Do

Judaism, the root religion from which Christianity developed, has many family-friendly home-based practices. The youngest child is cued to find the afikomen at Passover, older kids light the menorah candles at Hanukkah, and everyone participates weekly in inviting the sabbath with candle lighting and bread breaking.

Meanwhile, it sometimes feels like Christianity has largely outsourced observance to the professional places (churches) and the professional people (clergy). Time and time again, Molly has heard from parents in her church that they felt inadequate to the task of being "worship leaders" in their own homes. They don't know the stories well enough and don't feel they have the right to lead spiritually.

What follows is a sampling of progressive ways to observe the holy days and holidays of the Christian calendar at home. All of them take into account kids' ages and stages. None of these observances costs a lot of money, requires the creative skills of a Pinterest professional, or demands a lot of shopping or prep. They are kid-tested and approved and designed not to overwhelm already exhausted parents. In other words, you can't fail!

And not assuming any prior knowledge, we're going to offer you a beginner's explanation of each holy day and attendant practices. You can internalize these and teach your children about them in your own words. We can't say it enough: parents are their children's primary spiritual teachers. Just as you did when they were four and got into dinosaurs, or they were eight and got into trebuchets, if there's something you don't know enough about, you can learn together.

Advent, Christmas, and Epiphany

Advent is the monthlong season of preparation leading up to Christmas. It runs for four Sundays before Christmas Eve, and its liturgical color is purple or blue. Advent focuses on the events leading up to the birth of Jesus: from the prophecies from Hebrew scriptures about the Messiah that God's people were waiting for, to the birth of John the Baptist, the angel's announcement to Mary, the angel's other announcement to Joseph, and the long journey from Nazareth to Bethlehem by donkey.

Advent is a spiritual gimme for kids because they are already unbearably excited about the approach of Christmas.

Don't miss this opportunity to capitalize on their buy-in! The theme of Advent is waiting, expectation, and preparation.

Kids love Advent calendars, but most calendars don't tell the narrative very well, or at all. Molly puts together a family-friendly Alternative Advent calendar, which will be available on our website by Thanksgiving weekend every year. Each day suggests a simple activity with materials at hand, based on a Nativity-friendly theme (wonder, hospitality, resistance, making peace with the body, and so on).

Don't let perfect be the enemy of the good. If doing something every day of Advent on top of shopping and wrapping and baking feels overwhelming, mix it up. Ellen bought a reusable felt Advent calendar with a pocket for each day in December. Some get filled with the usual stuff—chocolates and tchotchkes. Others get slips of paper prompting activities pilfered from Molly's calendar. One Friday night is always reserved for watching the Griswolds' *National Lampoon's Christmas Vacation*.

Get yourself a sturdy crèche and have the kids help you set it up before the first Sunday in Advent. Make it dynamic: first set up Jesus far away, out of sight, since he's not born yet. Move the characters into different relationships as the story unfolds, week by week, as if they were a cast of characters and your whole living room the world they inhabit. Remember that the Wise Ones didn't arrive until January 6, Epiphany. Taking the long road to Bethlehem, from the Sunday after Thanksgiving to January 6, can help smooth out for kids the roller coaster of big expectations and the equally big letdown on December 26.

Get a simple Advent wreath, or make one: a candle for each Sunday of Advent in a circle, three purple and one pink, with a white candle in the center of the circle (the Christ candle, for Christmas Eve).

Each Sunday, light a new candle to build suspense toward Christmas and the coming Christ. Advent's candle themes, in order, are: Hope, Peace, Joy (that's the pink one), and Love. Talk or say a simple prayer at the dinner table about that candle's theme. Ask questions like "What do you hope for? What makes it hard to be hopeful? What places and people in our world need more peace? What sparked joy for you today?" Don't be afraid to pray out loud! For real! Fake it till you make it. Everyone feels awkward doing something new for the first time, but you get better by practicing, and the Prayer Police will not be listening.

Play religious Christmas carols on heavy rotation, so everyone learns them. Sing them as bedtime lullabies. Borrow a hymnal from church or print the lyrics off the Internet. Some beautiful theology is embedded in the little-known third and fourth verses of our favorite Christmas carols. Really listen to them, and learn. Sing the songs as a prayer or a family grace, wonder together about what the words mean, or change the words for modern contexts.

As Christmas approaches, have an intentional family conversation about gifts. What is your budget? In Molly's family, our kids write an old-school Christmas list. We ask the kids to make it comprehensive, and when it's done, it's done. Then we talk about what gifts are probable (the newest Amulet book), which gifts are improbable (airsoft rifle), and which gifts are out of reach. We heavily endorse the idea of gifts that will not break easily, gifts that are homemade, and experiences rather than things, without having a hard line on the very loud and very plastic things obviously made in sweatshops that the grandparents bring into the house. We're trying to create positive associations with Christmas, folks!

We don't want our kids to get the idea that gifts come by magic, à la the Santa mythology, or that receiving them (or not) is tied to goodness or badness (which we've covered already). So when we decided to do Santa in our house, we made sure the kids understood that stockings and their contents came from "Saint Nicholas" (an actual historical figure) and everything else came from their parents and family members. We were generous with one another, hoping that they would learn it from us and practice it themselves. We didn't want our kids going to school bragging to lower-income friends that Santa had done amazing things for them while apparently leaving their friends out of the loop.

Finally, Christmas doesn't end with Christmas, in an explosion of plastic detritus and remote-controlled trucks that make you want to go Incredible Hulk on your family. Christmas is twelve days long! (Generally, this is a good thing.) Consider holding back a small gift for each day of Christmastide, or at least a gift or two for Epiphany, known throughout South America as Three Kings' Day, when children traditionally get their gifts. This practice supports an alternate narrative that hews more closely to the Gospels, which is that we get and give gifts because Christ lives in us and it's his birthday. It also slows down and evens out the fun and the moods.

Other things you can do on the feast of Epiphany, January 6: move the Wise Ones to the crèche scene in a triumphant final tableau; put glow-in-the-dark stars on the dining room ceiling; give gifts to low-income families as a mirror of the Magi; light lots of candles (Epiphany is the season of light); take a trip somewhere you've never been (just like the Wise Ones); have a time of quiet prayer in which you ask God to send you in new directions.

Mardi Gras, Ash Wednesday, and Lent

Lent is the period of forty days (forty-six, actually) between Ash Wednesday and Easter Sunday that represents the forty days that Jesus spent in the wilderness after his baptism and before his public ministry began. It is a penitential and devotional season, which is to say that it's a season for cutting back, doing without, looking within. This is convenient for those who live in a part of the world where it gets dark at four p.m., or where no fresh food grows, a natural mirror to what the earth and sky are doing.

Mardi Gras, or Fat Tuesday, is a chance to eat up all the good stuff in the house before the fasting and self-denial of Lent. Pancakes are, of course, the traditional fare, but you can decide as a family what food you want to celebrate with in your last hurrah before Lenten discipline begins.

Ash Wednesday is one of the most kinesthetically engaging of the Christian holy days, and tailor-made for littles (yes, even with the emphasis on death and sin). At our church, we observe Ash Wednesday by getting ashes on our foreheads to remind us that "from dust we came, to dust we shall return" (from Genesis 3:19, the Creation story)—in other words, that life is short, is a gift from God, and that it is important that we make the most of it. We also write our sins on flash paper—that magical thin paper that burns up in a flash—and watch them go up in smoke, a sign that God can and does forgive us everything (yes, even *that* terrible thing you did).

We also "bury the alleluias." *Alleluia* is an ancient Hebrew word of celebration, and because we mute our celebrations during Lent, we put the word away until Easter, physically "burying" it (you can do this at home: under the couch cushions, or in the garden in a plastic egg) until Resurrection Day.

Ash Wednesday is also a good time for practicing the confession of sins (yes! Protestants can do this, too!). When kids start this as youngsters—telling how they hit their brother, cut off their sister's American Girl doll's hair (actual example), took a nip from their parents' liquor cabinet, shunned a friend in favor of the cool crowd—and then come into the cool grace and catharsis of knowing they have come clean before God and have a chance to do better next time, it sets them up for a lifetime of knowing how to make amends and choose differently.

The amazing Quinn Caldwell has summed up Ash Wednesday's purpose in an easily relatable, all-ages way:

> I'm human, imperfect, unfinished, and that's completely OK.
> I've made mistakes I feel badly about.
> I'm not afraid to ask for the help I need.
> I'm asking forgiveness from God and others.
> I'm hoping to start over and try again.

One way Molly describes the paradox of Ash Wednesday to children and adults is this: humans are made of God and dirt. God at Creation took earth, breathed God's own spirit into it, and made humans. God and dirt mixed so well that you couldn't separate them if you had the tiniest tweezers and a thousand years. You can illustrate this by taking some potting soil and sprinkling some glitter into it, then mixing it up. Leave it in the middle of your dining room table during Lent. Let your kids play with it, smell it, plant something in it, and see what happens.

The ashes of Ash Wednesday are traditionally made by burning last year's Palm Sunday palms in a nod to the cycle of life as the pendulum swings from triumph to tragedy, from celebration to crisis, and back again. You could have your own home observance of Ash Wednesday by burning leaves, mixing them with a little olive oil, and making the sign of the cross on each other's foreheads while saying the ancient words "from dust you came . . ." You could write your sins on paper and burn them outside (exciting!), and say to one another, parent to child and child to parent, while making eye contact, "God forgives you. God frees you to begin again."

Or get your ashes at church, as a family. Roman Catholic churches have a short early mass. A church near Ellen's hospital in Boston blesses passersby who want them with ashes on the sidewalk. Molly imposes "ashes to go" from the local coffeehouse in her church's neighborhood, something more and more Protestant pastors are doing.

It's surprising how nostalgic Ash Wednesday makes even currently nonpracticing adults for their childhood faith. It must be because Ash Wednesday allows us to linger with our shadow side a little bit, a recognition that sorrow, difficulty, and death are real and regular parts of human life. The other high holy days are about enforcing a joy and positivity we may not be currently experiencing, but Ash Wednesday meets us where we are, with our craving to acknowledge the reality of death, the brevity of life, and the mistakes we have made.

And that brings us to Lent, which means "lengthen," as in a time of lengthening light. Many Christians may claim that giving up things for Lent is negative, but we disagree. Humans are animals, and animals hew closely to the rhythms and cycles of the earth. As Ecclesiastes said, there is a time for everything: to plant, to reap, to laugh, to mourn, to dance. Lent gives us a good long opportunity to simplify, observe our habits and rhythms, and make necessary physical and spiritual shifts.

Kids love a contest, and Lent provides us with a way to have a contest with ourselves—to gamify, as it were, our religious observance. In our families, each person's Lenten practice is optional and autonomous. No one can make anyone do anything or give anything up, but each us of operates on free will and a practice freely chosen (intrinsic motivation at work!). Molly will often give up gossip and alcohol, as well as take on a new habit: for example, sending up a prayer for the addressee of every email she sends.

The family that observes Lent together can check in with each other in a supportive, not a judgmental, way about how things are going and any struggles. If we fall off the wagon, we help one another back on again, reminding each other that God gives second and seventy-seventh chances, but the important thing is to try. *Discipline* is related to the word "disciple," and *obedience* actually means "give ear to," to listen more closely to the voice of God in our lives. We wouldn't expect our bodies to get stronger without regular physical exercise. Our Lenten practices make us stronger spiritually, taking our flabbiness and turning it to muscle as we find out what we are really capable of, in our personal habits, diet, social behaviors, service to others, and spiritual mettle.

Because the time from Ash Wednesday until Easter Sunday actually constitutes forty-six days, Sundays during Lent are known as "Little Easters"—fasts from the fast—when swearing and sugar can be enjoyed in moderation. It is hard for kids (and grown-ups) to take on a new habit without any relief, so the Little Easter is a welcome respite. It makes Sundays special in a new and different way, and offers one more positive association with churchgoing if you do go to church!

Holy Week and Easter

Holy Week, like Lent, provides ample opportunities for spiritual practice that kids can totally get behind.

There are some hard and frightening themes in Holy Week: betrayal, abandonment, torture, and death. But these days are also an opportunity to have powerful conversations with your kids about power and privilege, jealousy, friendships that have soured, death and what's beyond it, and many other topics that feel taboo or hard to bring up. Then again, you may have a sensitive child, or a child at a sensitive age, and will need to modify your observance so that it supports their spiritual and emotional life and doesn't permanently put them off the incredible story of Jesus's last week.

That said, here are some easy, engaging practices you can do with your kids to observe Holy Week.

Maundy Thursday

- Read the Gospel of John, chapter 13. Teach kids about the story of footwashing and the Great Commandment Jesus gave the disciples to "love one another as I loved you." Do a foot-washing at home with a footbath! Molly's kids *love* this.

- Read the Gospel of Luke, chapter 22, about Jesus in the Garden of Gethsemane, feeling lonely, and the betrayal by his friends. Visit a cold garden and have the family sit scattered around, giving each person some alone time.

- Have an "agape meal" at home: an unconsecrated Communion that can be done by anybody. Take delicious bread and grape juice or pomegranate juice (tangy!) and share it in love.

- Write haikus about the scripture stories: foot-washing, the Last Supper, Judas Iscariot's betrayal of Jesus to the higher-ups, the desertion of Jesus by all his friends, Jesus alone and crying in the Garden, the arrest of Jesus, his cross-examination by the authorities, his crucifixion, his forgiveness of his enemies from the cross as he was dying, his crying out to God asking why God had forsaken him, his giving his mother and his best friend to each other, knowing he would no longer be able to care for either one.

Good Friday

· All four Gospels (Matthew, Mark, Luke, John) have a version of the Good Friday story. Read it aloud, taking turns reading. If your kids have stamina, compare the different versions to see what details are different.

· Have a "cold food day" or a day without hot water, because the light has gone out of the world—this can also be an alternative to fasting.

· Have younger children draw pictures of the stations of the cross, the fourteen moments on Jesus's last/worst day, and display them around the house.

· Hang up photocopies of great Good Friday–themed religious artwork for older children: crucifixions, pietàs.

· Learn how to make the sign of the cross: shoulder-shoulder-forehead-heart-forehead.

· Venerate the cross by putting it in a low place where your children can see it, kneel before it, and pray.

- Go to a church to pray—many churches are open all day for prayer, and especially at twelve noon, three p.m., and/or seven p.m. for special services. More and more churches are having kid-friendly Good Friday services.

Holy Saturday

- Prepare Easter outfits lovingly and carefully.

- Prepare special food, lovingly and carefully.

- Paint eggs and talk about how eggs are like Jesus's tomb: they look cold and dead but there's something with life, or that gives us life, inside them. Paint them with Easter words and symbols: "God is alive," "Jesus is risen," "Alleluia," empty tomb, empty cross, flowers, butterfly, lamb of God.

- Hang hollowed-out eggs from the chandelier: this is what was hung on a tree. It is Jesus, but resurrected!

- Holy Saturday is about baptism. Tell each of your children all about their baptism day: show them pictures; call their godparents. Talk about baptism as a new life every day, every morning when they wake up, a chance to let go of all their old mistakes and start fresh.

- Read the story about the women going to the tomb to anoint Jesus's body for burial (Luke 24:1–12; John 20). Walk a labyrinth (at a church, outdoors or indoors, at a school or community center—in our city there is one painted on blacktop on a local playground). Put an egg in the middle of it. You have found your way to the heart of all things. Put your nose into a bag of spices, like the women were going to use on Jesus's body. Rub some on your skin.

Easter Sunday

· Read one of the resurrection stories. Matthew, Mark, Luke, and John all have them. All four versions feature women prominently, and in John's version Mary Magdalene is the star.

· Make dressing a sacramental act—God is making all things new! In our house, the children always get new underwear and socks in their Easter baskets.

· Go to sunrise service! Kids adore it and will never forget it as long as they live. This is easiest to do when they are little and wake you at the crack of dawn daily.

· Easter baskets: Fill them less with toys and candy, and more with experiences and relationships (coupons for outings, hugs and kisses), signs of life (seeds, tools for digging in the garden, binoculars and bird books), and religious jewelry.

· Bring holy water (water from the Rite of Blessing) or holy fire (light a little votive from the candles on the altar) home from church, and put it in a central place in your home.

· Hide one of your Alleluia Easter eggs in your home. Whoever finds it gets a prize.

· Hide a fruit basket/fresh muffin basket in the home, and share it for breakfast.

· Bring bells to church, one for each person, and ring them every time you hear the word *Alleluia* sung or spoken.

· Be the hands and feet of Jesus by serving the marginalized in your community: volunteer at a soup kitchen or make a donation that will assist refugee families or those experiencing homelessness.

Easter Monday

· Take a "well day," go to Catholic mass, visit a body of water, and splash one another. Read the Gospel of John, chapter 21, and have an outdoor picnic (with sardines!).

· Read the Gospel of Luke, chapter 24:13–35, the story about Jesus appearing suddenly to the disciples on the road to Emmaus, and take an "Emmaus walk" with your children, asking them, "Where do you see God here and here and here? In whom or what do you see God? Is God appearing in any surprising ways?"

Pentecost Flames and the Birthday of the Church

One of the lesser-known but crazy-fun holy days of the Christian calendar (and one that corporate America has not yet figured out how to market) is Pentecost. Forty days after Easter, after hanging out for a bunch of parties and some further instructions, Jesus flew back up into the sky, waving goodbye. Ten days after that, on Pentecost, the followers of Jesus received the Holy Spirit. The Spirit appeared like little flames on top of the disciples' heads and conferred new powers on them. Suddenly they could speak in foreign languages they'd never learned, and even heal like Jesus healed!

The Holy Spirit has been described as "strength beyond ourselves." It's the power that allows us to do things we never thought possible. It's that little extra bit of something-something that arrives when we get quiet, pray, and dip a little deeper into what felt like an empty well. Or it arrives as the "peace that passes all understanding," as the Bible puts it.

Pentecost is called the "birthday of the church" because it was after receiving the gift of the Holy Spirit that Jesus's disciples began to get organized to do good in the world in the absence of Jesus.

We once celebrated Pentecost at our church by getting a giant sheet cake to mark the hundredth birthday of our church building. It was decorated with one hundred trick relighting candles. The kids clustered around the cake, awed, and bent over, trying to blow the candles out again and again. Especially the nine-year-old girls with long hair. Do you see where this is going?

Nobody caught fire that day. Not literally, anyhow. But Molly learned her lesson, and we all got a message we never forgot about figuratively—and literally—setting the church on fire.

Here are some ways you might celebrate that God has put in us a fire that will never go out:

- Read together the Pentecost story from Acts 2:1–18. Pretend to be a little drunk on the Spirit—since outsiders thought the disciples were drunk.

- Talk about what it means that Jesus didn't leave earth without giving us a gift: the Holy Spirit, which lives in us. We are ourselves—and also something more, invisible to others and often to ourselves.

- Learn to say "Holy Spirit" or "I love you" or "strength beyond ourselves" in a foreign language, and use it as a code word in your family when you need extra support.

Spiritual Practice, Not Spiritual Perfect

Whatever new traditions or rituals you adopt as a family, if at first you encounter resistance, keep trying. Treat new spiritual practices like broccoli. Encourage your kids to sample before deciding they don't like it, and to try it again later, because maybe their palates will change as they grow.

With any spiritual practice it's important to remember that kids are different from one another. Ah, temperament. And they may change as they get older. Molly's Carmen proudly dons a star costume each year for the all-ages pageant at Christmas Eve service while her Rafe, a thoughtful atheist, reluctantly may wear a shepherd's headdress or a Wise One's crown. Ellen's Luke loves to dress up in sweater and tie for holy days and go to church. Jonah, eight, wants to wear neon basketball shorts, starts asking when the service will be over five minutes in, and on occasion has come extremely close to becoming physically ill—some sort of hereditary allergic reaction to church. Ellen's uncle was known to vomit as a kid when the family knelt to say their nightly rosary, while her father was the ultimate altar boy.

Children will get involved differently, and their enthusiasm will vary from age to age. But plan these practices and traditions because you want to, or because one of your children wants to, and let the others choose their level of engagement. Always invite everyone in the family, never assuming that the morose fourteen-year-old who cries atheist doesn't secretly want to be asked and included. Something may shift—and he may suddenly know his need for ritual, community, and inclusion.

A Word about Churchgoing, If You Don't . . .

Maybe you've decided that churchgoing is not for you: you don't have time, your co-parent is not on the same page, you can't find a church that fits, or you think it's just too late: your kids would never accept the change in routine.

Here's the thing about good church: it is, like the Holy Spirit, strength beyond ourselves. It provides a community of people who will support your family through hard times, cheer you on through challenging times, and celebrate with you in good times. A good church can amplify and extend what you are teaching at home, spiritually and emotionally. It can provide your kids with other safe adults that they can turn to as they grow and naturally start to separate from you and your partner. It can provide logistical and emotional support (casseroles, kid care, prayer, and counsel) when your family suffers illness, goes through a divorce, faces a move, or encounters any other big life event. Our own church has saved our bacon countless times. In church we often say to one another, "How do people do life without a community like this?"

Look for a church that knows what to do with kids: it has rites of passage for children of different ages, has clean spaces and kind teachers, includes children as leaders in worship, and treats them with dignity and respect, not as "the future of the church" but as the present of the church, just as they are, and as they are becoming.

If your kids are older and set in their Sunday ways, remember that you are still the parent. Come alongside them to talk about the benefit to them of churchgoing. If they struggle socially in school, church can provide an alternate universe where the cruel rules of cool don't apply. Covenant with them to try the same church for three months running, to establish the habit and get past the initial resistance. Be consistent in attendance so they (and you) have a chance to develop relationships and get past the period of shyness. If you don't have a church, involve them in deciding which churches to visit and in evaluating their fit for your family: autonomy support for church-choosing.

And if, like Molly's son Rafe, your children claim not to be interested in God or even say they're atheists, tell them that positive-psychology studies have shown that even atheists benefit emotionally from going to church!

Not every church (not *any* church) is perfect, but a relatively healthy church that loves kids can make life a whole lot easier for modern families.

Other Rituals and Rites of Passage

Look for ways to effect a gradual release of responsibility for your kids in relationship to religious rituals as they get older. Let them hold the candle at church on Christmas Eve when they are old enough not to set their hair on fire (not the way any preacher wants things to go that night).

For Catholic kids, First Communion is a huge rite of passage often absent in other Protestant communities where anyone is welcome to receive Communion at any age. Talk to your pastor about offering fourth-graders some formal instruction—and then inviting them to help serve Communion after they have learned about it. Or have an agape meal (unofficial Communion, with bread and juice) at home, and let your children say some of the words, break the bread, pour the juice, or serve.

Send your kids to church camp! It's Christian spirituality pitched perfectly at them, intensive exposure to the stories and norms of Jesus. Molly's mom sent her to church camp at age thirteen, against Molly's will, and look at her now! Consider this quote from child development expert Michael Thompson on how camp counselors can outparent parents:

> As a so-called "parenting expert," I am struck by how often American parents think that the answer to their parenting dilemmas is for them to do more, or better, or to do something differently. I disagree. I often believe parents should do less, and should sometimes take themselves out of the picture, especially in the summer, when it's easy to stop battling and turn some of the toughest parenting challenges over to 20- and 21-year-olds who can perform magic with their children.

Here's another reason why church camp and church and Sunday school probably work so well for our kids. **They are hearing the lessons from someone other than us with ears different from the ones they listen to us with.** Jonah came home from second grade excited to show Ellen relaxation exercises he had learned in school to manage stress—telling her she should know them to help her patients. What?! She had been teaching Jonah breathing techniques since he was a baby. He didn't make the connection. It was novel, more compelling, and somehow more believable coming from someone else.

There's another benefit to inviting other spiritual teachers and experiences into our kids' lives. We can step back and watch them, unburdened by the anxiety of maybe not knowing exactly what to say and how to teach them ourselves. Watch for cues that they want to learn or do more. Luke used to quietly sidle up next to Ellen some Sundays after service to go through the receiving line with her, instead of rushing down to coffee hour with the other kids. It always seemed to be at a time when he was struggling with something. She eventually put two and two together and realized he needed a "blessing hug" from Rev. Molly. At family church camp (an overnight experience that young kids attend with their parents to grow into the norms and courage to go on their own), he equally surprised her by standing to go up for an optional laying on of hands at evening service.

Make Every Day a Holy Day

Somewhere along the line, Molly's kids got it into their heads that because they had a minister for a mom, they could get blessings for free right there at home. So now when they are stressed or cranky or just need extra courage, they will come up to her (even the giant sixteen-year-old) and say, "Mom, I need a blessing." She rubs her palms together, lays one on their forehead and one on their heart or back, and says a simple prayer:

> *God, please give Rafe focus and strength for the task ahead. Help him to learn what he needs to know tonight for tomorrow's trig test, and may all his neural pathways work on cue tomorrow when it's time to show what he knows. We pray in the strong name of Jesus. Amen.*

The power to bless with hands is not some great magic conferred by ordination. Molly didn't need to get a seminary degree to learn how to do this. It's just something we started doing. Now you know about it. Go and do likewise! The more you practice, the more comfortable you will get. And God will work wonders through you.

Turning Routines into Rituals by Ages and Stages

The Preschooler

It's usually pretty easy to set up routines for preschoolers. Without them you risk total meltdowns—by everyone. Preschoolers do best when each day looks pretty much like the last, or at least when every Tuesday looks like the next. Sometimes, though, parents of preschoolers can become so rigid about routines that they miss the opportunity for ritual. Take an example.

Ellen worked for a time in a program that provided guidance for parents who had cancer on how to support their kids through this tough time. Parents of preschoolers, knowing how much their kids need consistent bedtimes and specific, often monochromatic meals, worried most about routines being disrupted by their absence. They often feared that the co-parent, grandparent, or family friend there to support them when they were too sick or not home to care for their child would do things differently and at least temporarily traumatize their child.

Ellen would gently explain that, yes, preschoolers need routines. If they were going to be sleeping at Grandma and Grandpa's a few nights a week, be sure to send them with their lovey and info on their favorite brand of chicken nugget. But it was also more than OK for the youngest kids to develop their own, maybe different, routines with Grandma and Grandpa.

Even better if those routines were given room to develop

into ritual. Grandma and Grandpa had a different perspective on the trials of the time for their grandchild. They might incorporate their own song or prayer into the bedtime routine. Let them. It could well become a touchpoint for the child that would endure well past when treatment was over, no matter the outcome.

Even if your family is lucky enough not to have to face trials or trauma, try to be flexible enough in your routines to find ritual. Follow your child's lead as to what they want and need at bedtime or mealtime. Let them lead the prayer or song or story. Then replicate the best parts the next night. It could be the Lord's Prayer, a call and response, the story of their day, or all of the above.

The Grade Schooler

Making space for ritual in a household with grade-school-age kids is really pretty easy. Just follow their lead and look for opportunities to steer things in a spiritual direction. This will be easiest around holidays. You know that Elf on the Shelf doll that showed up a few years ago? The one who shows up the day after Thanksgiving and "magically" comes to life and moves every night, watching kids to report back to Santa on their goodness and badness? If you have no idea what we are talking about, say a thank you prayer this instant.

Another point to those advertisers marketing to our kids: What are you supposed to do when your eight-year-old builds a house and leaves treats for his elf? Explain that the elf is a doll designed by toy makers to make money and won't be showing up? Yes. But if, like Ellen, you didn't do that, try to find a way to make a stressful (for the parent) routine into a meaningful ritual for the child.

You remind him that neither Santa nor God gives gifts

based on goodness and badness, because we are all made up of goodness and badness mixed together. But the elf shows up in time for Advent, and helps us to mark the days until the joy of Christmas. Sometimes she makes us laugh along the way with her antics ("eating" all the stale leftover Halloween candy), and sometimes she leaves us notes with reminders of the magic of the season and the kind things she has noticed us do.

As grade schoolers begin to see the world as bigger and to appreciate others' perspectives, this is the perfect time to scaffold their spirituality through ritual. Take them to church when they want to go, even if you haven't set foot in one for a long time—or ever. Let them play and ask questions, and hold back the impulse to correct subtle inaccuracies.

The goal is to give them the space to figure out who their God is and to begin to develop their own relationship with Her. When you do talk about beliefs, preface them with "I believe . . ." or "Some people believe . . ." to give them a sense of autonomy and choice even while providing information and structure. Listen to how they work it out, and when you don't have the answer to a question, admit it.

The Middle Schooler

For most kids, a lot of the magic, mystery, and mysticality of holy days and holidays will seem to be gone by middle school. This makes it tempting to do away with a lot of the ritual of the preschool and grade school years. Yet even though most kids no longer believe in Santa coming down the chimney by age twelve, plenty still believe in Jesus being born in a stable to change the world. They, and we, still believe because this world is an infinitely mysterious place, and if we have decided to believe in God, anything is possible. **Rituals remind us of that, and of unseen forces of love, kindness, and tragedy over**

which we have no control. Routines and rituals give us a sense of order as well as awe. For this reason they are critically important to hold on to for our tweens and teens.

If you have younger as well as older kids, you will be more likely to see how much they really do want to hold on to the rituals of their childhood. It took us no coaxing at all to convince our older kids to keep the mysteries of Christmas alive for our younger kids. They help make lists, move elves, decorate, and pray even if they are not so sure of any of it anymore. The simplest thing you can do for your middle schoolers' spiritual growth is to stick to the routines and rituals developed earlier. And if you are late to the game, make subtle shifts to turn the secular routine into spiritual ritual. Pick one thing from this chapter to incorporate into the routines of a holiday you already celebrate, and expand from there.

The High Schooler

Remember how important having a sense of choice is to feeling autonomous and intrinsically motivated? By the time they are in high school, our kids are capable of choosing for themselves what to take and what to leave of our faith traditions and rituals, and of the beliefs that underlie them. This is the reason for confirmation in the Catholic and Protestant traditions. But too often, confirmation is presented as an expectation rather than a choice, probably because we fear that if we actually let our kids choose for themselves, they won't choose our God.

So we force them into confirmation. Or we continue the same rituals and routines of their childhood mindlessly, afraid if we make room for something different, everything will change. Let's be honest, when you have a teenager there is already too damn much change happening every day. Yet psychological science tells us that if we give them room, our teens may be more likely to *really* choose and confirm a belief that will be more real and long-lasting than anything we instill either by force or inertia.

Your teenager may begin dating someone with different rituals and beliefs and want to go to church with them on Christmas Eve. Let them. Maybe join them. Send them to the Bar and Bat Mitzvahs they are invited to. Invite the teen who has taken up yoga to find a Buddhist meditation to read at Easter dinner. Explain that a lot of people believe that each faith tradition is just a different way of looking at the same God, and talk about why your family takes the perspective you do. Remind them that they get to choose what to keep and what to leave of what they've been brought up with, the same way you probably did. Then support the choices they make and challenge them when you disagree, without undermining their autonomy. See what happens.

BIG IDEAS

- Children thrive on routine and ritual. Ritual is a form of spiritual play that helps concretize and embody spiritual meaning.

- You can practice all the holy days at home with very few props or setup. Which holy day is next—and how can you shift your observance toward the sacred from the secular?

- Gradually release responsibility to your children for rituals both at home and at church, so they take ownership of their own spiritual practices.

- You can bless your kids every single day. All you need is your warmed-up hands and whatever words God puts in your mouth.

- Send your kid to church camp! It may change their life.

Prayer

God, that next big holiday is looming. Give me the courage to pare down the habits that make us broke or stressed, and to start new traditions and rituals, even if it sets off some initial complaining at the change.

Amen.

PART III

Singular/Sacred Stories

CHAPTER 10

Worry Once and Worry Well

Brave Parenting

Jesus famously urged, in the Sermon on the Mount, "Don't worry about your life, what you will eat or what you will drink or about your body, what you will wear . . . [and] don't worry about tomorrow, for tomorrow will bring worries of its own. Today's trouble is enough for today." Jesus was great with the Whats ("Do Not Worry!"). He was not so clear with the How-Tos.

We both know worry. We worry about our children. A lot. To quote author Elizabeth Stone, "Making the decision to have a child is momentous. It is to forever have your heart go walking around outside your body."

Molly has survived cancer, and with it nightmares of dying and leaving her children motherless. Every day Carmen faces life-threatening food allergies. Ellen has type 1 diabetes and wonders if that ticking time bomb exists in Luke or Jonah, hoping that if it does, a cure will be found before it goes off. We have both lost close friends to early death. And we have, with tremendous relief, seen others survive the unimaginable.

In our work we have had the privilege of bearing witness for parents facing the reality that their children's lives are at risk. We have been right there in the middle of the mess when parents have lost children, or have lost the idea of the child they thought they had.

Ellen has sat with parents of children who have suffered second- and third-degree burns to most of their body, who have lost limbs, who have been diagnosed with diabetes or severe disabilities, who experience depression or substance abuse, or who were born into bodies that don't match their gender or into communities that won't acknowledge or accept them. Sometimes Ellen has to deliver the diagnosis. Molly has walked with families through suicide, addiction, serious mental illness, and every form of self-sabotage known to adolescents.

The harrowing reality is that you can follow every suggestion in this book and read a hundred more, heed the advice, and still have your child taken from you tomorrow. Bad things happen all the time, even to "good" people. None of us is immune.

We're not here to blithely tell you not to worry. **To let go of fear in parenting is not the same as never worrying. It is to find enough room *around* the fear that you refuse to allow worry to dictate your parenting.** This is brave parenting. And we are ALL capable of it.

Then, too, there is the way in which worrying has become a kind of competitive sport in certain parenting circles, proof of how much we love our progeny. When *should* we worry, and how much? How can we make worry work for us instead of against us?

First, we'll frame a theology of worry and loss. Then, we'll talk about what it teaches us about everyday worry. And finally, we want to leave you with stories from some brave parents who have faced very worrisome situations and found, in varying degrees, meaning, hope, redemption, joy, and a sense of God's guiding presence in the midst of the mess.

A Theology of Worry

Bad things will happen to you and to people you love. No one is going to get out of here alive. We know this, and some of us live in a state of low-level panic much of the time, wondering when the other shoe will drop. We are chronic worriers.

There is a difference between worry and prayer. Worry is thinking about things, keeping those thoughts to ourselves, and turning our anxieties over and over in our heads until they grow outsized and monstrous. Prayer is turning our anxieties over to Someone who has a broader perspective, who has information not available to us, and who can relieve our anxiety, even if the situation on the ground is essentially unchanged.

Worry says: I am master of my own universe, but I recognize that my power or know-how or skills are too limited to ensure the outcome I hope for. Worry is a petty tyrant of a failed state, an idol replacing God.

Prayer says: I am not in charge. I in fact *surrender* to the outcome. Things may take a painful turn, but I am not alone in this. God will send allies and angels who will strengthen me for anything life will send my way. And, in spite of my worst imaginings, things may turn out all right—or better than all right.

It's been said that courage is fear that has said its prayers. Praying doesn't mean we stop being afraid, or stop worrying altogether. But it does mean we recognize that we have a strength beyond ourselves, and that in spite of our fear, we can move ahead into the unknown.

The Bible says, "perfect love casts out fear." Molly has drawn on this short but substantial morsel many times in her life. It seems that love and fear cohabit. It is, in fact, our love for our kids that makes us so afraid for them. The thought of our children getting hurt or dying is at the top of the list of our worst fears.

But there is a point beyond which parent love, which is good and holy, becomes a grasping love, a controlling love. We are called to love our children the way God loves us: the kind of love that recognizes the free will and autonomy of every human, including our children. This love also recognizes that bad things do and will almost assuredly happen in our lives, but good often comes out of what at first seems evil to us. Cliché alert: we need to love our children so well that we surrender them (at the appropriate pace) to the One who is Parent to us all.

By now, we know this is consistent with all that we know makes for positive parenting. Controlling love will always backfire on us . . . and on our kids. **If we protect them too much from adversity, we will fail to give them the tools they will need when they face greater challenge, loss, and pain.**

Much is being made of resilience in popular parenting literature these days. There are many definitions of what it means to be resilient. The simplest means having the emotional tools to get through the tough times, to persist in the face of challenge, to keep getting up out of bed to fight the good fight even when everything seems to be working against you. To do this, it helps to have the spiritual tool of knowing that you not only have your parents in your corner, you also have a loving God— One who knows more.

At our church, every Sunday, the preacher starts the service by saying, "God is good," and the people answer, "all the time." This is a radical theological statement. It's one thing to say it on good-time sunny Sundays. It's quite another to say it after a beloved member of the community has completed suicide, or after the Boston Marathon bombing, both of which we have done. *It says: Things seem bad to us. But we don't know the whole story yet.*

The Bible also says, "All things work together for good for those who love God." This gem is a bit of a self-fulfilling prophecy. If you believe the wisdom of that statement, you will begin to see the world differently. You will begin to be on the lookout for angels and allies, God's co-conspirators. You will believe that everything turns out all right in the end. If it's not all right, it's not the end. This may sound like Pollyanna horseshit, but before you denounce it, try living it. Try practicing this worldview for a while and praying more frequently than you worry. We promise it will make you more resilient.

The God we believe in does not send adversity or tragedy, but She will take advantage of the crisis-in-progress for Her own holy purposes—to bring people together, to strengthen or teach them. Perhaps one of the most distancing and damaging things we can say to a person who is grieving is "God doesn't give us more than we can handle." It sure as hell doesn't feel that way a lot of the time to a lot of people, and it suggests God is the envoy of tragedy.

Similarly, "Everything happens for a reason." What reason is there for a parent to lose a child? We are pretty sure She already has plenty of angels.

Prayer doesn't necessarily change God's mind—but it can change ours. It can prepare us to bear anything and to find ourselves alive—even more fully and vigorously and joyfully alive—on the other side of whatever was trying to kill us and may have succeeded in killing someone we loved.

Everyday Worry: How to Worry Well

So, just how are we supposed to worry well? Like becoming a good enough parent, it is a process. It's one that parents of differently abled kids are often forced into sooner and harder than "typical" parents of "typical" kids. These parents often understand sooner and better that they do not get to decide who their child is or is not going to be. They are often forced to let go of expectations that others of us cling to for too long and let dictate our parenting.

One of Ellen's friends has a son who was born healthy, but just a few hours after his birth, he was struck by a virus that left him blind, deaf, nonverbal, and with cerebral palsy and autism. His parents had planned on a name but decided to change it. That baby and all the expectations they had for him were gone, replaced by this new one. To love him fully for who he was, they needed to grieve the baby they lost and receive the one they were given, with a name to match the strength he would need as he grew. So Max was born.

Ellen hears versions of this story every day at Shriners Hospital for Children in Boston, where she works. Children are brought from all over the world to Shriners for treatment of severe, life-threatening burns. These are injuries that frequently leave them severely disfigured, with amputations and prosthetics, without hair or noses or ears, or even with traumatic brain injury. Even when children live through life-threatening illness and injury, there is still grieving to be done, and a letting-go that has to happen.

A patient's mother, seeing her sixteen-year-old daughter for the first time, a daughter who had once been objectively beautiful by any standard, said to Ellen, "As soon as I heard her voice, her laugh, I knew my girl was still in there, unchanged. The rest we can deal with. I'm just so grateful to still have her." Together, they would have to grieve the loss of the daughter's appearance, of the identity she had built around how she looked, of an easy path to marriage and children and grandchildren. Things were undoubtedly going to be different. Expectations needed to be changed. That family still struggles. But the child that mom loves is still there, and that's enough.

"Typical" parents of "typical" kids can learn a lot from parents who have faced bigger adversities. To do so, we have to acknowledge that we could be them, and someday we might be. Some lessons will come easy and some will be very painful. Kids with able bodies can learn from kids with dis/ability and difference, too. Yet another plug for good church! Put yourself and your children in communities where you will be forced to be uncomfortable sometimes. You, and your children, have much to give and much to gain.

We can learn so much from kids who have faced tragedy and loss. They often are our best spiritual teachers. A boy Ellen worked with, who lost his father to cancer when he was in grade school, had this to say about death: "I think God is like a parent. He lets you out into the world to play and it's fun and it's awesome. And then he tells you when it's time to come home and back inside with him where it's safe." He made his own sense of the fact that we all go home at different times and ages, and sometimes we get called in before we feel ready to go—and almost always before our friends want us to leave.

Let's go back, for a minute, to Jesus's advice on worry: "Don't worry about tomorrow, for tomorrow will bring worries of its own. **Today's trouble is enough for today.**" Jesus is telling us to do our best to keep worries focused on what we know, rather than on what we don't know yet. Psychologists will tell you this, too. Veer too far into all the bad things that *might* happen in the future, and you make the cognitive error ("thinking mistake") of catastrophizing, which will make you a ball of anxiety. Ask yourself: "Bad things are always *possible*, but how *probable* is it that the thing you are worrying about will happen?" (Preview: This is a good question to ask a worrying kid, too.)

It's never wise to look too far into the future as a parent. Focusing on today still leaves us with plenty to worry about. But it is far more likely that we can actually *do* something about today's worries than we can about tomorrow's.

Here's an example of putting this into practice based on Ellen's experiences guiding parents facing "real" worry: Parents of children with intellectual disabilities often want to know what the future holds for their child. Will they ever hold a job? Get married? Have children? Live independently? Ellen's answer: We don't have a crystal ball. We just don't know. We can make guesses based on what we *do* know now, because that's really all we have to work with. For example, a daughter with a dis/ability might not be able to navigate a grocery store alone now at age eighteen, but it is not for us to limit her future with our expectations. It is our job to give her what she needs *now* so that maybe, possibly, she can shop for herself at twenty. Let's try to teach her how to shop. It is wise to plan for the future, too, but let's focus as much as possible on what we know now. It's enough for today.

Sounds easy, right? One day at a time. But it's damn hard. Here's a more personal, smaller worry example:

Ellen's Jonah has not been quick to learn to read. When he was in the first grade and getting extra help, the reading specialist was explaining to Ellen and Eric where Jonah was struggling and what they were doing to support and teach him in the now. It was great. Ellen knew that the teacher was using evidence-based interventions for kids with reading disabilities to bolster Jonah early—giving him the best prognosis for catching up to his peers.

Still, she worried. She said to the reading specialist, "If I were in the role of psychologist instead of parent, I would be telling myself that it's too soon to know if this is dyslexia. There is a huge range in reading ability in kids at this age, and that doesn't narrow until third grade, so he is not that far behind. We are doing all we can and should and we will just have to wait and see." The reading specialist replied, "You are giving yourself good advice." To which Ellen responded, "Yeah, but how do I follow it?"

Jonah is in third grade now and catching up—slowly but surely—and Ellen still worries. But she tries to put some spaciousness around that worry. She focuses on what she can do now: encouraging a love of books and scaffolding Jonah's reading and writing without pushing too hard out of worry and fear. She focuses on what he knows now, and she tries not to worry too much about what he will be able to do next week. And now, with more flexible expectations, there is no greater joy than peeking in Jonah's room early in the morning to see that he has picked up a book he is really into, all on his own, and is working hard to read to himself—whether it's a "typical" third-grade book or not.

Another key to worrying well: **Never worry alone.** Sharing our worries with God is prayer. Sharing our worries with others is a way to get answers to those prayers. At the very least, look for a friend with whom you can be totally honest about your parenting anxieties, or find a therapist for yourself to hash it out with. Don't let your worry dictate your parenting.

Recruit people who know more than you do about whether to worry, when, and how much. Ask your child's teacher, coach, aunt, uncle, grandparents, or friends' parents if they see what you see that is worrying you. Trust your gut. A good rule of thumb in deciding whether it's time to seek professional help for mental health concerns is the rule of twos and threes. If your child is struggling in just one area, give it some time. Ask for help from people in that one area. But if they are struggling in more than one area—at home, at school, with friends, on the playing field—you may want to seek more support.

Get professional help when your child needs it—tutors, therapists, doctors. You may be saying, "Well, obviously." But ask a parent with bigger worries—parents of a child with dis/ability and difference—and they will tell you this sounds a lot easier than it is. You may have to fight really hard to be heard. You may have to look really far to find the person who can help. You may also have to fight stigma and your own shame of your child's struggles. Having a community of faith can help, one where you and your child are fully accepted as you are. One that will support you as you work to get where you want to be.

Sometimes, having a diagnosis can help. Patti, whose son Nicky has autism, talks about the "shadow syndrome," her name for when your parent-gut tells you something is a bit off and you can't name it. You have no name for your child's struggle. How do you talk about it with others? You feel alone and unable to do anything about it because you don't know what it is.

Having a name gives you access to tools and resources. You can connect with a community of other parents who share the same worry. A diagnosis sometimes means you will be taken more seriously. You need one for medical insurance to cover therapy and to get access to support in school via an individualized education program (IEP). Parents often tell Ellen that they worry that a diagnosis will follow their child forever. But if it means getting their child what they need today, let's not worry too much about tomorrow.

Having a name can help us worry well in another way. It may be the first step toward acceptance. *Acceptance* and *dis/ability* are both loaded terms. When used in a certain way, they imply limitation, giving up, brokenness. But a progressive Christian theology of brokenness tells us that brokenness, as in the breaking of the bread at Communion, is a step toward blessing—because blessing always follows breaking. The Gospels tell a story about

Jesus rising from the dead *with* his wounds, and radiant. We can become stronger at our broken places than we would be if we had never encountered adversity.

Acceptance can help us worry well only if we know what acceptance is. Let's start with what it's not: acceptance is not becoming numb or refusing to feel difficult emotions. It does not mean you or your child can never feel sad, angry, hopeless, or frustrated. Acceptance is not a golden ring or an achievement; it is a process and a practice. Acceptance is a way of focusing on what we can do *now*. Think of the Serenity Prayer:

> *God, grant me the serenity to accept the things I cannot change,*
> *The courage to change the things I can,*
> *And the wisdom to know the difference.*

Oftentimes, parents of kids with type 1 diabetes (especially teenagers) come to Ellen distressed that their child "hasn't accepted" their diagnosis. When asked to explain how they know this is true, parents usually detail all the things their child isn't doing to care for themselves. They refuse to check their blood sugar and forget to take insulin when they eat. There is constant nagging and arguing about the things they *can* change, the things they *can* do. Why are their teens so resistant to the facts?

Probably, Ellen says, because they don't want to have type 1 diabetes. No one does. When Ellen meets kids with type 1 for the first time, she tells them right away that she doesn't have the magic wand to make this go away. She wishes she did. People are working on really good research for a cure, but it just isn't here yet. Having type 1 diabetes herself, she welcomes them to "the club no one wants to be a part of" and assures them there can be a lot of good that comes from being a member. But it takes time and struggle.

Acceptance is an act of surrender, of giving over the things we *can't* change so we can shift our focus to those we can. To surrender means to admit defeat. If your kid or your family is struggling, they need you to acknowledge (maybe many times over), the things that neither they nor you can change. And how frustrating, even infuriating, that can be. They (and you) may also need to get really angry before finding the serenity of acceptance. Acceptance is not an absence of emotion—it's a catharsis of emotion. Find healthy ways of letting it out. Ellen has had kids with type 1 and their parents break dishes, punch punching bags, and throw darts at a dartboard labeled with the worst parts of having diabetes—blood sugar checks, injections, low and high blood sugars, days having to sit out of sports, and nights sleeping in a hospital bed.

Another reason to name our worry, to feel all our feels, and to share our struggles is so that we might destigmatize dis/ability and difference, and build bigger and better communities for *all* our kids. Parents who have had to deal with big parenting worries are too often idolized, which has a distancing effect and denies the possibility that we who are ordinary might have to face something similar. When we say, "I could never do what you do each day," we leave parents of kids with dis/ability and difference feeling isolated and alone. What we are really saying is "I could never do that, and if God doesn't give us more than we can handle, then I won't ever have to. This won't happen to me or my kid."

Yet deep down we know that's a myth, a way of managing our own worry and fears. It's a myth that minimizes the fact that *all* of us struggle to be the parents we want to be, to accept and parent the kids we've been given. Show us *any* parent who hasn't at some time locked themselves in a room, screamed into a pillow, peeled out of the driveway, or run until they hurt to get out their anger and frustration and worry. If we let parents of kids with dis/ability and difference tell us their *whole* stories, we can learn about what acceptance really means.

Finally, without being a cliché or condescending, listening to stories of parenting children with dis/abilities and difference can shift our paradigm of normalcy, beauty, meaning, and happiness and give us a healthy perspective on our own situations.

Stories of Difference and Dis/Ability

Substance Abuse: Jamie's Story

Six years ago my wife and I confided to our friends at church that our youngest son was in jail, arrested for theft to support his drug use. One friend who had been in recovery for decades said, in her gravelly New York accent, "You guys get your butts to an Al-Anon meeting." Al-Anon is a spiritual program for those whose lives have been affected by another person's drinking or addiction. I didn't know that at the time. I figured it was a place where we would finally learn how to save our son. It was not. So we took her advice and went. That advice saved me and clarified my faith.

Before I went to Al-Anon, I thought I had faith. I had faith that everything was going to be all right. That was my statement of faith: "Everything is going to be all right." And I had proof. Everything *was* all right. My wife and I have three sons with five years between the first and the second, and five years between the second and the third. I could look over the shoulder of my oldest son as he approached adulthood and see that he had the capacity to travel his journey. And my next son, too. I could look over his shoulder and up the road on which he was traveling, and I could see potential for adventure, love, stability, and so on. Everything was going to be all right. But my third son? I looked over his shoulder and onto the road in front of him and it gave me great fear. We did everything we could to steer him onto another road or to fill in the potholes in front of him. The road got rough. I worried furiously, as if perhaps if I worried hard enough, I could fix this. I made myself sick with worry.

In Al-Anon I discovered that my obsession with my son was similar to his obsession with a substance. I couldn't stop. I went to bed worried, I woke up worried, and I was distracted by worry throughout the day. I suddenly feel the need to apologize to my close friends to whom I spoke endlessly about my worry. I needed recovery as much as he did. The first step in recovery is admitting powerlessness over your specific situation. For the alcoholic, it is powerlessness over alcohol. For me it is power-lessness over my son's addiction. In a way this step was fairly easy. I had spent years proving it over and over. Clearly, I was powerless. Powerlessness, by the way, is a great place to begin a spiritual journey.

We paid for stays at treatment centers, but we learned to let go of the outcome. We came to family night each week during the many months of his stays. We met some wonderful people in recovery and we began to see that these were the people who might be able to help our son. A friend who has been in Al-Anon for many years shared with me that he thinks that family members and loved ones are uniquely unqualified to help in some situations. I think that is true. More letting go. Through-out the years we heard from our son about his friends whom we had met who had relapsed or even died. We grew to understand the seriousness of this disease. We paid rent for sober living homes and we weathered the storms of our son's relapse and homelessness. We set boundaries and we held fast. All the while learning to let go.

Ironically, my son and I are on parallel spiritual paths of recovery. He is on a path of recovery from his addiction to drugs and alcohol. I am on a path of recovery from my obsession with his life. We don't talk about it with each other. I'm not ready to talk to him about his recovery. I'm afraid that I might try to take over. I might suspect that he is lying. I might slip back into obsessive worry. We talk about other things. Things that are not very important. And that's important.

When our children arrive, we parents do everything for them. We feed them, clothe them, and comfort them. As they grow, they do more for themselves. As we see them demonstrate ability, balance, and good judgment, we let go more and more. The *letting go* is just as important as the *doing*. Letting go of a young adult child who is not demonstrating good judgment is really hard, but it is just as important. Maybe more important.

I heard once at a meeting that "God doesn't have any grand-children." This is a clever way of saying that we are all children of God. My child is not God's grandchild. I am not the conduit through which my son is connected to God. My son has a di-rect connection to God just as I do. So why do I worry? More letting go. Still working on it.

The clarification in my faith statement came in the form of parentheses. "Everything is going to be all right (but I don't get to determine what *all right* is)." That's where faith comes in. I don't get to see it but in some way, and perhaps against all odds, everything is going to be all right. It may not be what I want. It may even be what I don't want. But it's going to be all right.

Depression, Anxiety, and Other Mental Illnesses: Kurt's Story

The first time we learned that our sixteen-year-old twins were cutting was at the ages of thirteen and sixteen, respectively.

Their explanation is that it gives them a sense of peace and calm. It's a feeling they can control.

A twenty-first-century coping mechanism for the chaotic post-9/11 world of a teenager in our society. The cutting, they told us, provides a momentary release from the anxiety-driven depression they are constantly fighting against when it comes to their grades, extracurricular participation, body image, clothing, hair, the future, their personal and online relationship status, everything.

Our daughter spent much of her early years retching as part of her morning routine. Our son spent a year and a half sleeping on the floor of our bedroom because he felt unsafe in his own room.

It would be eighteen months before we came to understand that our son needed professional help beyond the therapists, counselors, licensed social workers, and ADHD medication everyone was trying to put him on. This happened when he came downstairs for a snack with his arms and blanket covered in blood. His sister's illness culminated in a New Year's Eve inpatient admission following some cutting, the ingestion of nine acetaminophen, and a cry for help to friends on social media who immediately texted her mom.

By the time our children, yours and mine, will grow past their teen years, 50 percent of them will have self-harmed at least once, and 25 percent more than once. In 2015, nearly three million children between ages twelve and fifteen had at least one depressive episode over the year. Over six million children in the United States have some sort of anxiety disorder.

I'm telling you so my twins don't feel so alone.

I'm telling you so you don't feel so alone.

I'm telling you so I don't feel so alone.

What we've been told, what we've read, and the general sense we get from the way we live our own lives is that life today is very different than, say, twenty years ago. Most of that has to do with the level to which we are connected to it all—work, news, one another's lives—in ways most of us could never have fathomed even a decade ago. As a result of this connectedness, we are instantly aware of the pain and suffering of the wider world. We live in a world where threats of terrorism, natural disaster, warfare, and social unrest are made pervasive in the lives of those who are the least able to do something about it: our young children.

Because of our children's mental illness, my wife and I worry about a lot of things our parents never needed to worry about: anonymity in social media, which enhances isolation rather than connection; sharp objects in our home; every moment they are alone in their bedrooms.

We remind our kids consistently that they are each equally precious and worthy children of God in whom God is well pleased. It takes courage to hear that small, still-speaking voice of God, growing beyond self-rejection.

Queer Kids: Tom's Story

There wasn't one specific moment when we realized our child was transgender; no bombshell "coming-out" event or tearful announcement at the dinner table. The process was a gradual realization for our child and for us. Amazingly, alongside moments of worry, doubt, and confusion, there were also incredible moments of grace.

Based on all of the evidence available to us at the time, we assigned our middle child a female gender at birth. For more than six years, that's how life was lived. We did our best to not raise any of our children with traditional gender expectations and made sure that each child was welcome to play any sport or with any toy that they wanted. Even though we did our best to avoid having pink "girl" or blue "boy" clothes, our choices were often limited by what was offered in the stores. Our old pictures show that both older children were in dresses much more often than we remembered.

Gender roles began to be questioned in the first grade. When Grandma took the kids shopping, the oldest wanted dresses but the middle child began asking for suits and ties. Haircuts became shorter and shorter. One day while visiting a playground far from home, some other children asked, "Are you a boy or a girl?" When we talked about it later on, my child said to me, "I wanted to say I was a boy, but I didn't know I could do that."

I recognized God's hand in this situation when I remembered my sabbatical scheduled for that summer. This break would mean three months away from the church I serve and where my family attends: three months traveling on a grant that would take us far from home, an opportunity for my child to "try on" this new understanding of gender.

The summer was full of events rooted in family and in Christianity. It began when we traveled thousands of miles by RV to the Wild Goose Festival in North Carolina. Along the way, we reconnected with old friends and met new ones. Although many did not know my son's story, the ones who did were very supportive. It seemed that each tick of the odometer brought my son closer to his true self. Each mile away from home and each new face allowed him to be who God meant him to be.

Later in the summer, we flew to Ireland and Scotland and continued to grow more comfortable and confident understanding my child's identity. After a week with the Christian community on Iona, we wrapped up a phenomenal summer with a final weekend in Glasgow.

The sabbatical had been planned almost two years prior,

but it was apparent that God's hand had guided us along the way. While in Glasgow, we had a chance encounter with Eddie Izzard, a British actor who has been outspoken about breaking gender norms. He often wears makeup, heels, and dresses. "They're not women's clothes," he's been known to say, "They're my clothes. I bought them." He spoke with my family and my son for almost thirty minutes.

After we'd planned for years and traveled thousands of miles, our vacation concluded with one more amazing, unexpected experience. Our last weekend coincided with Pride Glasgow, Scotland's largest LGBTI festival. We were able to celebrate with a parade and a festival showing my son how much he is loved.

Of course, it hasn't been all sunshine and rainbows. After his return to school, some of the children who knew him "before" gave him a hard time by outing him to new students or teachers as "really a girl." The gossip spread around town quickly. No one seemed able to resist telling my child's story for him. One challenge has been the influx of new "friends"—people in the community who ignored us before suddenly wanted to show how understanding they were by adding a token trans family to their entourage. The other day when asked what he was thinking, our eight-year-old child said he always thinks about how his life is going to be a lot harder than other people's lives.

The process of discovering our child's true gender identity is ongoing and gradual. Almost a year after buying his first suit, we still don't know what to expect for the future. However, we vow to be by his side on the journey. Our understanding of a loving Creator who makes no mistakes reminds us that our child is exactly who God intended him to be.

In Matthew 19:12, Jesus says, "For there are eunuchs who have been so from birth . . . who have been made eunuchs by others, . . . who have made themselves eunuchs for the sake of the kingdom of heaven." It's not a direct correlation, but I believe this shows that God recognizes and accepts everyone regardless of where they fall on the gender spectrum.

Yes, we worry about the bigotry that our child will almost certainly face, but our love keeps us strong. We combat our fears by speaking out: telling our story and fighting for the rights of every person to live a full life as their true self. God's love has gotten us this far, and the hope of Christ's message of a better world keeps us going, moment by moment.

Autism Spectrum Disorders: Patti's Story

My son, Nicky, will be nineteen this week.

He was born without complications, ten fingers and ten toes, a beautiful baby. He met all the early milestones of sitting, rolling over, crawling, saying his first words on schedule. Then, somewhere after his second birthday, he started to lose language rather than expand his communication. By three, he was not speaking at all. An evaluation at the Yale Child Study Center followed, as did a diagnosis of autism.

That was when the interventions began. It was as if his development came to an almost complete standstill. I cut back drastically on my career plans in order to take him all over the state of Connecticut for therapy. We went to occupational therapy, physical therapy, speech therapy, audio integration therapy, applied behavioral analysis, and music therapy.

Many children on the autism spectrum respond to rigorous therapy and early education with amazing results. There are claims for success with diets, teaching approaches, and sensory-based therapies. For parents of a child with autism, there is a tremendous amount of pressure to bombard your child with as much as possible, because all the research points to the effectiveness of early intervention. It's a full-time job for at least one parent and it can bankrupt some families. It's absolutely wonderful when something works. It's unbelievably frustrating and painful when it doesn't.

Nicky's development has been very slow. He has severe information and sensory processing deficits. Practically speaking, his IQ is in the range of severe intellectual disability, and very low at that. Three years ago he started having seizures. He now has a secondary diagnosis of epilepsy. He does not have the ability to use language to communicate the most basic needs. I think that this inability to express his feelings is the hardest thing for us to deal with as parents. He can't tell me that he has a headache, or that he feels blue, or that he has a favorite color or a favorite food. We have to intuit everything with him because he lacks the language to describe what life is like for him.

The last three years have been particularly hard because of the epilepsy. Epilepsy medications are powerful, potentially toxic medications that slow the brain down intentionally in order to stop the neurons from overactivating. For a kid who already has cognitive processing deficits, this is disastrous. Without medication, Nicky would have full-blown tonic-clonic seizures. He has had seizures on bicycles, on airplanes, at concerts, in bathtubs, at school, and in parking lots. They can occur at any time without warning. It necessitates 24/7 supervision. It sometimes feels like he's barely treading water. Or that he's losing the skills we've fought so hard for.

I'm still trying to work out in my mind where it all fits in the "grand scheme of things" . . . I don't feel bitter about it. I mostly feel really bad for him because he is so limited in certain ways. I wish that he'd had the chance to develop normally, to have friends, to go to our local school. I wish that he didn't have to be on so many medications. I wish that his sister could have been able to confide in him, or didn't have to see him writhing on the floor in the midst of a seizure.

Despite his many, many deficits, he is a happy kid. As he has gotten older, we've relaxed a little and tried to focus more on keeping him happily engaged in day-to-day activities rather than on the intense acquisition of skills.

Nicky loves music and has learned to play the piano and even plays the cello well enough to play in a little community orchestra. He is so much more comfortable participating in nonverbal activities. He goes to weekly ballet classes and is part of a unified sports program at our local school where kids with disabilities and peer helpers play on the same team. His favorite sport by far is basketball, even though he has no concept of the competitive aspect of the game. And we are able to get an accurate read on him at times, like when he lights up with a big smile upon seeing a favorite person, or when he realizes we're going to go swimming or that it's someone's birthday. Those times feel like special blessings.

I have grown closer to my church as a result of being Nicky's mother. He has always been welcomed there, even if he occasionally makes noise during the quiet moments . . . As Nicky ages, I find myself struggling with the thought, "Who will take care of Nicky when I die?" He will always be completely vulnerable and unable to live independently. He will have to rely on the goodness of others for his survival and happiness when we are gone. Being part of a Christian community helps me trust that there will be people who care and who will help. Just being in the presence of others every week who want to do God's work is healing for me

I do my best to focus on what is good in my life and try not to become angry and frustrated about what is difficult. It sometimes feels like God put me on this earth to teach me the meaning of the word *patience*. The truth is that our lives have been blessed by Nicky's presence. He is completely nonjudgmental and living in the moment, a gentle soul who touches all who know him and who have worked or played with him. Our family has grown in ways we might not have because of our unique experience. We are more tolerant of differences, less competitive, and more tuned in to spending time together.

My heart cries for children who do not have what we are able to give Nicky. I think about children living in poverty or in countries where supports and education for the disabled don't exist. Over the past sixteen years I have gotten to know some of the most dedicated and creative clinicians and teachers. I have also made some deep friendships with parents of other children with disabilities. We are a tight community who advocate for and look out for one another's children. These are people I would never have met or gotten to know had it not been for my son. I am grateful beyond words for their life work, and for their friendship. Their presence is another gift from God.

My daughter Sydney likes to say that N/A or "not applicable" applies to Nicky regarding religion. He doesn't conceptualize things, so everything is very concrete, including his ability to understand God. He loves to be in church, but he doesn't really understand what is going on. He doesn't grapple with the larger issues of right and wrong, the dos and don'ts of the Ten Commandments that we all do. Interesting, isn't it? A part of him is an angel walking around on earth, simply and naturally good. He can inspire generosity and caring in others by being just who he is. God bless him!

Life-Threatening Food Allergy: Molly's Story

Our daughter Carmen made a dramatic entrance into the world via emergency C-section but didn't stop there. At five months old, the first time we gave her baby formula, she projectile-vomited. We noticed her face was bright red, and worried she'd somehow gotten sunburned, until we stripped her down to wash the vomit off and saw a red line moving down her body, the hives overtaking her.

We scrambled to the ER with her only to find out she was having an allergic reaction—turns out she was allergic to tree nuts, peanuts, sesame, soy, and dairy. We made the mistake of not clearing the house of offensive foods, and when a few months later she snagged a nut from her brother's cereal bowl and ate it, she started wheezing within minutes. We jabbed the Epi-Pen into her juicy baby thigh, called 911, and held her on the gurney in the ambulance all the way to the hospital. We finally came to terms with the seriousness of her condition.

By trial and error, we learned to parent her. It felt more like error alone at first. I was at a wake at the funeral home down the street when my husband called to alert me that she was having another attack and needed to go to the ER for the third time in three months. I ran home in heels, sobbing and shouting to my friend behind me, "How are we supposed to keep her *alive*?!?!"

Soon after, we discovered that at least some of those trips were due to asthma (much more easily treated), whose symptoms mirrored an allergy attack. This knowledge provided some relief, but it didn't change the bottom line, that her life was in our hands. I, as the grocery shopper and family cook, keenly felt the stress of being the single point of failure: the person who, if I let my focus slip for an instant, could kill our daughter. The sword of Damocles was forever hanging over Carmen's head, and I was the one holding it.

But God sent angels and allies to help us learn how to keep her safe: An amazing pediatrician who took us seriously but was never alarmist. An amazing allergist who was very conservative in his approach and helped us reform our hippie ways, at least in regard to ingredient labels. A naturopathic physician who gave us positive things to try to lower the level of reactivity in Carmen's body so we could feel we were doing something proactive instead of just waiting for catastrophe to strike again.

We learned to cook an entirely new diet, and saw our own BMI and cholesterol drop as we started eating more like Carmen: no processed foods (which were almost always made with an offending ingredient), only home-cooked meals.

We also learned to protect her without putting her in a bubble. We provided her with safe alternatives so she could go to social events, coached her in standing up for herself when adults were forcing food on her, and when she learned how to read, taught her to read ingredient labels carefully.

When she turned seven, Carmen suddenly became very anxious. It was as if she had just realized what the "life-threatening" part of "life-threatening food allergies" meant, and how it applied to her. When her mind invented an imaginary enemy named Throwup who wanted her to die, we found a skilled therapist who helped her develop coping strategies, like using worry beads she'd made herself, "changing the channel" when anxious thoughts overtook her, and cataloging her worries into things she could control and things she couldn't control. I taught her the Serenity Prayer.

Today, Carmen is twelve. She has learned to cook simple meals for herself in an act of empowerment. She has survived more Epi-Pen sticks and ambulance rides and has become a pro at the ER, always charming the staff with her detailed knowledge of the human body. Apart from feeling left out on occasion when we find ourselves gushing over whatever dairy-filled deliciousness we're cramming into our pie holes, she has made relative peace with her allergies. And in her best moments, Carmen understands that the allergies that make her different, and sometimes left out, have also made her a stronger self-advocate and given her more empathy with other kinds of difference. God didn't give her allergies. But God is using them.

Helping Our Kids to Worry Well

So far, we have been talking about when our kids are the cause of *our* worry—when we worry about and for them. To sum it all up, the most important thing your child needs to hear from you, through your words, your actions, or both, is this:

> *God doesn't make any junk. Of everything God made, in the Creation story, God said this and only this: It's good. It's real good. That includes you. You are not broken. You are not bad. You are not a burden. You are beautiful through and through, and made in the image of God. I love you so much, and my life would be different and worse if you were not in it.*
>
> *God didn't make this happen to you (give you this burden, diagnosis, illness, disability, and so on). But God has used and will use this challenge to bring all kinds of awareness and gifts and goodness into your life, into our family's life, and into the lives of many people that your life bumps up against.*

When Kids Are the Worriers

Anxiety disorders are the most common mental health problem experienced by Americans. About one quarter of thirteen- to eighteen-year-olds will experience anxiety at some point in their lives, and about one in twenty teens will experience severe anxiety. Even kids without anxiety disorders face anxiety-provoking situations all the time, including challenges that seem too big for someone who has seen and experienced so little.

Here is a distillation of what we have learned (through both professional and very personal experience) about helping kids with worries big and small:

1. **The worst thing anyone can do when facing something anxiety-provoking is to avoid it.** Avoiding our fears allows them to grow and gives them power over us. So if your child is worried about something, don't give them a total pass. Don't throw them into the deep end without teaching them how to swim, either. Good psychological research on anxiety tells us that gradual, step-by-step exposure to the things that we fear is better than "flooding" with anxiety. Baby steps. Scaffold so your child experiences just enough anxiety that they feel it but can manage it. And when that gets easy, help them try the next hardest thing.

2. **When you have something scary or anxiety-provoking to tell your child, at any age, don't hide it, at least not for too long.** We make it a rule never to lie to our kids. Ellen doesn't lie to her patients, either. No matter their age or ability, most kids are incredibly emotionally attuned. They are evolutionarily wired to be so. If cave children didn't quickly sense the adults' alarm when danger appeared, they wouldn't run. Left to worry alone, they become balls of anxiety with no help to cope. And they often imagine that whatever they *aren't* being told is much worse than it actually is.

3. Related to #2, **remember that your child's perspective is uniquely hers. Don't dismiss worries as silly, because from her point of view they aren't.** Equally, when having to share a big worry, don't

assume your children see it in the same way you do. Ellen worked for several years with the Parenting at a Challenging Time (PACT) program at Massachusetts General Hospital, providing guidance for parents with cancer on how to talk to their kids. Many times, parents would tell their children about their cancer, expecting tears and anguish, only to be surprised by sighs of relief. Kids would say things like "Oh, thank God. I thought you were going to tell us you guys were getting divorced . . . you lost your job . . . we have to move." Just as things that are a big deal to them are not always so big to us, it goes the other way, too.

4. **Consider, too, how your child's worries and reactions to worrying news will be shaped by their age and stage of development, and their temperament.** Some kids will be very concrete, seemingly self-centered, emotional, or not, depending on who they are and where they are. It's a good idea to familiarize yourself with how kids your child's age generally think and to reflect on who they are when helping them to worry well. Prepare to be surprised by an unexpected reaction.

5. **A conversation about a big worry is never a one-and-done.** Remember: acceptance. Expect multiple conversations, follow-up questions, a resurgence of emotions, an ebb and flow of anxiety. Maybe they were able to get up in front of the class today but next week could be back to square one. Managing worry and anxiety is *always* at least two steps forward and one step back along a winding path. Follow their lead. Don't

answer questions they don't have yet, or give more information than they are ready for.

Several years ago, one of our mutual mom friends was struggling to help her anxious kid, and sick with worry about him herself. She wanted to know how to help him through the weepy panic attacks he was having, and how to talk to him afterward in a way that didn't discredit or discount him but also didn't reinforce his anxiety. How could they avoid stopping everything, focusing only on him and letting the anxiety have all the power, while still acknowledging that he was hurting? Here is an edited version of Ellen's email answer:

> *First, in the same way you shouldn't avoid the worry, don't avoid talking about it. In fact, go ahead and give it a name. Your very own worry monster. Talk about the "worry part" of their brain. The worry part is not a bad thing. We need it. It keeps us safe, tells us when to be cautious. But it is not always super smart. Sometimes it tells us to worry a lot about things that we really only need to worry about a little (e.g., having missed a few more days of school than the other kids) or tells us to worry when we don't need to at all (e.g., that there is someone at the window when it is the wind). It might even send signals to other parts of our body that we need to run so that we feel hot and sweaty and sick and panicky. We all need to learn how to question our worry part and challenge it sometimes. That lets us take risks, try new things, have new experiences—all important things to do.*
>
> *The challenge for a parent of an anxious kid is walking the tightrope of support without enabling the worry monster. Don't provide too much reassurance—so that he starts to need that from you as opposed to being able to reassure himself. But, mama to*

mama, the biggest challenge is managing your own anxiety: your worry that your kid is not OK and is never going to be OK.

Speaking as a psychologist and from lots of personal experience, there is something I know 100 percent. It's that if your kid is sensitive, is socially attuned, cares about doing well and being his best self, and is prone to thinking big and deep about things—he will always be that way. It may also leave him a little more prone to anxiety and depression. It is also what makes him the loving, successful, beautiful person he is and always will be. The key is helping him to learn how to manage those thoughts and feelings—in the good times and bad—so they don't keep him from doing and being all the things he wants and needs to do and be. Learning to do that is a lifelong process. So take a deep breath with him. Slow it all down. Know you are doing all of the right things, taking this as seriously as you should be, and also know you may need to give him a little time.

When a Parent Gets Sick: Molly's Story

Nine years ago, when my kids were four and eight, I was diagnosed with an aggressive cancer. After the cancer took out half a lung and the doctors had blasted me with eight months of chemo, I was pronounced done with treatment.

I am lucky and blessed that I have not had a recurrence, and these days, cancer is so far in the rearview mirror that I don't think about it very often. But during that difficult year, it was hard to think about anything else; the laborious nature of treatment, the side effects and symptoms, and the looming ogre of my mortality were always with us.

One of the hardest things about being sick with small kids was helping them manage their fears while not lying to them about the reality of what we were facing. But the children in my life—my own, and others—also helped me manage my own fears. Ellen's Luke was six at the time, and he came right up to me at coffee hour and said, "At school they told us about this bike ride for kids to raise money to help people who have cancer. And I said to myself, 'Molly's having some cancer! I could do that.'"

I liked Luke's idea that I was having "some cancer." It somehow cut down to size the vast, monolithic power of cancer. It's not Cancer. It's, you know, some cancer. There's choice implied, and moderation. *Like going to tea at the Ritz: "I'll have some crumpets, a little prosecco, and some cancer, please—I'm watching my figure."* Luke then invited Rafe (eight at the time) to do the PMC Kids Ride, which made Rafe so proud and gave him some agency over this new challenge we were facing.

We didn't tell Carmen and Rafe about the cancer until after surgery and biopsy—why worry them with abstract possibilities? But when the diagnosis came in, Peter and I sat them down on the bed and told them the doctors had found a ball of cells that was growing really fast inside my body. They had taken it out, but just in case there were a few cells still floating around, trying to start new balls, they wanted to give me some strong medicine. The medicine would make me really tired, it might make me sick to my tummy, and it would make all my hair fall out. (Carmen, four years old at this point, laughed out loud.)

That was it, more or less. The children nodded gravely, we talked a bit more about when my hair would fall out and how other people would be taking them on playdates, and sometimes picking them up at school, because of my chemo schedule. We told them if they had any questions they wanted to ask, any funny feelings they wanted to talk about, they could ask us anything. And if they didn't feel like asking us, they could talk about it with another adult they felt close to. "Who are some adults you feel close to, whom you could ask?" They named an epic list of adults they loved. Then they were done and scampered off.

They didn't ask if I was going to die. I wasn't fooled. Rafe has been obsessed with death since he was two, and there was no way the omission was accidental. But kids process things in their own way, at their own pace, according to their own temperament.

A couple of days later, Rafe woke up very early in the morning, about four a.m., came to our door, and said simply, "I need comfort." It turned out he'd been reading *The Lightning Thief* and the mother gets killed off early in the book. For real? Later that day, as we lolled on the couch, Rafe said, "I needed comfort last night because I was reading that book, and then I fell asleep and dreamed that you died."

"That must have been scary," I said.

"It was," he said. "You know how, when I was little and I asked about death, and said how I didn't want you and Dad to die, you'd say you were most probably going to live to be old; that a lot of things had to happen before you would die, like I would become a teenager, then go to college, then fall in love and get married, then have my own children, then have different jobs, then get a little bit old myself and maybe stop working, and maybe I'd even become a grandfather?"

"Yes," I said.

"Well, you might not. You have cancer. You might just live a short time."

"You're right about that."

"Sometimes I think you are going to live a long time, and other times I think you are going to die, and other times I just don't know."

I said, quietly, "That's about where I am."

I wished my kid were not so smart, sometimes, because then I could not *lie* but *conceal* a little more. I didn't and still don't lie to my kids, mostly because I am a terrible liar, but also because I think kids deserve the truth, at their own pace, which means not burdening them with more information than they have sought or answers to questions they haven't asked.

But I also believe that kids notice more than we think they do. Knowing that they know more than we imagine, it is a disservice to them to lie outright or even conceal information that affects their lives directly—and could hurt their trust in us. Kids are much more resilient than we give them credit for. We need to start preparing them for death early—the most natural, holy thing, and deeply a part of life.

I told Rafe the truth—that most of the time I thought I was going to live a long, long time, and then I brought him over to the computer to show him the vast list of emails with prayers embedded in them. Together we counted the number of clergy who said their communities of faith were praying for me. We did the math.

Carmen took a couple of extra days to get around to the question. Being four, she was very concrete, and narcissistic, and all about ensuring her own security. Even before cancer, she had developed a line of questioning to make certain that I would never abandon her. "Will you still be my mom when I am a grown woman? Will you still be my mom when I am a mom? Will you still be my mom when I am crabby, or when I cry, or when I hit?" There were many variations on this theme. I always assured her that I would be her mom, no matter what, no matter when.

There was a new one the week after diagnosis. We were in the car on the ride to daycare. "Will you still be my mom when I am a teenager?" she asked.

"Yup, Carm, I will be your mom when you are a teenager. You may wish I weren't, then," I said.

Then her rejoinder: "Will you still be my mom when you are in heaven?" she asked.

Thunk.

"Yes, Carm, I will be your mom even when I'm in heaven."

A street sweeper cut off our progress through an intersection. "Hey, Mom, what's that?!" She had already moved on, with typical four-year-old in-the-momentness. I, meanwhile, managed to hold it together until I dropped her off, but eight blocks later I was crying so hard that when I stopped at a red light, the kind man in the car in front of me got out and asked me if I was all right.

The thing about having young kids and being in cancer treatment was that while the poignancy was almost too much at times—the terrible daymares about dying and Carmen having only the vaguest of memories about me, wondering if Rafe would feel always cheated and a little bit bereft—I was and am very, very grateful for the dozens of ways every day that having young children forced me during such a difficult time to stay in the present, grounded, incarnated. I couldn't go off into the stratosphere ruminating all day long about death. There were still permission slips to sign, lunches to pack, dinner to fix, homework to check, bottoms to wipe, asthma medicine to puff, stories to read, nightmares to suck out of ears.

The curse of being a parent in cancer treatment was: the poignancy. The blessing of it was: the poignancy.

Self-Care

Before we end this chapter, here's one more reason to cut back on worry: your worry itself could negatively impact your kids. Anxiety can lead to overprotection. Depression (the shadow side of anxiety) in parents can lead to distant parenting.

Both depression and anxiety are highly heritable. For depression, heritability estimates range from about 40 to 50 percent and probably higher for severe depression. Same for anxiety. This means that about 50 percent of the chance of experiencing depression or anxiety in your lifetime is genetic. Put another way, if a parent of identical twins has anxiety, chances are very good at least one of them will have anxiety.

But, and this is a big *but*: genetics account for only our *chances* of having depression or anxiety. Environment matters just as much. Remember all those high-reactive-temperament kids from Chapter 2 who went on to be relatively nonanxious successful kids (at least on the outside)? They learned the tools to manage and challenge their anxiety so that it didn't overwhelm them. We can teach and model this ourselves.

If you were looking for a mandate to spend more time and energy taking care of yourself so that you can take care of your children, this is it. You've heard it a thousand times: put your own oxygen mask on first. We owe it to ourselves to heal ourselves, modeling healthy self-care strategies both for our own sake and so we don't pass our anxiety on to our children.

Once, on vacation, and still in the throes of chemo brain, Molly poured Carmen the wrong milk. Within seconds she was going into anaphylactic shock. Molly and Peter gave her the EpiPen and got her to the ER in time, but she had a breakthrough reaction, her tiny face swollen and red, and had to be hospitalized overnight for observation. Molly held it together all night long, checking Carmen's breathing, but the next morning she ended up sobbing in the hallway, afraid to even be in the same room as her sick daughter, and afraid of ever feeding her again. Molly left her in the able care of Carmen's extremely competent father, and went to spend the next day and night with a dear friend.

When all else fails, discern. Step back, calm down, say a prayer. Try an open-ended one like this: "God! I have no idea what to do next! But You do." Slow your breathing. If you are really anxious, try the "Four-Five-Eight Breath": breathe in for a count of four, hold for a count of five, breathe out for a count of eight. (This works great with anxious kiddos, too).

Get quiet enough to hear what God has to say, and God will have a fighting chance to guide you to the right decision, resources, and people (another good reason to go to church: the presence of people who pray, can make referrals or casseroles, and throw spaghetti supper fundraisers when those medical bills roll in). Getting quiet to listen to God may mean tuning out messages from your family and your culture about what they think you should do, in order to hear a very different Voice. You'll know it's the right Voice because it will calm you down. It will be altogether wiser than you, and know things you don't. It will ask you to suspend your fear and pride. And in their place it will offer you something much better: grace, and peace that passes all understanding.

BIG IDEAS

- Jesus said we shouldn't worry past today. Worry is an attempt to control the future. Prayer runs parallel to it and disarms it. "Courage is fear that has said its prayers" (Dorothy Bernard).

- The key to building resiliency and gaining emotional strength is not to be stoic but to be vulnerable, feel your big feelings, allow your children to feel theirs, and live forward, looking for what God might be working amid the difficulties and dangers that happen in life.

Prayer

God, I hate this thing that is happening right now. I'm scared and sad and lost in the dark. But You are light on my path, leading me forward. Scripture says, "All things work together for good for those who love You," and I'm trying. Show me the blessing inside what's broken.

Amen.

Epilogue

Still Becoming

For many reasons, this book took us much longer than we anticipated to write, not the least of which is that our patients, our parishioners, and most of all our own kids kept giving us new material to work with. Eventually we had to call it "good enough" and put the pen down.

As a result, we have no neat and tidy ending for you. We are still in the messy middle of our children's and our own unfolding. At this very moment, Molly's Rafe is finishing his high school career out-of-state, having new adventures in an alternative outdoor learning curriculum designed to support kids with ADD. It's a path that Molly and her husband, Peter, never imagined for their child, but after more deeply attending to his "grain," it was a decision all three of them made together. Molly's Carmen has (mostly) learned to manage her food allergies and the anxiety that comes with them. She still loves church (for now) and has a flair for the dramatic, often standing in for Molly to do the announcements in worship, with jazz hands. She is tiny in stature and huge in heart, wondering if and when she might grow so that her outsides match her insides.

Meanwhile, Ellen's elder son is at the start of his high school career, also small for his age and playing tackle football for the first time, against every instinct Ellen had as a psychologist. She cheers from the sidelines and silently prays and monitors kids for signs of concussion. The philosophical debates over the value (or lack thereof) of homework continue. Jonah (his dyslexia now confirmed) is becoming a stronger reader day by day but recently has eschewed books for video games, and Ellen wonders how it is that the bookworm gene seems to be missing in both boys. He still complains that church makes him ill but asks for prayers at bedtime. Luke asks her daily when he might grow in height to match his shoe size. "Who knows?" Ellen says. "You are still becoming. We will have to wait and see."

Madeleine L'Engle said that we are all every age we've ever been. We are also all we might yet grow into. Only God, who lives outside of time, knows the whole.

We took you on a journey through this book to impress upon you your primary task as a parent: to get to know and love your children as God does, with all their beauty, flaws, and imperfections. Like Dorothy with her ruby slippers, perhaps you didn't need the journey of our book to come home to this truth. You had the grace to live it all along. But the journey, and the spiritual practices it teaches us, can help us get to grace a little bit faster when it doesn't come naturally, or when circumstances conspire to make us angry or anguished.

The Holy Trinity of Parenting scaffolds us toward that grace. To really know our children, we need to practice involvement. To do this nonjudgmentally, we need to practice autonomy support. This doesn't mean that we should ignore our hopes and dreams for our kids and for their futures. But it does mean we should work to be aware of how our fears and biases might be dictating our parenting. Structure gives us a way to do this that sets boundaries. We have a responsibility as parents to put up guardrails on the highway of our children's heroes' journey, if not railroad tracks toward a specific outcome.

We will not always like our children. We will not always be "in love" with them. But, as theologian Richard Rohr said, both partnering and parenting are a kind of Love School. "Again and again, you must choose to fall into a love that is greater with both friends and children. It is all training for the falling into The Love that is the Greatest." We are called to love our children as they are. Not our idea of them, nor our hopes or projections, but they themselves. This is how we will train them in the way *they* should go, and this is how we ourselves will grow spiritually and discover the best that Love can offer.

Long before they had kids, Ellen's husband asked her to define God. She had no prepared answer and to this day is unsure where her response came from: "God is love. God exists in the space between people. She is there when the distance between them is great and when it's small, when it's beautiful and when it's awful. She's *always* there. It's just a question of whether or not we will reach for Her."

Scripture comforts us that "neither death, nor life, nor angels, nor demons, neither the present nor the future, nor any powers, nor height nor depths nor anything else in all Creation, will be able to get between us and God's love (Romans 8:38–39)." We might paraphrase this core truth: if we love our children as God loves them, not with a grasping, fearful, transactional, or desperate love, but with the warm, wondrous, and relaxed grip of a Godly love (which we might manage for only a few blissful moments a year), nothing can tear us apart.

We may at times feel distant from our children, lost on our own parenting journey without a map. But the Really Real—another name for God—teaches us that the space we feel is a fiction, because as long as we reach for that Godly love, nothing can separate us. Not the latest craze that has them locked in their room for hours, or their oppositional struggling that makes us crazed. Not test scores or their testing ways. Not anxiety or depression (theirs or ours), not addictions, not life-threatening illnesses. Not even death can truly, permanently, separate us from this being God has given us to love.

Our hope in writing this book is that you, our readers, will walk away with some useful nuggets of parenting advice, have some laughs along the way, and find yourselves with a framework for parenting that will guide you through any storm. But most of all, we hope you are coming away with a soul-sense that love—the love between you and your *real* child and the Really Real God who loves you both—really is enough, if you reach for it.

If you love in this way, your children will teach you to have faith in them . . . and maybe even a greater and more perfect faith in the One who made them.

Notes

Before We Begin

4 **Besides, new data suggest:** "It's Good for Girls to Have Clergywomen, Study Shows," Religion News Service (blog), July 17, 2018, https://religionnews.com/2018/07/17/its-good-for-girls-to-have-clergywomen-study-shows/.

Chapter 1

9 **Some years ago:** Sarah Miller, "New Parenting Study Released," *New Yorker*, March 24, 2014, https://www.newyorker.com/humor/daily-shouts/new-parenting-study-released.

Chapter 2

19 **There *is* some evidence:** See the research and writing of sociologist Phil Zuckerman.

19 **As an example:** Jean Decety et al., "The Negative Association between Religiousness and Children's Altruism across the World," *Current Biology* 25, no. 22 (November 2015): 2951–2955, https://doi.org/10.1016/j.cub.2015.09.056.

20 **Much of this research:** Lisa Miller, *The Spiritual Child: The New Science on Parenting for Health and Lifelong Thriving* (New York: Picador, 2016).

24 **Kagan piloted:** Jerome Kagan, *The Long Shadow of Temperament* (Cambridge, MA: Belknap Press, 2004).

30 **When we are able to see:** The phrase "our little masterpieces" comes from our inspiration: Wendy Mogel, *The Blessing of a Skinned Knee: Using Jewish Teachings to Raise Self-Reliant Children* (New York: Scribner, 2001).

31 **Self-determination theory is based:** Richard M. Ryan, *Self-Determination Theory: Basic Psychological Needs in Motivation, Development, and Wellness* (New York: Guilford Press, 2017). This is the most recent summary of a large and influential body of work first developed by Richard Ryan and Edward Deci at the University of Rochester.

33 **This is the core of:** Attachment theory originated with John Bowlby in the late 1960s and was expanded upon by Mary Ainsworth. It is one of the most

influential but frequently misinterpreted psychological theories. For a recent summary of the wide-ranging research on attachment, see Jeffry A. Simpson et al., eds., *Attachment Theory and Research: New Directions and Emerging Themes* (New York: Guilford Press, 2015).

39 **Dr. Grolnick describes:** Wendy S. Grolnick, *The Psychology of Parental Control: How Well-Meant Parenting Backfires* (Mahwah, NJ: Erlbaum, 2003), xi. See also any of the other excellent articles and chapters by Dr. Grolnick on how self-determination theory applies to parenting.

Chapter 3

46 **School-based bullying:** Joshua R. Polanin, Dorothy L. Espelage, and Therese D. Pigott, "A Meta-Analysis of School-Based Bullying Prevention Programs' Effects on Bystander Intervention Behavior," *School Psychology Review* 41, no. 1 (2012): 21.

46 **And even though:** "Student Bullying Is Down Significantly," *US News & World Report*, March 15, 2018, https://www.usnews.com/news/data-mine /articles/2018-03-15/student-bullying-is-down-significantly.

46 **Still, more than:** "Bullying Statistics," Pacer Center, December 27, 2017, https://www.pacer.org/bullying/resources/stats.asp.

48 **Pioneers like:** Ronald Duska, *Moral Development: A Guide to Piaget and Kohlberg* (New York: Paulist Press, 1975), and Lawrence Kohlberg, *The Meaning and Measurement of Moral Development: Heinz Werner Lectures, 1979* (Worcester, MA: Clark University Press, 1981).

50 **In the 1930s:** Fred Newman, *Lev Vygotsky: Revolutionary Scientist, Critical Psychology* (London : Routledge, 1993).

51 **From the ZPD:** David Wood, Jerome S. Bruner, and Gail Ross, "The Role of Tutoring in Problem Solving," *Journal of Child Psychology and Psychiatry* 17, no. 2 (1976): 89–100, https://doi.org/10.1111/j.1469-7610.1976.tb00381.x.

63 **But here's the rub:** "The Best Predictor of Future Behavior Is . . . Past Behavior," *Psychology Today*, January 3, 2013, http://www.psychologytoday.com /blog/witness/201301/the-best-predictor-future-behavior-is-past-behavior.

64 **The popular books:** Rosalind Wiseman, *Masterminds and Wingmen: Helping Our Boys Cope with Schoolyard Power, Locker-Room Tests, Girlfriends, and the New Rules of Boy World* (New York: Harmony Books, 2014), and Rosalind Wiseman, *Queen Bees and Wannabes: Helping Your Daughter Survive Cliques, Gossip, Boyfriends, and Other Realities of Adolescence* (New York: Crown, 2002).

69 **It takes opioid addicts:** Lela Moore, "Clean, Sober and $41,000 Deep in Out-of-Pocket Addiction Recovery Costs," *New York Times*, October 3, 2018, https://www.nytimes.com/2018/07/26/reader-center/costs-of-drug-rehab .html.

72 **Research psychologist:** Paul Bloom, *Descartes' Baby: How the Science of Child Development Explains What Makes Us Human* (New York: Basic Books, 2004).

73 **For a fun song:** Bryan Sirchio, "Holy Spirit Fruit," https://www.youtube .com/watch?v=awvdpUNP3zc.

73 **Or check out this summary:** Jerome Berryman, "Sacred Story: The Ten Best Ways," 2014, https://s3.amazonaws.com/childformation-2015-16/GPSacred Story/10_The+Ten+Best+Ways.pdf.

Chapter 4

83   **"The inclusion of":** Mogel, *The Blessing of a Skinned Knee*, 62.

89   **A theory of:** Edward L. Deci, *Intrinsic Motivation and Self-Determination in Human Behavior: Perspectives in Social Psychology* (New York: Plenum Press, 1985).

91   **Lest you fear:** John Santelli et al., "Abstinence and Abstinence-Only Education: A Review of U.S. Policies and Programs," *Journal of Adolescent Health* 38, no. 1 (2006): 72–81, https://doi.org/10.1016/j.jadohealth.2005.10.006.

93   **Dr. Kagan's research:** Kagan, *The Long Shadow of Temperament*.

95   **Find a new:** Walter Wink, *The Powers That Be: Theology for a New Millennium* (New York: Doubleday, 1999).

96   **Marriage and family:** Susan Stiffelman, *Parenting without Power Struggles: Raising Joyful, Resilient Kids While Staying Calm, Cool and Connected* (New York: Atria, 2012).

104   **But here is:** E. Mark Cummings and Patrick T. Davies, "Effects of Marital Conflict on Children: Recent Advances and Emerging Themes in Process-Oriented Research," *Journal of Child Psychology and Psychiatry* 43, no. 1 (2002): 31–63, https://doi.org/10.1111/1469-7610.00003.

Chapter 5

117   **And social science:** Christian Smith and Hilary Davidson, *The Paradox of Generosity: Giving We Receive, Grasping We Lose* (New York: Oxford University Press, 2014), http://nrs.harvard.edu/urn-3:hul.ebookbatch.GEN_batch: EDZ000088681420160622.

122   **Data collected by:** See Jennifer Breheny Wallace, "Why Children Need Chores," *Wall Street Journal*, March 13, 2015, https://www.wsj.com/articles /why-children-need-chores-1426262655, for results of the Rossman study and other studies supporting kids doing chores.

124   **Personal finance columnist:** The column led to this excellent book: Ron Lieber, *The Opposite of Spoiled: Raising Kids Who Are Grounded, Generous, and Smart about Money* (New York: Harper, 2015).

125   **Even these days:** Katie Lobosco, "One Thing You Should Know about Your Spouse, but 43% Don't," CNN Money, June 24, 2015, https://money.cnn .com/2015/06/24/pf/married-couples-salary/.

126   **It is true:** Jamie Ducharme, "This Is the Amount of Money You Need to Be Happy according to Research," *Money*, February 14, 2018, http://money.com /money/5157625/ideal-income-study/.

126   **Positive psychology:** Smith and Davidson, *The Paradox of Generosity*.

129   **There is good:** See William Deresiewicz, *Excellent Sheep: The Miseducation of the American Elite and the Way to a Meaningful Life* (New York: Free Press, 2015), for a summary and commentary on this phenomenon.

130   **In her documentary:** Vicki Abeles, *Beyond Measure: Rescuing an Overscheduled, Overtested, Underestimated Generation* (New York: Simon and Schuster, 2015).

131   **In 2017:** "Employment Characteristics of Families Summary," Bureau of Labor Statistics, April 19, 2018, https://www.bls.gov/news.release/famee.nr0 .htm. See also "Raising Kids and Running a Household: How Working Parents Share the Load," Pew Research Center, November 4, 2015, http://assets .pewresearch.org/wp-content/uploads/sites/3/2015/11/2015-11-04_working -parents_FINAL.pdf.

132   **Glennon Doyle:** Glennon Doyle, "2011 Lesson #2: Don't Carpe Diem," Momastery (blog), January 4, 2012, https://momastery.com/blog/2012/01/04/2011-lesson-2-dont-carpe-diem/.

135   **In 2009:** "Marketing to Children Overview," Campaign for a Commercial-Free Childhood, https://www.commercialfreechildhood.org/resource/marketing-children-overview (accessed January 18, 2019).

136   **This, unsurprisingly:** Joe Pinsker, "Why Kids Want Things," *The Atlantic*, August 30, 2018, https://www.theatlantic.com/family/archive/2018/08/kids-materialism/568987/.

Chapter 6

143   **Richard Weissbourd:** "Making Caring Common," Making Caring Common, https://mcc.gse.harvard.edu/ (accessed January 18, 2019); "Richard Weissbourd," *Psychology Today*, https://www.psychologytoday.com/experts/richard-weissbourd (accessed January 18, 2019); Rick Weissbourd, *The Parents We Mean to Be: How Well-Intentioned Adults Undermine Children's Moral and Emotional Development* (Boston: Houghton Mifflin Harcourt, 2010).

145   **In his book:** Bruce Feiler, *The Secrets of Happy Families: Improve Your Mornings, Rethink Family Dinner, Fight Smarter, Go Out and Play, and Much More* (New York: Morrow, 2013).

151   **Po Bronson:** Po Bronson and Ashley Merryman, *NurtureShock: New Thinking about Children* (New York: Twelve, 2009).

Chapter 7

163   **A Pew research study:** "America's Changing Religious Landscape," May 12, 2015, http://www.pewforum.org/2015/05/12/americas-changing-religious-landscape/.

164   **Amend that to:** Frederick Buechner, *Wishful Thinking: A Seeker's ABC*, rev. ed. (San Francisco: HarperSanFrancisco, 1993).

166   **Rabbi Abraham Joshua:** Abraham Joshua Heschel, *The Sabbath: Its Meaning for Modern Man* (New York: Farrar, Straus and Giroux, 2005).

166   **Christian pastor:** MaryAnn McKibben Dana, *Sabbath in the Suburbs: A Family's Experiment with Holy Time* (St. Louis: Chalice Press, 2012).

169   **As a young doctor:** National Institute for Play, http://www.nifplay.org/ (accessed January 18, 2019).

170   **The skeptical mystic:** Simone Weil, *Gravity and Grace* (London: Routledge, 2002).

173   **According to psychologists:** Paul K. Piff et al., "Awe, the Small Self, and Pro-social Behavior," *Journal of Personality and Social Psychology* 108, no. 6 (2015): 883–899, https://doi.org/10.1037/pspi0000018.

181   **A lot of research:** See Anne K. Fishel, *Home for Dinner: Mixing Food, Fun, and Conversation for a Happier Family and Healthier Kids* (New York: American Management Association, 2015), and "The Family Dinner Project," https://thefamilydinnerproject.org (accessed January 18, 2019), for data and ideas.

185   **atheists have reported:** We may be extrapolating a little, but listen to this: Gretta Cohn, "Does Religion Make You Happy? (Ep. 176)," Freakonomics (blog), July 24, 2014, http://freakonomics.com/podcast/does-religion-make-you-happy-a-new-freakonomics-radio-podcast/. Or read

this: Harry Cheadle, "Can an Atheist Church Make Nonbelievers Nicer?," *Vice* (blog), July 5, 2013, https://www.vice.com/en_us/article/vdy5y4/can-an-atheist-church-make-nonbelievers-nicer.

187   **Many middle- to upper-middle-class:** "Here's the Insane Amount the Average Parent Will Pay for After-School Activities," *Money*, http://money.com/money/4425114/parents-rising-costs-after-school-activities/.

Chapter 8

193   **Take "Just say no":** Scott O. Lilienfeld and Hal Arkowitz, "Why 'Just Say No' Doesn't Work," *Scientific American*, January 1, 2014, https://doi.org/10.1038/scientificamericanmind0114-70.

193   **A 2009 meta-analysis:** Wei Pan and Haiyan Bai, "A Multivariate Approach to a Meta-Analytic Review of the Effectiveness of the D.A.R.E. Program," *International Journal of Environmental Research and Public Health* 6, no. 1 (January 2009): 267–277, https://doi.org/10.3390/ijerph6010267.

194   **A 2002 study:** Pim Cuijpers et al., "The Effects of Drug Abuse Prevention at School: The 'Healthy School and Drugs' Project," *Addiction* 97, no. 1 (2002): 67–73, https://doi.org/10.1046/j.1360-0443.2002.00038.x.

206   **Brené Brown:** See any of her talks or writing, but for these specific quotes listen to Brené Brown, "Listening to Shame," TED2012, March 2012, https://www.ted.com/talks/brene_brown_listening_to_shame?language=en.

211   **If you need:** Glennon Doyle, "A Mountain I'm Willing to Die On," Momastery (blog), March 26, 2013, https://momastery.com/blog/2013/03/26/a-mountain-im-willing-to-die-on-4/.

212   **There is good:** "Experts: Mom Has Biggest Impact on Girls' Body Image," *USA Today*, August 23, 2013, https://www.usatoday.com/story/news/nation/2013/08/23/moms-daughters-influence-body-image/2690921/.

213   **Families that eat:** Krushnapriya Sahoo et al., "Childhood Obesity: Causes and Consequences," *Journal of Family Medicine and Primary Care* 4, no. 2 (2015): 187–192, https://doi.org/10.4103/2249-4863.154628.

213   **Boys are not:** Sarah Marsh, "Eating Disorders in Men Rise by 70% in NHS Figures," *The Guardian*, July 31, 2017, https://www.theguardian.com/society/2017/jul/31/eating-disorders-in-men-rise-by-70-in-nhs-figures.

223   **On average:** Patricia A. Cavazos-Rehg et al., "Age of Sexual Debut among US Adolescents," *Contraception* 80, no. 2 (August 2009): 158–162, https://doi.org/10.1016/j.contraception.2009.02.014.

Chapter 9

226   **In a study:** Mary Spagnola and Barbara H. Fiese, "Family Routines and Rituals: A Context for Development in the Lives of Young Children," *Infants & Young Children* 20, no. 4 (October 2007): 284–299, https://doi.org/10.1097/01.IYC.0000290352.32170.5a.

Chapter 10

261   **It's one that:** Throughout this chapter we use the term *dis/ability* to make it clear that having a disability is not all or nothing and does not define the person who has one . . . or even many. Parents of children with many quite severe disabilities would often love for you to ask about their child's abilities.

282   **About one quarter:** "Any Anxiety Disorder," NIMH, November 2017, https://
www.nimh.nih.gov/health/statistics/any-anxiety-disorder.shtml.

291   **For depression:** Falk W. Lohoff, "Overview of the Genetics of Major Depressive Disorder," *Current Psychiatry Reports* 12, no. 6 (December 2010): 539–546,
https://doi.org/10.1007/s11920-010-0150-6.

Epilogue

296   **But, as theologian:** Richard Rohr, *Breathing under Water: Spirituality and the
Twelve Steps* (Cincinnati: St. Anthony Messenger Press, 2011).

Acknowledgments

We thank God first of all—for the gifts of life, kids, spouses, and callings that stretch us and make us happy (almost) every day.

Thank you to our families who learned how to make their own school lunches perhaps 1.2 years sooner than they might have otherwise, and who ate a lot of questionable leftovers for dinner while we were writing early and editing late. We love you Eric, Luke, Jonah, Peter, Rafe, and Carmen! Thank you for giving *us* room to grow and keep becoming as well.

Thanks to our friends who told us your parenting struggles and wisdom, read early drafts, and listened to endless minutiae about Da Book for the six-year gestation period that it took to hatch it (consider it: a pregnancy three fetal elephants long): Sue Donnelly, Katie Kavanaugh, and Angela Jernigan. Thanks to our people who helped it find a path to publication: Tina Villa, Matt Laney, and our awesome agent, Joy Tutela, who first read the manuscript cover to cover the day after Christmas in the midst of an explosion of plastic detritus, no doubt.

So much gratitude to the people who love books, who know how to midwife them into being, and help them thrive given the high infant mortality rate of print these days: from Mary Reynics, who first heard this book's heartbeat, to Ashley Hong, who did vitals checks all along, to our editor, Gary Jansen, unfailingly kind, supportive, and wise even as he told us our baby needed to bake a little longer (you were always right). Thanks to Nick, Sharon, and the whole marketing and publicity departments at Convergent who are teaching us how to get our ideas into the world in a bigger way!

We both have countless fabulous mentors—bosses, other parents, and the churches full of people whose wisdom we have magpied into our parenting and into our work as pastor and clinician: First Church Berkeley UCC, First Church Somerville UCC, Second Church in Beverly, Silver Lake Conference Center UCC, Wendy Grolnick and the entire Clark University graduate psychology program, supervisors and colleagues at MassGeneral Hospital and Shriners Hospital for Children, Boston. Words fail us when we think of the countless children, teens, parents, and families who have let us into their pain and their joy, their mess and their struggle, their trial and triumphs. It is the grace of witness to these families' stories that allowed us to write this one.

We love you and have learned so much from you and your beautiful kids, Leslie Chaison and Sam Stegeman, Sue and Jason Donnelly, Sarah Neidhoefer, Robin and Christopher Junker, Terri Lupoli, Sue Brandies, Jennifer Wokoske, Katy Finkenzeller, and a thousand more who deserve space in this acknowledgment, but we are already over our word limit (surprise surprise). Warm love to our own parents, George, Kathleen, Wendy, Sarah, Claudia, and Ed: for all you have taught us by word and by deed.

We owe a debt of gratitude in writing this book to psychologist Wendy Mogel's excellent book *The Blessing of a Skinned Knee: Using Jewish Teachings to Raise Self-Reliant Children*. When we read it, we knew the world needed the same sort of resource for Christian parents.

We've also seen the benefits for parents and families of a new "vulnerability revolution" born out of that great revealer, social media, and the specific voices of early parenting bloggers/authors like Glennon Doyle and Brené Brown. Mommy blogs have succeeded in large part because their writers have been honest about the hard stuff, at risk to their own egos and even careers in the era before it was okay to overshare. Thanks for making it culturally relevant to talk about epic fails, ugly cries, and just how hard this totally wonderful job really is.

Index

About the Authors

Rev. Molly Phinney Baskette, M.Div., is the senior minister of the First Church Berkeley UCC in California and the author of several books, including grief workbooks for children and practical how-tos for church renewal. She is a popular speaker and conference leader but known for making workshop attendees get out of their chairs and dance. She lives in Alameda, California, with her husband and two teenagers, where she loves to march in the streets, bike the Bay, or read in the hammock, depending on God's agenda for the day.

Ellen O'Donnell, PhD, is a child psychologist at MassGeneral Hospital for Children and Shriners Hospitals for Children, Boston, and an instructor at Harvard Medical School. She has authored numerous articles and book chapters on topics in child psychology, such as learning disabilities, coping with a child's or parent's medical illness, and positive parenting practices to prevent depression and anxiety in children. Ellen lives in Concord, Massachusetts, with her husband and their two boys, who find ways to pull her away from reading books and doing yoga to learn to ski, fish, paddleboard, hike, and build stuff in the woods.